W9-BVY-391

THE DEVIL AND SONNY LISTON

ALSO BY NICK TOSCHES

Country

Hellfire

Unsung Heroes of Rock 'n' Roll

Power on Earth

Cut Numbers

Dino

Trinities

Chaldea

THE DEVIL AND SONNY LISTON

Nick Tosches

LITTLE, BROWN AND COMPANY

BOSTON · NEW YORK · LONDON

First Edition

Library of Congress Cataloging-in-Publication Data

Tosches, Nick.

The Devil and Sonny Liston / Nick Tosches. — 1st ed.

p. cm.

Includes index.

ISBN 0-316-89775-2

1. Liston, Sonny, 1932–1970. 2. Boxers (Sports) — United States Biography. I. Title.

GV1132.L53T68 2000

796.83'092 — dc 21 99-42098

Q-FG

10 9 8 7 6 5 4 3 2

Printed in the United States of America

TO A BENCH IN THE OLD NEIGHBORHOOD,
AND TO A STAR THAT OVER IT SHONE
IN THE HEAT OF THE SUMMER NIGHT

This is a song
for the one who is doomed,
a blow to the heart that breaks the mind.

—Æschylus

FROM NOTHING

THE CORPSE WAS ROLLED OVER AND LAY FACE down on the metal slab. It was then that the coroner saw them: the copper-colored whipping welts, old and faint, like one might imagine to have been those of a driven slave.

To say that Charles Liston had been a slave would be to render cheap metaphor of the life of a man. And yet those scars on his back were as nothing to deeper scars, the kind that no coroner could ever see, scars of a darkness far less imaginable than those from any lash. Charles Liston, the most formidable of men, the most unconquerable of heavyweight boxers, had been enslaved by the forces of that darkness: enslaved, conquered, and killed by them.

Born with dead man's eyes, he had passed from the darkness of those scars on his back to the darkness of the criminal underworld, to a darkness beyond, a darkness whose final form was the last thing his eyes ever saw.

I remember the figure of Sonny Liston from my boyhood: distant, ominous, enigmatic, alluring. It now strikes me as odd — looking back at that boyhood — that a black man could have fascinated me so. In 1962, the year that Sonny won the heavyweight title, I was in the eighth grade of P.S. 24 in Jersey City. The school was predominantly black, and intramural racial conflict was the foremost extracurricular activity. There were skirmishes every day, full-blown gang fights every Friday afternoon: black against white, white against black. The mutual hostility had always been there, but in the fall, winter, and spring of 1962–3, the brew of that hostility boiled over. Friendship between black and white was driven underground, or ended. The punishment for consorting with the enemy was to be beaten, damned, persecuted, and ostracized, not only by one's own kind but by the enemy's kind as well. To black and white alike, such behavior was *contra naturam,* an assault and a crime against all that was as it should be.

At this same time, LeRoi Jones was writing a novel about the evil spirit of those days. In *The System of Dante's Hell,* published in 1965, it was as if Jones, setting out to exorcise evil, was overtaken by it, and his book emerged as one of the most powerful and beautiful expressions of blind hatred and its wages since the Pentateuch. The hell he chose in which to set his story was the city of Newark, where he had his roots, and where I was born and partly raised. I must have read the paperback in 1966, and I was in Newark in the summer of 1967 — the Summer of Love, those hippie assholes called it — when the riots flared. For me, it was like the force of Jones's vision erupting from the underworld regions through the streets. I loved it. It had nothing to do with black and white, it merely was: an emanation of all that destroys us from within, wild and deadly and beyond the lie of law. I remember the old Jewish shopkeepers fleeing, painting the words SOUL BROTHER on their storefront windows, in the vain hope that their enterprise would be perceived as black and therefore spared.

But no one, black or white, was spared. There was much talk about "black rage" — a catch phrase that was brought to us by the same mass merchants who brought us "summer of love" — and blacks themselves bought into it, for the black is no less a fool than the white and will cling to any rationalization that masks or justifies, however fatuously, the part of our nature that seems to belie our humanity: the part of our nature that, in our vanity and denial, we have come to call inhuman, a word that has barely changed since the Latin *inhumanus* of the ancient Romans, whose empire was built upon slavery.

As I remember those old Jewish shopkeepers hurriedly painting their windows, so I remember the self-proclaimed black radicals, like Jones, having their dashikis made by those same old Jewish tailors. It was as close to Africa as they had ever been, the corner of Broad and Market in downtown Newark. A little old Jewish tailor stitching raiments of polyester pride for a bunch of guys who were suddenly talking about slavery as if it were a personal experience and about Africa as if it was their true home. It was a minstrelsy skit of a new age: the angry young Afro-American and his tailor.

LeRoi Jones, 1964: "Sonny Liston was the big black Negro in every white man's hallway, waiting to do him in, deal him under." Liston, wrote Jones, was "the bad nigger," the "heavy-faced replica of every whipped-up woogie in the world."

But nobody ever saw Sonny Liston in a fucking dashiki. Sonny Liston knew — you could see it in those dead man's eyes — that there was no black and white; there was only that hallway: your hallway, my hallway, Jones's hallway, the unlighted hallway of the world.

I think now that my boyhood fascination with Sonny Liston had to do with his being as feared and hated by blacks as by whites. He was the ultimate outlaw. Man, those narrow-lapelled sharkskin suits, that felling left and that slaughterhouse right, and that scowl: his badness transcended race.

As years passed, the more I learned of boxing, and the more

fighters I saw fight, the more I knew that there was no other fighter like Sonny Liston. There never had been, and there never would be. And the more I lived and learned of other things, the more I began to feel that the secret history of Sonny Liston would reveal one of the greatest Mob tales ever told, a tale that ended in a murder mystery whose solution seemed to be lost forever, as gone as that night when Sonny's dead man's eyes went dead for good. I did not know that it would also reveal the forces of another, unexplored darkness, an underworld unto itself. And I did not know, above all, that it would reveal a soul that, even amid the darkness in which it dwelt, eluded all concepts of good and evil, of right and wrong, of light and dark themselves.

A GUY WHO KNEW SONNY ONCE SAID, "I THINK HE died the day he was born." Nobody, not even Sonny, knew exactly when that day was, or where he was born. Only he and the men who killed him knew the date of his death. His life began and ended in a blur.

A wind through the savanna, a rustling through scrub, through big trees' shadows never to be seen again; the eye of one's own kind more terrible than the eye of the leopard cat.

The Oyo enslaved the Oyo and the Dahomey, and in their freedom the Dahomey enslaved the Dahomey and the Oyo and the Ashanti, and in their time of might the Ashanti enslaved the Ashanti and the Oyo and the Dahomey and all men of free-born ancestry.

When the leopard drenched the grass and dirt with the blood of one's life, one's soul returned to the spirit of the river of his father. But to be wrenched from the land was to lose all ancestral power. It was to be forsaken by all that was immanent in the places of that power, and it was to know that, upon death in a strange land, the soul would never return to the river of its kind. To know these things was to know fear and was to bear in life the fate of the soul in death, which was that of an ended sigh. If it was true that evil dwelt in the branches of the odum tree, then it must be from the souls of man that the roots of the odum drank.

Those who were taken downriver to the sea by their own kind knew this. It was a knowledge that reverberated like the thunder of Shango. The gods had been vanquished by powder and guns. No man was free.

The sea was the color of the odum tree's leaves. The color of the leaves of Mississippi was the same.

The state of Mississippi was carved from the Mississippi Territory, which also included Alabama, in 1817. Thirteen years later, the Choctaw who lived there were dispossessed of their land through the 1830 Treaty of Dancing Rabbit, which opened much of Mississippi to white settlers. Most of the Choctaw were relocated in Indian Territory, land the government reserved for them in what was to become, in 1907, the state of Oklahoma. Their chief, however — Greenwood Leflore — stayed behind, acquired much land, much wealth, and many slaves. He is known to have bought a hundred slaves on one day alone in the spring of 1839, and in 1850 his real estate was valued at $80,000. He lived and died on a 15,000-acre estate called Malmaison — "Evil House" in the tongue of his French-Canadian father. He was not alone among the Choctaw in owning slaves. In the Civil War, it was for the Confederacy that the Choctaw nation fought.

Choctaw County, Mississippi, formed in 1833 from the ceded Choctaw lands, lay between the rich alluvial brown-leaf loam and loess of the Yazoo-Mississippi Basin and the flatwoods of Oktibbeha County to the east. It was a land of short-leaf pine, of few souls and infinite shadows amid dark blue-green foliage.

Sonny Liston's ancestry was a haunted whisper through the savanna, a hainted whisper through those pines.

•

The name of Liston, which represents English, Scottish, and Irish bloodlines, is ultimately of Norman origin, and it is believed that the first Liston to leave Normandy for England came with William the Conqueror, the first Norman king of England, in the invasion of 1066. This progenitor settled in the Essex lowlands, where to this day the parish of Liston and, within that parish, lands designated Liston Manor commemorate the Listons' presence as a knightly family.

In the twelfth century, in one of the early invasions of Scotland, some Listons settled in the East Lothian region of that country. (Centuries later, the first minister from Great Britain to the United States after the British acknowledgment of American independence was Sir Robert Liston, who died in Edinburgh, the administrative center of the Lothian region, in 1836, in his ninety-fourth year.)

It was later in the twelfth century, in 1171, that a Liston accompanied Henry II to Ireland and was granted land in Limerick, the richest agricultural area in the country's south. The Listons held the land for almost five centuries, until 1655, when the subjugator Oliver Cromwell confiscated it and gave it to the Bishop of Limerick. The Listons dispersed then to the various outlying townships and beyond. By 1665, there were Listons in America.

Martin Liston was born in Virginia in December 1798. He moved to Georgia, where he married Caroline Elmira Tranum, who was born there in 1813 and who there gave birth to a son, Henry, in 1837. From Georgia, the Listons moved to Mississippi.

The western division of Choctaw County, where the Listons settled, became Township 17, Range 7, of Choctaw County, in the area that in 1870 came to be known as Poplar Creek.

But back then, when Martin Liston was drawn to the rich soil south of the Big Black River and east of the Mississippi floodplain, it was a place without a name, a land of hills and open meadows, wild piney woodlands, and swamp overgrown with cane; a land of panthers, bear, wolves, and deer. The Big Black flowed as clear as springwater in those days, and there were no towns. The future Montgomery County seat and self-styled "crossroads of North Mississippi," the town of Winona, on the "yan" side — that is to say, north — of the Big Black, would not be incorporated until 1861; Poplar Creek not until 1870; and Kilmichael, an outgrowth of one of the region's earliest settlements, also on the yan side of the Big Black, not until 1890. These were the places, unnamed and then named, that circumscribed all that branch of the Liston family.

Martin Liston was one of the founding members of the Bethel Methodist Church, established in the 1840s about seven miles southeast of what was to become Kilmichael. He was also one of the founders of Biddle School, organized twenty years later, about two miles east of Bethel Church.

Caroline Liston bore six children in Mississippi: Robert, William, H.J., Susan Emmaline Amelia, Fanny, and Martin Liston, Jr. The son known as H.J., barely thirteen, died in the fall of 1870.

The oldest of them, Robert C. Liston, was born in October of 1845. In 1878, he married a twenty-six-year-old Poplar Creek girl named Eudora Wilson. They brought into the world six children who died at birth, in infancy, or in youth. But others survived beyond childhood: Verdie, Wiley, Alma, Edith, Willie, Renfro.

Martin Liston died, age seventy, in the spring of 1869. His wife, Caroline, died, age seventy-four, in the last cold days of 1887. Their son Robert C. Liston died in the spring of 1913, five years after the death of his wife, Eudora. Robert C. Liston's son Wiley, born in 1882, came to own much of the land around Bethel Cemetery in Poplar Creek, and was a member of the Masonic lodge there; Robert C. Liston's son Willie, born in 1890, was appointed postmaster of Kilmichael in 1935 and was also a member of the

Masonic lodge there. He and his wife, Hester Loraynne Jordan, had five children. One of them, William Harry Liston, Jr., born in 1931, co-founded the Winona law firm of Liston-Lancaster and is today the eldest member of the only family to bear the Liston name in Montgomery County.

Bill Liston remembered his father telling him what he had been told of those days before the Civil War. "They had a few slaves. When they were freed, they stayed on the farm."

Of the ten or more million Africans sold into slavery from the early sixteenth century to the middle of the nineteenth century, few were brought to market in the land that came to be called the United States — far fewer than a million — while Brazil and the Caribbean colonies alone accounted for more than seven million.

Nevertheless, when England and the United States abolished slave trading in Africa in 1807, it was much to the disappointment of the West African *alaafin,* kings and chieftains who thrived on their harvest of flesh.

The first federal law prohibiting the importation of slaves from outside the United States came into effect in 1808, nine years before Mississippi became a state. While slave-smugglers continued to operate downriver in New Orleans, Mississippi's involvement in the foreign-slave trade was slight, and most of her slaves came from other states, either through direct purchase, professional traders, or the migration of their owners.

By 1840, there were more slaves than white folk in Mississippi. Yet less than ten percent of those white folk were slaveholders, and Choctaw County was among the Mississippi regions where slavery was rare. What few slaves there were in Choctaw County were found on the small farms of the settlers.

The Martin Liston homestead was one of those farms, valued at a meager $290 in 1850, the year that Choctaw chief Greenwood Leflore's real estate was valued at $80,000.

A proper surname was a nicety that few slaves knew, and upon Emancipation, it was the common practice for freed slaves to adopt the family name of their former owners. Thus, the few slaves that had worked the Liston homestead came themselves to bear the name Liston after the Thirteenth Amendment was ratified in December 1865.

Alexander Liston was born into slavery on the farm of Martin Liston in October 1840. Fannie, his wife, was born into slavery in March 1838. They dated their marriage to 1866, the first year of their freedom, although by then they had four children: Ned, Rachel, Joseph, and Frank, all of them born into slavery on the Liston farm.

Although courthouse fires in 1874 and 1881 destroyed most of the old records of Choctaw County, Montgomery County land records of 1884 show that Robert C. Liston laid hold of almost forty acres in Poplar Creek in the fall of that year. United States Homestead Certificate Number 10768 shows that Alexander Liston laid hold of a little over 160 acres of land neighboring that of his former master's son in the fall of 1896.

White Liston, black Liston: they remained together, in a once nameless place of pine and cotton that became Beat 5, Poplar Creek, Montgomery County, Mississippi.

By the end of the century, Fannie Liston had given birth to nine children, six of whom survived. Among the survivors was Sonny Liston's father, Tobe, born in January 1870.

In 1889, Tobe Liston married a woman named Leona, also known as Cora, who in the span of the next twenty years bore him thirteen children, seven of whom survived: Ernest, Bessie, Latt, William K., James, Helen, and Cleona.

•

Ned and Mary Baskin were born into slavery on the nearby Liston farm. Both of them were sixteen when they had their first child, Willis, in 1858. A daughter, Martha, was born in 1860.

Martha Baskin got pregnant by a man named Joe McAlpin. The child, a daughter named Helen, who became Sonny Liston's mother, was born in 1897. Another child by Joe, a second daughter, named Ida, was born in 1900.

Joe up and left when the girls were very young. Martha later married Charles Berry, a farmer from North Carolina who was eighteen years her senior and by whom she had a third child, again a daughter, named Lesla, born in 1917.

Jessie Hemphill Golden, one of the elder sisters of the local black community, laughed fondly when recalling Charlie Berry, who she said was known, for reasons that were not known, as Spodge. "He was a tall, ugly man with a round, hard head." She told of a storekeeper in Kilmichael who kept two big, heavy-staved barrels outside his shop. One of these big barrels was empty; the other was full of flour. If you could knock over the empty barrel by butting your head into it, you got the full barrel for free. Charlie Berry, with that round, hard head of his, brought home a lot of flour that way. And once, on a bet, a man took a two-by-four to the crown of that head.

Martha's eldest daughter, Helen, grew up wanting nothing to do with the curse of these men's names, neither the father that had abandoned her nor the stepfather with the round, hard head. She chose to be known by her mother's maiden name and called herself Helen Baskin.

•

As they had taken the names of their masters, so their religion as well. The forgotten gods and spirits of Africa were a vague and underlying ancestral presence in the palimpsest Christianity that slaves had created from the church-stuff religion of their Baptist and Methodist masters. Most of those masters never knew that the word "religion" was not to be found in any bible or that the pagan Latin word *religio,* whence it came, denoted the supernatural powers of magic and of sacred place, concepts much closer to the purer spiritualities of Africa than to the debased and pious spirituality denoted by "religion" among America's settlers.

Though great Shango was forgotten, the power of his thunder lingered. It reverberated in the blood when the Mississippi sky broke open with a blast and a serpent of lightning; and it reverberated in the Word. The risen Christ was mighty *vodu,* and in His cross there was more of meaning, more of *religio,* than any bible-toting bossman ever knew.

Bethel Methodist Church, founded by Martin Liston and other settlers, was out on Bethel Road. From its earliest years, in the 1840s, a section of the church was reserved for slaves. Nearby on Bethel Road was a black Baptist church called Pinkney Grove, founded after the Civil War; and east of Poplar Creek there was another black church, called Shiloh Missionary Baptist. Amid the graves marked only by rocks in the little Shiloh cemetery, several headstones, including that of the pastor, the Reverend S.H. Winfrey (1866–1963), bear Masonic symbols.

It was at the Shiloh church in 1914 that Helen Baskin met a man named Colonel Ward, the son of a Poplar Creek farmer named Gerard Ward. As her own father had done her mother, Ward got Helen pregnant and then up and left. The child born to her, on August 6, 1915, was given the name Ezra Baskin Ward.

I found Ezra Baskin Ward, age eighty-three, living with his

wife Mattie at a nursing home in Arkansas. Of all the children Helen had, he, the first-born, was now the sole survivor. Nobody called him Ezra anymore. For most of his eighty-three years, he had been known as E.B. or as Ward. That is what his wife called him: Ward.

Whatever happened to that father who ran off on him and Helen?

"I think he got poisoned by a lady," he said. It was while Ward was still a baby, barely two years old.

Children born out of wedlock were common, and Ward made no pretense that his mother and father might ever have been married. Things were different in those days, Mattie said. As *she* saw it, propriety overtook licentiousness, not the other way around. "I didn't know but one girl that got pregnant until they was married. Go to church, keep that dress *down*."

It was soon after Ward's birth that Helen Baskin became the second wife of Tobe Liston. Her mother, Martha, advised her against it, telling her that she should stay free and single and not marry this man. Helen did not listen.

IN THE OLD DAYS, THERE HAD BEEN NO BOLL WEEVIL in Mississippi. The ugly little long-snouted creature and its fat white maggot larvae, first found in Central America, were unknown. But they had put an end to cotton farming in Mexico, and in the early 1890s had spread across the Rio Grande to Brownsville, Texas, and thence outward, wherever cotton was grown, at a rate of about seventy miles a year. The boll-weevil infestation brought blight to Mississippi cotton farming in 1916, the year in which the demagogue Theodore G. Bilbo became governor of Mississippi.

Tobe Liston heard that a better crop could be made farther north, on the other side of the Delta; and so it was that he and Helen moved northwest across the Mississippi River into Arkansas, taking with them a rag-tag load of Tobe's children, siblings, and his seventy-six-year-old father, Alexander. Tobe's mother, seventy-eight-year-old Fannie, moved to Arkansas as well, but lived apart from her husband, with the family of her daughter Maggie.

Both Helen and her mother, Martha Berry, agreed that Helen's baby boy, Ezra Baskin Ward, should stay behind with Martha rather than risk mistreatment by a stepfather in a strange land. Besides, Martha said, she "didn't have no boy," and she was "gonna keep this boy and raise him up right." And she did.

"She was crazy about him. He was almost spoiled. But she whup him, though, take him to church," said E.B. Ward's wife, Mattie. "He loved her, he really cared for her."

Ward remembered the little church, Pinkney Grove, and, across the rutted road, its small patch of a cemetery where his and Sonny's grandmother, Martha Berry, now lies buried in an unmarked grave, close to the unmarked grave of Ward's first "wife," the mother of the bluesman B.B. King.

As for Martha's husband, Charles Berry, "All I know is he's just a man," Ward said. "A man who come in up there in Kilmichael who married my grandmother."

The first child that Helen bore to Tobe Liston up in Arkansas was a daughter, Clara, born in the summer of 1919. She would not survive, but others did: the daughter Clytee, then Leo and Shorty, who was also known as J.T. After them came Annie, Alcora, Curtis, and, last-born, Wesley, who would be remembered always as the baby.

And, somewhere among them in that brood, the son named Charles L. Liston.

Charles Liston, after the world came to know him as Sonny, would often say that he was born in Pine Bluff, Arkansas. He would also say that he was born in Little Rock; and on one legal document he would state his place of birth as Memphis, Tennessee.

His mother would say that her son claimed Pine Bluff as his birthplace because "his manager told him to give a big town," and Pine Bluff was bigger than Forrest City, where, according to her, he was in fact brought into this world. "He was never in Pine

Bluff," she would say, "and I never been there either." But the "big town" of Pine Bluff lies about sixty miles from Forrest City, no closer than the state capital of Little Rock, and is but thirty-four miles west across the Mississippi River from Memphis. Today Pine Bluff is the shadow of a town. One of the military's eight chemical dumping grounds on the mainland, the Pine Bluff Arsenal, eight miles long and three miles wide, is the storehouse of over 10 percent of America's stockpile of chemical weapons, and since 1963 has cast an ever darker pall of desolation over this forsaken town on the Arkansas River. Like Forrest City, like Poplar Creek — population 350 in 1960, current population reckoned at fewer than a hundred of the sparse twelve thousand or so who now inhabit Montgomery County — the places where Sonny Liston's past existed, and the places where he claimed it to have existed, when he owned to any past at all, are places of ghosts.

More than anything else, that is what this is, I now feel: a ghost story, a haunting unto itself. A whisper through the savanna, a whisper through the pines, a whisper unto itself through the dark of the blood.

Forrest City, the county seat of St. Francis County, Arkansas, lay on the western slope of Crowley's Ridge, between the L'Anguille and St. Francis rivers: a town of a few thousand souls that had risen from a working camp of the Memphis & Little Rock Railroad in 1867. It was named for the Confederate general Nathan Bedford Forrest, a former Tennessee slave trader who served after the war as the first leader of the original Ku Klux Klan, an organization which, in 1869, he tried to disband in disdain of its increasing violence.

During the Civil War, Cross County, to the north, had been formed in part from the older county of St. Francis and named for the Confederate colonel David C. Cross, who was the largest landowner in the area. Its county seat, Wynne, also located, like Forrest City, on the western slope of Crowley's Ridge, grew from the wreckage of a train derailment in 1882: a box car, overturned and without wheels, was set upright and named Wynne Station, in honor of yet another Confederate veteran, the Forrest City banker Jesse W. Wynne.

The cotton plantation of George Morledge straddled both counties, encompassing some twenty-five hundred acres. The Morledge house — it was called different things: the Big House, Headquarters, the Main House — was located near Wynne, in Cross County. It was there that George Morledge lived with his wife, Mary. Nearby were a barn, cotton gin, and commissary.

It was in the sector of Morledge Plantation that lay in Johnson Township, St. Francis County, that Tobe Liston and his family came to live and farm, on a low patch where a rill of muddy water, a mile and a half or so long, dribbled dead to its end in a slough of sandy dirt where nothing could grow. The place had a name, but it was not to be found on any map. They called it Sand Slough.

It was there, in Sand Slough, on the Morledge plantation — not in Forrest City, not in Pine Bluff, not in Memphis — that Charles L. Liston was born, on the fifty acres that Tobe rented from the Man.

Helen remembered the house where Sonny was born: a cypress-board shack. "It had no ceiling. I had to put cardboard on the walls to keep the wind out." He was given the name Charles L. not by her or by his father, but by the "old woman who delivered him." If the "L." stood for anything, the old woman never told, or if she did, no one recalled.

"I noticed his big hands when the mid-lady brought him to me," Helen said.

As to Charles L. Liston's date of birth, at least half a dozen have been set forth. Liston himself, who in 1950 gave his age as twenty-two, and in 1953 gave it as twenty-one, finally settled on May 8, 1932, saying that anybody who doubted it "is callin' my mama a liar." Testifying before the Senate in 1960, he said, "I was born in 1933."

After Liston had settled on May 8, 1932, his mother settled on January 8, 1932. This date, she said, had been duly recorded in an old family Bible, but the Bible, she added, had been lost somewhere along the way. At times, she gave the date as January 18. "I know he was born in January," she said. "It was cold in January." While corroborating the year of birth her son had come to claim, she seems to have once inadvertently recalled the year as 1929, then 1930, before correcting herself to confirm Sonny's chosen year of 1932. He was, Helen said, the ninth of ten children she bore to Tobe. This places his birth between that of Curtis, who may have been born in the summer of 1929, and that of Wesley, "the baby." Annie and Alcora, who came before Curtis, are believed to have been born in the summer of 1925 and the fall of 1927, respectively. One of Liston's closest friends, the boxer Foneda Cox, who was born November 2, 1929, felt that Sonny was older than he, but not by much.

Ultimately, the precise truth may never be known, since there was no record filed at the time of birth. (It was not until 1947 that Arkansas mandated the filing of birth certificates, and then only for hospital births; and it was not until 1965 that the state enacted mandatory filing for every birth.) The only record is one filed, for legal reasons, in 1953, when Sonny put forth the date of May 8, 1932. He was almost certainly older than that, and he knew it, but it is doubtful that even he knew by how many years he was lying. Where May 8 came from is anybody's guess. As to Helen's date of January 8, it is interesting that of the two Liston siblings whose births were officially recorded, one of them, Sonny's brother Curtis, was registered as having been born on January 8, 1928. Though Sonny and his mother disagreed on the number of children she bore — Helen remembered eleven, including her first-born, Sonny's half-brother E.B. Ward, while Sonny said "my mother had either twelve or thirteen children" — they both agreed that Curtis was older and that only "Wesley, the baby," was younger than Sonny. As United States Census records are not accessible until seventy-five years after the year of census, the stated age of the boy named Charles Liston in 1930 or 1940 must wait until 2005 or 2015 to be revealed.

Conceived and born under stars no one remembered, Sonny himself never knew how old he was, only that he was most likely older than he claimed. According to ancient astrology, the day of one's death could be foretold only when the astronomy of one's first breath was known.

Sidonius Apollinaris, a bishop in fifth-century Gaul, told of a friend, an orator called Lampridius, whose death by violence was presaged to him by African astrologers, down to the year, month, and very day, on which it came to pass that Lampridius was murdered by his slaves.

"I know he was born in January," Helen Liston said. "It was cold in January." It was in January, too, that life was known to have left him: the starless astrology of the soul of a man that "died the day he was born." January, the month of Janus, who beheld beginning and end at once.

The plantation owner George Morledge quit farming in 1955 and died, age eighty, in the spring of 1966. His wife, Mary, passed on, age eighty-three, in the spring of 1975. Their son, George, Jr., born in the summer of 1923 and today the lord of the land that was his father's, is the only one from the plantation who remembers the Listons.

The elder George Morledge was known as the Man, or the

Captain. His son, from about the age of ten or twelve, was known as the Little Captain. Big George and Little George, they called them, too.

There were perhaps fifty to sixty families, roughly two hundred people, black and white, working the Morledge land. The humblest of them were the day hands, who labored in the fields for thirty-five or fifty cents, later seventy-five cents, a day. Then there were the tenant farmers and the sharecroppers.

The Listons were tenant farmers, not sharecroppers. The difference was in the breakdown of pay and expenses. Sharecroppers worked the land with seed, fertilizer, beasts of burden, and equipment furnished by the farm operator, and when the crop was sold, they got fifty percent. Tenant farmers rented their acres, either with cash or a promised portion of the crop to come. They furnished three-quarters of their farming expenses; the owner furnished the rest. When the crop was sold, the tenant farmer got three-quarters of the money, the owner got the rest. Throughout the year, sharecroppers and tenants ran accounts at the commissary — "the farm was seventeen miles from town," Morledge said. "It took a wagon all day long to go to town and come back" — and if the crop brought enough money, the commissary accounts were settled. Not everybody settled. "They might be there for ten years, move off in the middle of the night and owe you three or four hundred dollars," Little George recalled.

And ten years was nothing. There was one family of five generations that made the Morledge farm its home. "So it wasn't too bad," George said, "or they wouldn't have stayed." In fact, he said, it was all "like family." The Big House was left unlocked. If anyone, black or white, got sick, the Morledges would fetch a doctor, and if the stricken family couldn't make good on the bill when the crop came in, "we'd take care of it." If anyone got thrown in jail, behind too much liquor or for whatever else, the Morledges would bail him out.

There was a little church for white folk, Morledge Church, in the northwestern part of the plantation. There was a little Baptist church for black folk, known as New Sardis, on the bank of a lake in the southwestern part, and, a few miles down the dirt road, there was a second, Methodist church for black folk that was known as Jones Chapel or simply the Sand Slough church. New Sardis and the Sand Slough church each held services twice a month, on alternating weeks. So it was that many of the black families on Morledge were Baptist one week, Methodist the next; and so it was that while Helen Liston held that Sonny had taken religion in the Methodist church, his half-brother E.B. Ward held that Sonny had been raised a Baptist. However he had been raised, on the one known occasion when he professed himself to be of any religious denomination at all, Sonny professed himself to be a Baptist.

The churches were churches only on Sundays. The rest of the time, they were one-room schools that housed classes from the first to ninth grades.

"If their mother and father wanted to send them to school, they sent them to school," Morledge said. "If they didn't want to send them to school, they didn't." One way or the other, there was no school during the cotton-chopping months of June and July or during cotton-picking time, which could stretch from September to March, depending on the weather.

The black preachers were Morledge Plantation laborers during the rest of the week. "We did not enter into there. That was theirs," Morledge said of the little church on the lake. But often, when a black sharecropper or tenant farmer died, George, like his daddy before him, was asked to come down to say a few words in eulogy. George was asked as well to attend "many a baptism" in the lake. "They take 'em down there," he said, "and they all dress in white, and they back up out of the water." He remembered it as "one of the greatest social events of the year" for the black church folk of Morledge Plantation.

George Morledge, Jr., said that he could not recall the Listons all that well, no more than he remembered any other family that worked the land. By the time in his youth that he had become the plantation's Little Captain, Tobe Liston and his kin had been there for the better part of twenty years.

Tobe, he said, "was a little fella," maybe a hundred and forty or a hundred and fifty pounds, maybe five-feet-six or five-feet-seven. Helen, he said, was big, two hundred and thirty-five pounds or thereabouts, and maybe five-feet-ten. Everybody called her Big Hela, pronounced *Heelah*.

"Her name may have been Helen," Morledge said, "but the niggers on the place called her Hela."

"They had I don't remember how many children," he said of Tobe and Big Hela. "They had several inside, several outside."

Several inside, several outside. "Well, the terminology in the southern plantation days was, if the children were not of the mother and father, then they were outside, and if they were, they were inside children. That's terminology. Y'all wouldn't understand that, but that's what it was."

Inside, outside. "I don't think she ever saw anybody that wasn't a friend," Morledge said, laughing. "You are not in with the black community whatsoever, the dark ones, are you? They were very" — he seemed to search for a word that did not come. "As I said, she never saw anybody that wasn't her friend."

The boy who came to be known as Sonny was close to none of his kin. They were accidents of the blood, like himself, without known age or meaning or even the senseless animal bond of kindred familiarity. From savanna and pines to the rut of a destiny in a slough of sandy dirt where nothing could grow, neither cotton nor love nor hope, that whisper in the dark of his blood told him not that he had come from anywhere or anything, and not that he was or could ever be anything, but, simply and fatally, that he was alone and doomed so to be.

Later in life, he would be unable, or unwilling, to name more than a few of his brothers and sisters. In 1962 and 1963, before and after Sonny became the heavyweight champion of the world, the Little Rock reporter R.B. Mayfield was paid by *Newsweek* magazine to file several reports on Liston's background in Arkansas. When Mayfield interviewed Helen Liston for one of these unpublished background reports, she told him that Sonny knew only "two or three" of his half-siblings, and of the six surviving children she had while living on the Morledge farm, Sonny had always been the loner.

Clytee died in the forties.

Leo was shot to death by another man in Michigan some years after leaving Arkansas.

J.T. Liston — Shorty — remained on the plantation after the rest of his kin were gone; then he himself moved on, his whereabouts unknown.

Annie Liston lived in Gary, Indiana, as did Curtis Liston.

Wesley was a farmer near Cherry Valley, Arkansas, near the plantation where Sonny and he and the rest of them were born.

"He never talked much," Helen said of Sonny, "and still don't." He was "big and strong" as a boy, and he kept to himself.

In Arkansas, countless bodies of water left by the shifting courses of rivers and streams bore the name of Horseshoe Lake. The Liston shack in Sand Slough was situated near one such Horseshoe Lake, and Charles "loved to swim, and to ride his mule named Ada."

George Morledge, Jr., had no idea of when Sonny was born. It may have been around the time the old Big House burned down, back in 1929 or 1930 or so. The Captain rebuilt it, and it burnt down again many years later, after Morledge Plantation had come to be known as the St. Francis River Plantation.

He recalled the adolescent Charles Liston as "big, overgrown, never too bright, and pretty much of a loner."

That is what he told the reporter from Little Rock many years ago. I wanted to know more.

"You want a truthful impression?"

Yeah.

"He was just a little nigger kid. That's the way it was in those days. Just another little darky."

The grandson Martha had raised, Helen's first-born child, E.B. Ward, was known in Poplar Creek as something of a blues singer and guitar-player. He had taken up, as man and wife, with Nora Ellen King, the mother of another, younger blues singer, who would come to be known as B.B. King. Nora Ellen had died in 1935, when E.B. was twenty.

Ward made a living as a farm worker: "'Workin' for wages,' you called it," as one old-timer said. "They gave you a place to live, three meals a day, and a salary."

Mattie Mae Ratliss, who was about two years older than Ward, had been married to a man named Walter Flowers, by whom she had six daughters and a son. They lived off in the hills, a few miles from Poplar Creek, across the Choctaw County line, in French Camp.

"It was a real poor place," Mattie said. "There was a white lady, she was real sweet, lived next door to us," who gave Mattie food and brought good water for her children. The white lady, Dorris Collins, told Mattie: "You're gettin' too skinny. You got to go to your people." But Mattie's mother and father were dead. Her husband, Walter, said that the white lady was right. He told her to take the daughters but leave him the son. Mattie went to her Auntie Sophie Robertson, whose family was making a good crop in Sumner, up in Tallahatchie County.

Ward at that time was working for wages right down the road from Sumner, on a farm in Webb. He and Mattie met in Sumner and were married at the courthouse in Webb on the first day of 1941.

Ward had been brought together with his and Sonny's mother, Helen Liston, at the funeral of his grandmother, Martha, in Poplar Creek in 1940. Not long after that, Ward and Mattie and Mattie's six daughters moved to a shack not far from the Listons on the Morledge plantation in Arkansas. They had two children on the plantation: Ezra, born in 1941, who survived little more than two months, and Ezraline, born in the spring of 1943.

In 1944, they moved to a plantation that was co-owned and run by a white man named Riley McCorkle, south of Parkin, about fifteen miles west of Wynne, on the St. Francis River. Unlike Tobe Liston, who rented land at Morledge, Ward sharecropped — "workin' on halves," he called it. "If you had ten bales of cotton, the white man got five."

Lone, brooding Charles Liston was, as certain funny-looking and funny-talking white folk of the day had lately come to say, a problem child. Looking back more than half a century, Ward remembered Big George Morledge as a "real nice" man. But things were different for kids in those days. "You stayed in your place," Ward laughed. "If you didn't, Mr. Morledge gonna whup you, and when you get home, your daddy gonna whup you again."

Helen said, in 1962, that Sonny as a child "was a good, obedient boy" who "never gave me any trouble, never." In 1963, she saw the past differently. Young Charles was, in his quiet, lonesome way, "always a rough boy," she said. "He like the rough side of life." He took to mean and sinful ways, fell in with the wrong crew — "running around with bad boys," as Ward said.

According to Mattie Ward, Big Hela "didn't know but to go to church and chop cotton, that's all I knowed of." She could not set her son aright. She tired of seeing him whipped, and she tired, too, of a growing hatred between father and son, or, as it sometimes seemed, between son and all the flesh of this world. For his part, Tobe would just as soon be quit of him. Sonny was sent to live with his older half-brother, Ward, in Parkin. Ward remembered the year to be 1945 or 1946 and reckoned that Charles was about sixteen years old at the time. Ward was around thirty. The boy stayed with Ward and Mattie for about a year.

"He was all to hisself," Ward said. "You know, he was off in hisself."

There was no radio or phonograph in the Ward home. As Mattie put it, "We would do good just to have a piece of bread." But Ward still sang and played the blues. Those blues and the fierce, lovely hymns of church were all of music that Charles Liston knew.

"Sonny liked blues music," remembered Ward.

He and Mattie took Charles to church regularly, and, according to Ward, "He got better when he was around me."

Mattie remembered a letter she got a few years later. "When he went down to the penitentiary, he sat down and wrote me a letter." It was likely the first of the letters that Sonny, throughout his life, would "write" through another's hand. She recalled the gist of it: *"Miss Mattie, you sure was nice to me. When I get out of here, I'm gonna make you proud of me. I'm gonna make you proud of me. You just watch and see. I'm gonna make you proud of me. I'm gonna be good from now on till I die."*

"And then he went to boxing," she said, and that did indeed make her proud. "It did. It sure did."

George Morledge, Jr., left home for the service during World War II. He ended his duty stationed in occupied Germany because of his fluency in German, and he did not return to the plantation until 1946. When he returned, the Listons were gone, save for one of the sons, Shorty. "He was a brother, or a half-brother, or maybe a fourth-brother. I don't know. He had the name Liston, and I couldn't tell you whether he was inside or outside."

Shorty Liston, the remaining Liston — "that crazy Liston boy" — worked for George, Jr., as a tractor driver. "He was nutty as a fruitcake, but he could drive a tractor."

"That was the last of the family. All the rest of them were gone."

Bringing her son Curtis with her to the McCorkle farm, Helen Liston had joined Charles and Ward and Mattie and their children, little Ezraline and newborn Clint, and Mattie's daughters by her first husband. Helen made one crop there with her sons and daughter-in-law. By then, Tobe Liston was over seventy-five years of age, and in time would be trucked off to the Forrest City hospital where he would breathe his last.

"He taken sick," was all Ward said. "Taken sick and then died." It was all that needed to be said.

Except for his big brother Shorty, who stayed behind on the plantation where he was born, and his daddy, Tobe, who lay beneath the dirt in Forrest City, Charles's kin had dispersed and gone the way of four winds, many of them joining him to live with the Ward family before moving on.

"I really can't place nobody but Wesley and Uncle Sonny, I guess, because he turned famous. But all them other people, I just can't place them," said Ezraline, who was little more than a child at the time. "I don't know if it's because I got beat upside the head or what, but I can't place those people" from the days "out there in the country."

His sister Alcora Liston had gone off as a teenager. By the end of the war, she was married to a man named Jones and living some two hundred miles north, across the state line, in the city of St. Louis, Missouri.

At the end of the war, after that last crop at the McCorkle farm, Helen Liston followed her daughter Alcora to St. Louis. As if in phonetic conflation of her plantation name, Big Hela, and her proper Christian name, the 1946 St. Louis city directory lists her as Healon Liston.

In time, Ward quit the cotton fields and moved his family to Forrest City, where he worked as a carpenter. Ezraline remembers that she was sixteen when they left the farm and got their first real house — with a real address, 220 North Beach Street — in a real town. From that first Forrest City house, they moved to another, at 114 Union Street.

By then, Charles L. Liston was a feared and mighty man who was known to the world as Sonny.

Writing in the year before the March on Washington that led to the Civil Rights Act of 1964, the Arkansas reporter R.B. Mayfield, in the first of his unpublished background reports to *Newsweek*, observed, "The average Eastern Arkansas Negro is still virtually a slave, and was even worse off during the depression days."

Charles Liston was a child of those depression days in eastern Arkansas, and the child, too, of a slight, scowling man whose small breath of freedom, cold and cruel as any bossman's, was drawn through the only tyranny that was afforded him, over the only living chattel allowed him, the chattel that his God had given him the power to create from his own soulless seed.

"He who is by nature not his own but another's man, is by nature a slave," said Aristotle. While acknowledging that "others affirm that the rule of a master over slaves is contrary to nature," Aristotle concluded that "some men are by nature free, and others slaves, and that for these latter slavery is both expedient and right."

Aristotle, pillar of Western Judeo-Christian thought, tutor of the conqueror Alexander the Great, lived and spoke in the fourth century before Christ. The society that he knew, like every society that had come before and would come after, was a society of slavery, a universal practice older than history itself: in Mesopotamia, India, China, Egypt, Greece, and Rome; among Jew and Muslim, pagan and Christian alike.

Again: "some men are by nature free, and others slaves, and . . . for these latter slavery is both expedient and right." Note that "right" follows "expedient." This sleight of synapse is the Aristotelean fallacy, the Aristotelean legacy that has shaped, or misshaped, human thought.

Aristotle owned fourteen slaves, and kept a slave woman, Herpyllis, as wife, by whom he had a son, Nicomachus. He saw himself, of course, as one of those deemed by nature free; and he was a great expounder of freedom and democracy, much as, in Martin Liston's day, Thomas Jefferson spoke loftily of liberty and strongly against miscegenation while owning slaves and fathering a son, in 1808, with one of them, Sally Hemings, the slave girl half-sister of his wife, Martha. Of what Aristotle called the "three corresponding perversions — tyranny, oligarchy, and democracy," he judged that "democracy is the most tolerable of the three." But democracy precluded slavery no more than did the other perversions of government. A nation without slavery, a world without slavery, was unimaginable; and in the end the helix of Aristotelean rationalism became lost in a swirl of equivocating subtleties:

"Enough," he declared, ending his treatise on slavery in the first book of the *Politics*, "enough of the distinction between master and slave" — as if throwing up his hands before a suddenly glimpsed truth to which the tide of his logorrhea had delivered him, a truth that was beyond philosophy and logic, greater than philosophy and logic, and therefore unutterable: that there was no distinction by nature of slave and master, that they were by nature the same.

No race, no people has been free from slavery, either as slave or as master. Every race and every people ever enslaved became at every opportunity enslavers themselves: Greek enslaved by Greek in the time of Aristotle, black enslaved by black since time immemorial in Africa and in the nineteenth-century American South. Slavery was never predicated on race except as circumstance rendered it. Many of the vast number of slaves of ancient Rome were fair-haired, fair-skinned Germans and Anglo-Saxons.

The universal truth of slavery, that it has been throughout history one of the defining manifestations of human nature, has been suppressed both by that history and by that nature. The enduring myth that slavery was imposed upon Africa by outside forces, that it was introduced by the Portuguese in 1444, is belied by the fact that slavery and the slave trade were ancient and commonplace within Africa long before the arrival of any white slaver. (The trans-Sahara slave-trade route between West and North Africa likely had its beginnings as early as 1000 B.C., hundreds of years before the Ethiopians, long enslaved by Egypt, conquered and gave to Egypt its Twenty-Fifth Dynasty; hundreds of years before Homer wrote in the *Iliad* that half of the soul of a man was lost when "the day of slavery" came upon him.)

"Slavery was widespread in Africa," writes Professor John Thornton in *Africa and Africans in the Making of the Atlantic World, 1400–1800*, "because slaves were the only form of private, revenue-producing property recognized in African law." To the *odehye* — free-born — elite of West Africa, the outside forces of Europe, England, and the Americas imposed no evil, but merely presented a new market, increased demand, and lucrative new export opportunities that the indigenous powers welcomed and readily exploited.

We bewail our past as slaves — experienced or ancestral, real or fancied — but never commemorate our enslavement of others. Only circumstance separates slave from master; and for much of history, freedom and the will to enslave have been one. The oppressed in the blessing of their deliverance will become the oppressors.

"The ox" — Aristotle again — "is the poor man's slave."

Sonny Liston knew nothing of Aristotle. But he knew more about slavery than Aristotle said or did not say. And that was because he knew Tobe Liston.

To Tobe Liston, who was born four years to the month after the Thirteenth Amendment abolished slavery, the passel of children he bred were younglings of burden. If they were big enough to go to the dinner table, Helen remembered him saying of his children, they were big enough to go to the fields.

She recalled the one-room plantation schoolhouses, and said that Charles "went a little bit, whenever his daddy would let him." But he never learned to read or write, and by the time Charles was eight, Tobe had him laboring full-time.

"He wasn't a mean man," recalled E.B. Ward of his stepfather, Tobe. But he had known Tobe only in adulthood, and it was to protect Ward from possible abuse by Tobe that Helen had left him behind with his grandmother all those years before. In further conversation, he said that, yes, Tobe was mean to Sonny, and the two of them, father and son, did not get along.

It is impossible to tell how big the figure of small, slight, slaving Tobe Liston loomed in the solitary estrangement and taciturn brooding of his son. What little the son knew of his past he would leave behind him in the Arkansas dirt, where it belonged. But in that greater part of the soul that had nothing to do with knowing or leaving behind, he would never be shut of that past, as he would never be shut of masters or slavers or those who, like his father, gave life and cast a curse upon it at once.

"The only thing my old man ever gave me," Sonny would say, "was a beating."

He never said more than that, and he never said elsewise. In fact, that was about all he would ever say of his childhood. And, just as those copper-colored welts the coroner discerned years later were the scars of something more palpable than any figurative or virtual slavery, so these few grim words evinced wounds that deepened unseen beneath those other, mere welts: wounds that left him not so much the brute beast that the world at large perceived him to be, but a man as hurtful as he was hurt, as deadly as he was deadened, and whose soul beneath the layers of its scar tissue was to others hidden and unknowable, to himself a dark and dangerous place rarely to be visited and never to be delved.

UNKNOWN NEGRO #1

ARRIVING IN ST. LOUIS IN 1946, HELEN LISTON found a job at a shoe factory and a place to room, at 1017 O'Fallon Street, in the black part of town near the waterfront of the Mississippi. In time, her son Charles fled as well, seeking her.

"One morning," he said, "I got up early and thrashed the pecans off my brother-in-law's tree and carried the nuts to town and sold them. That gave me enough money to buy a train ticket to St. Louis. I figured the city would be like the country, and all I had to do was to ask somebody where my mother lived and they'd tell me she lived down the road a piece. But when I got to the city, there were too doggone many people there, and I just wandered around lost. But one morning, I told my story to a wino, and he says I favor this lady that lives down the street. He took me over to the house."

In a variation of the tale of the pecans, young Sonny arrived in downtown St. Louis in the dead of night. Some cops found him, lost and wandering. They took him to an all-night cafe. Someone there knew where his mother lived, on O'Fallon, and the cops took him there.

"I say, 'Sonny, why you come here?' And he say, 'Mama, I got tired of that cotton patch.'"

That is the way she would tell it. But by some accounts, nobody, including her, called or knew him as Sonny back then. That name did not come until later, after other cops delivered him to another place.

There were stories later that Charles tried to go to school in St. Louis, but that the kids in the elementary class shamed him, laughed at him, because he was so much bigger than them, like a grown man from the backwoods set among them to learn to read and write. And his mother claimed that he held jobs, at a poultry-packing plant, at an ice-house. But the earliest documentary evidence of the existence of Charles Liston shows no sign of school, no sign of dead chickens.

By the early winter of 1949, Liston had fallen in with another, younger Arkansas native, Willie Jordan, who lived on North Tenth Street, not far from the two-room place where Liston and his mother then lived, at 1006 O'Fallon Street. There was a third man, whom they knew only as James, who then joined up with them. The three of them hung out at a tavern, a cheap beer and ribs joint, down the street from the home of Charles's mama.

The St. Louis police first became aware of them on December 30, 1949, the Friday night after Christmas, when a young clerk, Anthony Bonmarito, filed a report at the Fourth District police station.

> The victim reported that about 8:45 o'clock this P.M., he was walking west on Biddle street and when on the southwest corner of 8th and Biddle streets 3 negroes who are described on the reverse of this report came up behind him and pulled him into the vacant lot on the southwest corner of 8th and Biddle streets and took from his person his brown leather billfold which was in his left hip trouser pocket and which contained about $45.00 in various denominations of currency, personal papers and 1 Yale lock

key, after which time they ran north on 8th street making their escape.

The Description of Persons Wanted, on the second page of Complaint Number 94710, lists the strong-arm offenders as #1 Negro, #2 Negro, #3 Negro, the latter two reduced to ditto marks beneath the first.

Biddle Street lay one block south of O'Fallon, in the Mississippi waterfront area where the downtown black and Italian neighborhoods merged. The lot where Bonmarito was robbed was at the corner of North Eighth Street. Three nights later, at about a quarter past five on the evening of January 2, 1950, Anthony Tocco, a fifty-nine-year-old Italian immigrant who lived on Biddle Street, had just closed his vegetable store on North Seventh Street and was walking north on the west side of Seventh when "three negro men" emerged from an alley between Cole and Carr on Seventh Street.

They "threw dirt in his face, and then beat him and dragged him into the alley where they knocked him down and kicked him, and one of the men took from his right side trousers pocket $9.00 consisting of nine one dollar bills, and they ran west in the alley towards 8th Street, making their escape. Tocco refused medical attention when offered."

In the space designated Means of Attack on the offense report, Complaint Number 346, Girard G. Dorsey, the Fourth District captain in command, typed: "Dirt — Fist — Feet."

The Description of Persons Wanted, on the second page of Complaint Number 346, describes the strong-arm offenders simply as "Three Negro Men."

At about ten past seven on the Friday night of January 13, an eighteen-year-old white dockhand named William James was approached by "three negroes" while walking near his home on North Eighth Street.

"The #1 Negro struck him in the mouth knocking him to the street," whereupon "all three negroes held him down" and robbed him. James pursued his attackers as they ran north on the west side of Eighth Street, then west on Mullanphy to Tenth Street, then south on Tenth, into an alley, where James lost sight of them.

The take: six dollars in folding money, a buck-fifty in change. Description of Persons Wanted: #1 Unknown Negro, #2 Unknown Negro, #3 Unknown Negro, the latter two once again reduced to ditto marks beneath the first.

Later that night, at the tavern on O'Fallon, the "#1 Negro," Charles Liston, was drinking with his cohorts and another neighborhood character, thirty-five-year-old Sterling Belt, originally of Louisiana. Belt had a second-hand 1948 Mercury sedan that he had bought for $1,395 from the Goldstein used car lot less than eight weeks before. Willie Jordan suggested that they could take down some easy money by robbing the night attendant at the Wedge Filling Station nearby at O'Fallon and Broadway, and Belt agreed to be the driver in his fine new second-hand sedan.

Belt drove to Broadway and Biddle, parking the car on the east side of Broadway, about twenty feet north of Biddle. It was going on midnight. Liston, Jordan, and James walked to the next corner, O'Fallon and Broadway, and went round back of the gas station. They looked through the rear window and saw that the attendant, Frank Moran, was alone. A drunken soldier in uniform walked haplessly their way. Liston took him by the neck from behind with a right-arm stranglehold and curved him backward like a sapling. Jordan went through the soldier's pockets. He found one nickel, which he kept; and they sent him on his way.

Liston, Jordan, and James went round front, entered the station, went to the toilet, then left. They returned minutes later, and Jordan asked the attendant to sell him a quart can of gasoline. When the attendant stepped toward the door to get the gas, Liston took him from behind as he had taken the soldier boy. James went through the attendant's coverall pockets, and Jordan removed the metal money changer from his belt. Liston let him loose, and Jordan told him he had best not call the cops. The three men ran down Broadway to the waiting Mercury, and Belt drove back to the tavern at Ninth and O'Fallon, where they divided the money: about ten bucks each for Liston, Jordan, and James; three bucks for Belt. Liston bought a bottle of whiskey, and they drove across the river to East St. Louis, Illinois, in the early-morning blackness.

Late the following night, Saturday, January 14, Liston met Jordan and Belt again at the bar on O'Fallon. Sterling not only had his fine sedan with him this night, he also had with him a fine Hopkins and Allen .32 caliber break-top revolver. Jordan suggested they take a ride and look for — the phrase is from the report of Jordan's subsequent interrogation by the police — "a likable place of business to hold up." Driving west on Market Street, they came upon a joint, at 1502 Market, called the Unique Cafe. Inside there was a lone counterman, whose name was Leroy Andrew Nelson. Belt parked nearby, at the corner of Fifteenth and Market. He took the gun out from under the front seat, gave it to Liston, told him he could use it. Liston took the gun from him and shoved it in his pocket. Again, Belt stayed in the car. Liston and Jordan entered the diner. Liston pulled out the gun, but Jordan grabbed it from him, stuck it toward the counterman, and announced, "This is a holdup." Liston took what there was to take from the cash register, and they ran out the door to the car. They came away with twenty-three dollars in paper money, fourteen in coins. This time, Belt's cut would be doubled to six bucks.

The night, motherfucker, was theirs. They drove north, came upon a filling station at Easton and Prairie avenues. There was only one attendant, a black man named Wilson Miller. Liston held the gun, then handed it to Jordan and cleaned out the register.

Two joints in under twenty minutes. They returned to the tavern at 901 O'Fallon, and recommenced drinking and divvying the take.

In the Saturday night cigarette smokehouse neon dark of that dive, Charles Liston, who neither knew his age nor felt any ties of blood upon this earth nor saw any future beyond the drink in front of him and the smoky dark spare refuge of this barroom from the bone-cutting, river-heavy dank and freezing chill, knew only that he was nobody and that he had come from nowhere and that he was nowhere. He did not see that one could be nobody with a capital "N." It was the name that Odysseus took — Οὖτις, Nobody — when he killed the great Cyclops.

Maybe, for Charles Liston, a big fine car like Belt's, a big fine gun like Belt's to get it with; a fine silk suit, maybe, and a fine store-bought bitch to wear with that suit — the vista of his future extended that far, maybe. But beyond that, nothing. For the truth, and the young stick-up man Charles Liston knew it, was that Charles Liston was not good for a damned thing in this world except for chopping cotton and robbing people. He could not read, he could not write, he could not do much of anything else that this world demanded in exchange for what it called good, honest pay. It was not to labor, like his mama, on an assembly line that he had fled the dirt roads and cruel poverty and cotton fields of Arkansas. It was not to find here, in some white man's downtown sweatshop factory, the same bitter seed of bare existence that God — Methodist or Baptist or whatever His white ass was — had tossed him in Sand Slough. It was not to find here, amid the fancy paved avenues and asphalt and radio music and electric lights and pretty, white folk parks of this place, another Morledge Big House; not to find here, instead of one hated father, a world of hated fathers. All he had were his body and his wits, that sum of self which in the end is all that anybody has, though few are stripped down to it alone; and his wits failed to perceive that his body — his body, which was bigger and stronger and tougher than any other man's, either in the backwoods and farmlands of Arkansas or the big city of St. Louis; his body, which had allowed the child to haul a man-load of bales and which allowed the man to bend other men backward, like Sand Slough willow switches, with the force of only one arm — could be used for anything else other than hauling or strong-arming. And that was because these things were what he knew and what he could do. He was not a fool. No. But what there was of wisdom in him told him that, between breaking one's back and breaking the backs of others, between being the victim of sinful injustice and being its deliverer, it was better to break than to be broken. Fuck right and wrong, neither of which had been a friend to him; and fuck that honest-pay shit. Let others get it, and he would take it from them. For Charles Liston knew one thing: it was easier to rob folks than it was to chop cotton.

In a hallway near that beer and ribs joint, sheltered from the freezing rain, was twenty-four-year-old Patrolman David Herleth.

"I decided to stake-out down in that area and see if I could catch this sucker," he said many years later of his pursuit of the Unknown Negro.

From where he was, Herleth could see the tavern — a "rib station," he called it; a "beer joint that sold ribs."

"It was a cold January night," he remembered.

"Now here's about four, five, six jobs," Herleth told me, "and the guy" — he was talking about Liston — "wore the same clothes all the time. Dumb street kid. Yellow-and-black-checked shirt. He got the name of the Yellow Shirt Bandit."

(The January 14 police report of the Wedge Filling Station robbery described "#1 Unknown negro" as "wearing black chauffeur cap, yellow shirt & brown trousers." Other, earlier reports gave other descriptions.)

It was going on two o'clock in the morning. "I was about to give up and go to the station and get warm," Herleth said.

> I don't remember whether a car stopped or what, but he come runnin' over from this rib station towards his house. I walked out of the hallway, put a .38 on him, said "Whoa, hold it," all that good stuff, "hands against the wall." Shook him down for a weapon. No weapon, but he had rolls of nickels in the hammer pocket of his overalls. He was wearing bib-type overalls as I remember, and this yellow shirt.

One roll of pennies, one roll of nickels, twenty-four loose nickels, ten dimes, and twelve quarters: seven dollars and seventy cents. That was the exact accounting of what remained of the fruits of the criminal career of the Yellow Shirt Bandit, Charles L. Liston, Unknown Negro Number One.

"So I marched him up to the station" — which was close by, on Carr Street — "with his hands on his head, or behind his head, or what the hell. Walked behind him with my .38 out."

At the Fourth District station, Liston was "booked, placed on the holdover, charged held pending further investigation, suspected of being implicated" in the Wedge Filling Station robbery. Police reports of January 15 and 16 recount the information that Liston gave under questioning after Herleth brought him in. As Herleth said, Liston was "big": "six-something, hands like hams." And yet, within an hour of being brought in, "CHARLES LISTON, colored, 22 years of age, born in Arkansas, Single, a Laborer, residing at 1006 O'Fallon Street," made a detailed confession and ratted out both Jordan and Belt "and a man known as 'JAMES.'"

"I won't go into how they talked to him," Herleth said.

At a quarter past three that Sunday morning, led to him by information got from Liston, Officer Herleth and Sergeant Jesse Miller arrested at his home Sterling Belt, "colored, 35 years of age, born in Louisiana, Married, a Laborer, residing at 1241 North Ninth Street." At the time of his arrest, he had six .38-caliber cartridges in his left trouser pocket.

"Upon questioning" — an ominous phrase in St. Louis law enforcement of this era, as David Herleth's wry implication attested — Belt, within forty-five minutes, corroborated what Liston had said and went further, confessing to the Market Street diner holdup as well. At about four o'clock in the morning, the Market Street counterman, Leroy Andrew Nelson, arrived at the station, "where he viewed Charles Liston and positively identified him as the man who removed the money from the cash register, while his companion held a pistol on him. Liston then related in Nelson's presence how they had planned and enacted the holdup and also identified Nelson as the man he had robbed."

Later, at about half past one that Sunday afternoon, three Fourth District patrolmen arrested Willie Jordan, "colored, 18 years of age, born in Arkansas, Single, a Laborer, residing at 1018 North 10th Street." He was brought to the station, "where he was questioned" and further corroborated the information given by Liston and Belt regarding the Wedge Filling Station and Unique Cafe stickups. Like Belt, he went beyond what had already been established by his previous confessor, giving account of the second filling-station holdup, at Easton and Prairie. By then, the Hopkins and Allen .32-caliber revolver was found at Belt's home and identified by Liston and Jordan as the gun used in the Market Street and Easton Avenue holdups.

At about half past seven that Sunday evening, Frank Morgan of the Wedge Filling Station, Leroy Nelson of the Unique Cafe, and Wilson Miller of the filling station at Easton and Prairie "positively identified Willie Jordan as the man who was in the company of Liston at the time they were robbed." In turn, "Liston and Jordan identified the aforementioned men as being the men that they held up."

Liston, Belt, and Jordan were booked that Sunday night on three counts of robbery, with warrants to be applied for on the following morning.

When morning came, Liston, Jordan, and a third man confessed to the robbery of William James. It is curious that here, and repeatedly hereafter in the Supplementary Report of Monday, January 16, as well as in the Continuation Report of January 17, the third person's name was subsequently blacked out — "redacted," as they say in law enforcement. Sterling Belt had never been implicated in the strong-armings prior to the Wedge Filling Station holdup; no mention had ever been made of a possible fourth assailant; and the same redacted report stated that the third man accompanying Liston and Jordan in the attack on William James was known to Liston only by the name of James, his identity thus presumably still a mystery. It may have been that the police had wanted a third man and found him through "questioning," a man arrested at his home the night before: "██████, Colored, 21 years of age, born in Missouri, Married, a Laborer, residing at 1521 O'Fallon Street."

Charles Liston was, of course, the motherfucker they really wanted: the big bad nigger who looked at you like he didn't know whether to drink your blood or spit on you, or, worse, like he didn't even see you with those deep dark grave-dirt-colored dead man's eyes of his; the big bad nigger who come up here from way down there and took people round the neck from behind like a beast. Even old Tocco — around the neck from behind. Dirt, fist, feet. They looked at him and they saw not only something that was inhuman, but also something in which humanity was not even vestigial. He was worse than a predator, worse than a cop-hater: a man-hater. And not one, not two of them could take him alone without a gun, and they knew it, and they hated him for that, the very fact of his existence. Big bad niggers weren't supposed to be that big and that bad, not in St. Louis, anyway.

That first hour at that station, in that desolation between two and three in the morning on the Lord's given day, when he, Charles Liston, Unknown Negro Number One, confessed as openly and wildly as any mourning-bench Baptist beset with the speaking in tongues — it must have been an hour of brutality as awful as any that Charles Liston himself had brought down upon another. An eye for an eye, maybe, a tooth for a tooth, one cold January night for another. He was a man who had forsaken wrong and right, and in that desolate station, he did not know what hit him, wrong or right, justice or vengeance, or just that sort of shit that happens when animals get to mixing, a pack of one kind against a stray of another. He had hunted lone defenseless prey with his little pack, all right, attacking from behind, silent as a big nightstalking cat. Dirt, fist, feet. And now he was the prey.

Helen Liston remembered how her son got the scar between the thumb and forefinger of his left hand. It was back on the plantation, and he was splitting stove wood. "I told him to be careful with that ax, and I just walked into the house when he hit his hand and cut it bad. We soaked it in coal oil to stop the bleeding." But she never knew where those other scars came from, the one on his cheek, the one on his forearm.

"They say he confessed," she would say. "I don't know."

Captioned "Man Caught 25 Minutes After $37 Cafe Holdup" and describing him as "a bandit," a small item in the *St. Louis Globe-Democrat* of January 16, gave "Charles Liston, 22, Negro," his first notice in the press. A *St. Louis Post-Dispatch* item of that day began: "A flamboyant yellow lumberjack-type shirt worn by a young Negro walking in the 1000 block of O'Fallon street early yesterday attracted the attention of Patrolman David Herleth."

On May 23, he pled guilty on all counts to three charges of first-degree robbery and two charges of larceny, and was sentenced to five years on each charge, the terms to run concurrently, at the Missouri State Penitentiary in Jefferson City.

David Herleth, who now advocates boot camps or tent towns for young criminals, never saw much good in sending them to prison. "Shit," he said, prison was where "they learned to do the job right." Charles Liston knew the job: it was to survive, any way he could. But as for doing it right, he had not a clue.

Upon entering prison, on June 1, 1950, Liston stated his age to be twenty and his residence to be Wynne, Arkansas, which appeared misspelled as "Wynn" on the prison identity card that carried the first pictures ever taken of Charles L. Liston, right profile and facing front, with a tag around his neck: Mo. State Prison 63723, dated 6–2–50. His weight was recorded at 199 pounds, his height at six feet, his build as Heavy; his complexion was described as light brown, his hair as black, his eyes as dark brown. In the pictures, those eyes say nothing.

"I'm not sure how he happened to get into so much trouble," Helen Liston would say. "You know, it's sometimes the company you keep which run your luck into a bad string. He was just a country boy. He didn't know to do nothing." She simply could not understand it, she would say. He had, after all, taken religion in the Methodist church down home in Arkansas. "I heard him confess. I used to tell him he had to cultivate his religion. He said he would."

All things considered, she said, "He was about as good a conditioned child as I had."

By the time Charles entered prison, Helen was gone again, off to another daughter, in Gary, Indiana. She and Charles were never to see much of one another from that time on. And by the time he got out of the joint, Charles was no longer a bandit. He was a boxer named Sonny.

Charles Liston fucked with no one in Jeff City, and no one fucked with him. "I didn't mind prison," he would later say.

The prison population was about two-thirds white, one-third colored, and the three dominant gangs were white. After Liston became the heavyweight champion of the world, he was mythologized into a hero of the Jeff City cultus. There was the legend about the time the prison gangleader Hank Calouris gave shit to some black kid, and Liston walked across the yard, smacked Calouris across the face with the back of his hand, and told him, "I'll do that every time I hear you touched a colored boy. If you don't like it, I'll see you in the Hole" — a storage room beneath the cellblock — "at six"; about how he went to the other prison gangleaders, Nick Baroudi and a guy named Frankie, and told their white asses the same damn thing; about how when he emerged from the Hole that night, he left the three of them lying battered behind him on the concrete floor.

In reality, his disciplinary record showed only three minor violations: shooting dice, wasting food, and "chewing gum rubber bands in his cell." He was enrolled briefly in the prison school program, but he dropped out.

William P. Steinhauser, who worked at the prison during Liston's term and later became the assistant warden, told the sportswriter Andrew Sturgeon Young that "as well as I can remember, Liston was assigned to the kitchen and worked on the docks — where they bring the vegetables in and unload them from the farm." He remembered him as a formidable character all right. "I don't think you could hurt the man," and if he hit you, "it's just too bad." But, as long as nobody fucked with him, "he didn't fuck with nobody." "He was a reserved sort of fellow," Steinhauser said. "He was the sort of fellow you almost had to draw a conversation out of. We had no trouble with him at all. He was all right."

Though men have claimed to know where Liston's nickname came from, and some have taken credit for bestowing it on him, no one knows for sure who it was in prison that gave Liston the nickname of Sonny. But the man who first put gloves on his fists was the Reverend Edward B. Schlattmann, the prison chaplain.

Born in 1909, Father Schlattmann was retired and in his eighty-ninth year when I spoke to him. He clearly recalled Liston's arrival at the Missouri State Penitentiary in the spring of 1950.

"The Catholic chaplain," he explained to me, "was also director of athletics. No extra pay, of course." Liston "was a big husky guy and always getting in fights with other men."

Like other brawling inmates, he was put into the main-yard ring by Father Schlattmann. "After four weeks of fighting, nobody in the penitentiary would get into the ring with Sonny."

From the outset, there was the problem of gloves. It was a problem that would remain for years to come. Sonny's hands were bigger than other men's. Almost all heavyweight fighters have fists that measure a foot or less in girth. But Sonny's fists — which gave pause to men merely on seeing them — were between fourteen and fifteen inches around. Aside from the poor, pitiable giant Primo Carnera in the early thirties, the only heavyweight champion for whom a fourteen-inch fist was claimed was Jess Willard, the six-and-a-half-foot champion of the late teens. Standard boxing gloves simply were not made for fists like Sonny's. They did not fit. His hands could be forced into the biggest of them, but then they could not be properly laced and tied. Eventually, there would be money for custom-fashioned gloves from the Sammy

Frager Company in Chicago. Until then, he would use what he had to use.

Father Schlattmann was the first of several Catholic priests who became important in Liston's life. He was drawn to men such as Schlattmann — the real ones, the rare ones who devoted their lives to God through their devotion to other men — and their voodoo over him was strong. He showed to them a side of himself that few saw. It was not a hidden side, but it revealed something in that it was a manifestation both of how he wished to be and how he wished to be seen. In many respects, the priests knew and loved a Sonny Liston that did not exist. It was part honest and heartfelt desire to be otherwise and part con job, the way of a half-wise man: wise enough to sense beatitude, fool enough to think it could be boosted with the right line of shit.

"He never drank," Father Schlattmann said, as every priest who knew Liston would say. "He never used cuss words. He was a good Joe." And then, for a moment, it was as if Father Schlattmann had always known that there was another Liston, the one beneath, or apart from, the Liston that Sonny allowed the priests to see, the Liston, part wishful and part real, that they drew from him. And it was as if, in that moment, he still saw something good. Liston, he said, had "no religion." But, in a way, "he had his morals."

Schlattmann said that while Liston beat every opponent in the prison, he had no proper knowledge of boxing. His first "trainer" in the joint was another black prisoner who had boxed on the outside. Schlattmann vaguely recalled that this other prisoner may have been called Sonny and that the nickname of his conquering protégé may have been passed from the one to the other, either directly or as Sonny's Boy, then Sonny Boy, then simply Sonny.

Liston watched the prison heavyweight champion and strongman, a man called Booker, go down before him and a crowd of nearly three thousand howling inmates, and he very nearly killed another convict, a man called Earl.

Later, when Liston was on the outside, he never forgot the priests. "Every fight that Sonny had," said Schlattmann, "he invited us to come to the fight. We had free tickets. That was Father Stevens" — Schlattmann's successor at Jeff City — "and myself. We'd go to his dressing room before the fight." The fights got bigger, and still Liston never forgot. "We both tried to pay our way, our airline and all that, and his manager at that time, I forget who he was, he spit on the sidewalk and said, 'It's like that in the ocean.'"

When Father Schlattmann was transferred to a parish, he was replaced at the prison by Father Alois Stevens, who previously had been chaplain at Algoa, an intermediate reformatory nearby. Monsignor Jack McGuire, who at the time was an assistant at the Jefferson City parish, remembered the day Father Stevens came to him about Sonny.

"He told me that there was this great big monstrous convict over there that they couldn't get anybody else to fight; they had to put two men in the ring with him at the same time." Stevens told McGuire that he thought Liston "could have a very successful career as a pro boxer, but they couldn't get him paroled because he couldn't even sign his name," and they would thus never be able to line up a promise of gainful employment for him.

Father McGuire, born in 1924, had been a sportswriter for the *St. Louis Star-Times*, a UPI stringer, and a publicity director for the St. Louis University athletic department. He knew Robert L. Burnes, who was the sports editor of the *Globe-Democrat* and an active Catholic layman.

"So one day Father Stevens and I drove down to St. Louis to see Bob Burnes in his office." Burnes called his friend Monroe (Muncey) Harrison, a thirty-two-year-old former boxer who had become a coach and trainer.

Harrison went to Jefferson City in late February 1951, in the company of his partner and fellow trainer, William (Tony) Anderson, who ran a gym with Harrison on Olive Street. They brought with them thirty-two-year-old Thurman Wilson, considered to be the best heavyweight fighter in St. Louis.

At this time, Sonny's trainer in prison was a fellow inmate, Sam Eveland, a young 1950 Golden Gloves champion who had been sent from Algoa to Jefferson City for aiding the attempted escape of two fellow prisoners.

"I was in the pen with Sonny," Sam told me. "I had just won the Golden Gloves in Kansas City. They gave him to me to teach him how to box, and I was his coach in the pen."

"There was a bunch of trainers in there," Sam told me, "but none of them was ever a champ. They was just guys helping out." Father Stevens "didn't know nothing about boxing." One of those "guys helping out" was an inmate named Joe Gonzalez, who claimed to have given Liston the ring name of Sonny Boy. Sam himself believes that Liston got his nickname from "his grandma." He is not alone in believing that the nickname dated to childhood. George Morledge, Jr., said that Liston was known as Sonny back on the plantation.

Eveland remembered Harrison and Anderson coming to the joint. They were "short heavyset black people. Good people." And he remembered Liston's fight with Thurman Wilson. "Sonny destroyed him. I mean, there was no contest."

Wilson is said to have gone two rounds with Sonny, then called it quits with the words "I don't want no more of him."

When I asked David Herleth, the cop who busted Liston, to describe him, he thought awhile, his words wandered, and then, plainly and firmly he answered: "Big overgrown kid." Father Alois Stevens had described him as "big but very much a boy, just barely dry behind the ears."

I asked Sam Eveland what Sonny was like back then. Was he a good guy?

"He wasn't a guy," Sam said affectionately. There was a hard-edged sort of sympathy in his voice. "He was a kid. Yeah, he was an animal, all right. He was still a kid, though. A good kid. He had a good heart."

And, as fighters go?

"Nobody could beat Sonny," he said, "and they knew that."

From between two pages of a tattered scrapbook, Sam handed me an old Christmas card from Sonny, the three-cent stamp on its envelope postmarked Philadelphia, December 8, 1961. He showed me a note from around that same time: Sonny had learned to write his name longhand, and the note opened to reveal one of his first autographs, which he wanted Sam to have.

"Yeah, poor Sonny," Sam said, at the end of a long talk. "Poor kid."

Monsignor McGuire remembered Liston much as Father Schlattmann had: "an enormous man," but a basically good and kind and simple man — simple, he added, "in the best sense of the word." But he also echoed the epitaph of Sam Eveland's description: "the poor man," said the good monsignor with an elliptical sigh; "the poor man."

On the night of February 22, 1951, Muncey Harrison rushed grinning into Burnes's office at the *Globe-Democrat*. "He was breathless," Burnes wrote many years later.

"You finally found me a live one," Harrison told him.

It was Burnes's hope that his friend Muncey Harrison would become Liston's manager, but his friend knew that he could not do it alone.

Monroe Harrison was respected well and widely as a trainer. He had been Joe Louis's favorite sparring partner, and he had trained Archie Moore, who learned from Harrison the "shell style," or "turtle defense," that became his greatest fighting maneuver. But his career brought him less money than satisfaction, and he worked as a school custodian to make ends meet. Harrison knew that he lacked the capital to manage alone a fighter of Liston's astounding potential.

He turned to Frank W. Mitchell, the forty-five-year-old publishing heir of the *St. Louis Argus,* which was founded in 1912 and was the oldest and most respected of several weekly newspapers serving the local black community. No stranger to boxing, Mitchell already maintained a small stable of several black fighters. He had raised Charley Riley, the St. Louis featherweight, from anonymity in the mid-forties to a shot at Willie Pep's title in 1950. He managed the man who became Liston's friend and sparring partner, the light heavyweight Foneda Cox. Another of Mitchell's light heavyweights was young Jesse Bowdry, who would begin to make a name for himself in 1955, with his professional debut at the age of sixteen.

Together Harrison and Mitchell, with the blessing of Father Stevens and Bob Burnes — church, white press, black press — campaigned for Liston's release. Meeting with officer Richard Niles of the parole board, Mitchell promised that he would see to it that Sonny would receive a job and proper training as a boxer.

"I didn't really want to get involved with Sonny," said Burnes, "and my publisher kept telling me not to get involved. This may sound like preaching, but I saw Sonny and said to myself, 'Here's a man who has his one chance, his only chance; no other way in God's world to make anything except with his fists.' I tried to help him."

Father Stevens, too, had been advised not to become overly involved with Liston, and he later made it clear that Sonny was paroled to Frank Mitchell and Monroe Harrison, not to him. "I usually had to stay out of those things," the priest said.

Sonny fought what may have been his last fight in prison on July 4, 1952. He was paroled to Mitchell and Harrison on October 30, 1952. Mitchell got him a job as a laborer at a steel plant and a room at the Pine Street YMCA.

In March 1952, the tenor saxophonist Jimmy Forrest, a thirty-two-year-old son of St. Louis, broke the R&B charts wide open with a brooding, tough-rhythmed evocation called "Night Train."

Duke Ellington had written and recorded a song called "Happy-Go-Lucky Local" in 1946. Forrest had played in Duke Ellington's orchestra in 1949 and 1950, and he had stolen "Night Train" directly from the Ellington composition. He had dragged it down to the gutter to behold the starless heavens magically anew; had transformed it, yes, into a brooding, tough-rhythmed evocation, a wordless siren's song, a summoning, slow and wild at once, of vague and dangerous beauty. But he had stolen it outright none the less.

How fine and fitting it was that this act of inspired robbery should become the favorite record of Sonny Liston, who at the time was in the joint for a lower form of robbery. It was the record that he would play, again and again, at every workout, until it echoed within him, the soundtrack of blow and heartbeat, until the end. It was the music, faraway and seductive, of that animus, that place inside him rarely to be visited and never to be delved, and of that scar tissue too. He had always been on that night train, had been born to it. And now, released to the dream of a golden new morning, he was about to enter the darkest tunnel of all.

BIG
TIME

THEY WANTED TO ENTER SONNY IN THE GOLDEN Gloves as soon as possible. There was no age restriction in the Golden Gloves, but legal proof of age, any age, was required. In Arkansas in those days, an affidavit from an older family member sufficed to establish a record of birth. And so it was, in 1953, that Charles Liston, by way of a "Delayed Birth Certificate" filed with the Arkansas Bureau of Vital Statistics, came to be born on May 8, 1932; and so it was that Sonny Liston, who had been twenty-two in January 1950 and twenty in June of 1950, turned twenty once again in the spring of 1952.

Harrison gave him a brand-new background to go with his brand-new birthday. His life of Sonny presented a young and innocent boy whom the police found sleeping one night in an alley at Twenty-Third and Cole. He was cold and hungry and could not go home because there was no one there to let him in. Their compassion for him was such, and he so deserving of compassion, that they embraced him as their own.

"The police liked the boy," Harrison would say. "He was handy around the station, washed cars, did everything. He was big for his age. Finally they found his aunt, and she came and claimed the boy. But it was the same thing. There was Sonny: hungry, no money, no place to eat or sleep. He saw a boy with five dollars — money the mother had given him to buy groceries — and he took it, strong-armed him for it when he was only fifteen years old."

It was Harrison who said that Sonny had attended school for a few days and been driven to quit because the other children laughed at him. Again, however, there was never any record of his attending school, and it is unlikely that he would have fled the mockery of smaller children. As Bob Burnes later declared, "Sonny never went to school." Liston himself cottoned to Harrison's tale, but in delivering the new revised version as autobiography, he sometimes let slip morsels of revelation about an earlier and more youthful criminal career. Telling one time of how the other schoolchildren had ridiculed him, he ended the poignant performance with the point-blank afterthought: "So I wound up in the wrong school."

"What school did you wind up in?" his interrogator asked.

"Well, the house of detention."

"How old were you then?"

"I was about fourteen."

Age, according to the endless flux of the Liston calendar is, of course, highly subjective, but according to the birth date he had finally settled on, he would have turned fourteen in 1946.

"How long did you stay there?"

"My mother, she got me out; and then, well, I figure — she got me out, and I went right back for the same things."

"You did what?"

"I went back to the same thing and wound up in a bigger school this time."

In what seems to be his most straightforward account, published in 1961, Liston said:

> I got to running with the wrong crowd. We broke into this restaurant about two in the morning and got away. But after we had gone

ten blocks we decided to get some barbecue, and then the police came along and barbecued us. I got out on probation. I was sixteen then, weighing over two hundred pounds. I was in a lot of street fights. I used to punch first and ask questions later, that's the way those guys do. I guess I was the biggest, strongest guy on the corner. None of the other gangs would mess with me, and so I started to strut with this gang and wound up in a bigger house.

Some sucker sold me a gun to be shot only on Saturday night, that's the only time you needed it. I never shot a gun before, so I held it up in the sky and pulled the trigger. The gun lit up and I, thinking it was on fire, threw it in the mud. After that I started running with this guy who had a car. We made a few stickups, got away with the first, tried a second and it didn't turn out. This time, they sent me away to Jefferson City for five years.

As much as they tried to cultivate for him an image of innocence, he inspired in Mitchell and Harrison themselves images of the predatory, the beastly, and the savage, which they expressed years later. In telling a story to illustrate the speed and stealth of the fighter's hands, Mitchell recounted the day when Sonny reached down and scooped a moving pigeon from a St. Louis sidewalk. "Man," Mitchell told him, "turn that pigeon loose. Everybody looking, think you a cannibal."

"He's like a leopard," said Harrison, "that animal out there in the jungle — leap at an animal, kill it, but he don't need it."

Sonny had not yet achieved much refinement of boxing style. He did not finesse his opponents; he simply obliterated them, usually without ever even using his right fist. "He had absolutely no right hand at all at this time," recalled Jim Lubbock, a *Globe-Democrat* reporter who was involved in that newspaper's sponsorship of the

Golden Gloves. "He just slapped with his right hand. He really didn't know how to fight." But, in Lubbock's phrase, "he had a left like a pile driver."

That February 1953, Liston swept the competition in the open-and-novice heavyweight division of the *Globe-Democrat*'s eighteenth annual Golden Gloves tournament. He went with the other local winners to Chicago, where, emerging as the sole surviving victor of the St. Louis team, he wiped out all comers and took the Midwestern Golden Gloves title from Ed Sanders of Los Angeles, the heavyweight champion of the 1952 Olympics. At the national matches in March, Liston defeated Julius Griffin of New York to become the Golden Gloves heavyweight champion of America. And his right was becoming less idle.

> When sports-minded St. Louisians turn out for the *Globe-Democrat*'s International Golden Gloves matches a week from tomorrow night, [wrote Jim Lubbock on June 14, 1953] chances are they'll be coming as much to see one St. Louis fighter as they will the 10 all-European champions who make up the visiting team.
>
> The local larruper is a big, quiet, amiable heavyweight named Charles "Sonny" Liston. Virtually unheard of in fistic circles a year ago, he is currently bearing out predictions that someday soon he'll be "another Joe Louis."
>
> Within just a few months of formal boxing training, "Sonny" has batted around with comparative ease the best of the amateur fighters. One of his victims is World Olympic Heavyweight Champion Ed Sanders of Los Angeles.
>
> In fact, he has so completely outclassed most of his opposition that Chicago coaches have selected him to fight as their heavyweight when the Europeans battle here Tuesday night in their only other matches in this country.
>
> Possessed of no astounding amount of boxing skill as yet,

> "Sonny's" technique is simply to push his opponent in the face with a long, powerful jab, and occasionally crash home with a ponderous but even more powerful right.
>
> This rudimentary approach to the noble art of self-defense succeeds so well principally because the young man employing it is one of the strongest, fastest amateur heavyweights ever seen in a St. Louis ring, according to veteran boxing coaches who have seen them all for many years.
>
> Since last January, Liston has smashed and bashed his way to heavyweight championships in the *Globe-Democrat's* St. Louis Golden Gloves, the Midwest Golden Gloves and the National Golden Gloves, the latter two tourneys in Chicago. He has also won the Ozark A.A.U. title here.
>
> Just 20 years old, Sonny weighs 204 pounds. He works at the St. Louis Ordinance Plant, 4300 Goodfellow Boulevard, and trains in the evenings at Tony's Gym, 4525 Olive Street. His heavy punching makes sparring partners hard to find.
>
> What luck he'll have battling West Germany's Herman Schreibauer, the hard-hitting European heavyweight, remains to be seen. Most ringsiders expect to see him win. They feel they are watching the early stages of what could well be a truly great ring career.

On June 22, Liston wiped out Herman Schreibauer of West Germany in less than a round, thus becoming the Golden Gloves champion of the world. According to the *Globe-Democrat,* "His victory over Schreibauer was so impressive that it left the 7489 fans in Kiel Auditorium Monday night convinced that the amateur ranks no longer can contain him."

In four months, he had risen to the height of the amateur standings, and few who saw him doubted that there was a man alive he could not bring down. "Gloves King Liston Ready to Turn Pro," declared a headline in the *St. Louis Post-Dispatch* two days after the Schreibauer fight:

> Charles "Sonny" Liston climaxed the show with a quick technical knockout [reported the *Post-Dispatch*] in the first round of the final heavyweight bout.
>
> Obviously unworried, Liston whistled as he went about his work, stalked his opponent and then floored him with a solid right. When Schreibauer rose, he was unsteady and Referee Vic di Filippo quickly signaled the end of action after 2:16 of the round.
>
> This probably was Liston's final appearance in the amateur ranks. He is expected to sign a professional contract within the next few days.

His contract with Harrison and Mitchell granted the two men half of Liston's purses and held them to pay all his expenses. The managers soon discovered, however, that it was difficult to find anybody willing to fight him, and when they could, the purses were small. Expenses included all his meals; and, as Mitchell's mother, Mrs. Nellie Mitchell Turner, said, "That Sonny is an eater."

The first professional fight they lined up for him — the contract was signed on August 26 — was a four-round preliminary match against Don Smith, a newcomer from Louisville who had won his two previous matches, both in St. Louis, with impressive early-round knockouts. Liston's rise through the amateur ranks had been so fast and so fulminous — such a sudden, attention-commanding burst of neon lightning and Shango thunder — that the price negotiated for his professional debut was two hundred dollars, about four times the going rate for a preliminary novice.

The Liston-Smith fight, held in St. Louis on September 2, 1953, lasted thirty-three seconds, ending in a knockout by Liston with the first punch of the first round.

Those thirty-three seconds, that one single blow — the same

blow that had felled robbery victim and Olympic champion alike — brought Liston more money than he had ever seen.

Fifteen days later, he beat Ponce de Leon, a stiff from Spokane who was in the fifth year of a dead-end career laden with losses and draws. On November 21, Liston beat Benny Thomas of Memphis. In his first fight of the new year, on January 25, 1954, he beat Martin Lee; and on March 31, he beat Stan Howlett for the Missouri state championship. These are men whom boxing history has all but forgotten, but who never forgot their nights in the ring with Liston.

By the spring of 1954, Liston had fought five fights, all of them in St. Louis, all of them against nobodies, all of them victories. Every good fighter with smart handlers is given many lambs to slaughter, easy fights that build a record that looks good on paper while giving the experience in the ring that will prepare him for bigger, tougher, and more seasoned game.

Liston's first big fight, his first out-of-town fight, his first televised fight, was on June 29, 1954: a main-event match in Detroit against the Michigan state heavyweight champion John Summerlin, a veteran fighter who had lost only once in a career of twenty bouts. That loss, several years before, had been to another St. Louis fighter, Wes Bascom, who was among the top ten light heavyweight contenders of his day and with whom Liston had sparred in St. Louis.

Summerlin was a hometown hero and generally considered to be Michigan's finest heavyweight. Local bookmakers had Liston as an off-the-board twenty-two-to-one underdog. But those odds meant nothing to Sonny, except for the nickel he had laid on himself; and he was the victor that night before the near-capacity crowd of twelve hundred at the Motor City Arena.

Six weeks later, in a rematch, on August 10, in the same ring, also televised by WWJ-TV, Liston won again. "Sonny Liston," stated the *Detroit News* the next day, "could claim the Michigan title without dispute, if he resided here."

Before the fight, the *Detroit News* had scoffed at growing comparisons of Liston to Joe Louis. "His home town," wrote Harry Stapler, "is paralleling his rise to that of Joe Louis, a bit of wishful thinking often engaged in on behalf of other heavyweights since the mid-thirties."

After the fight, the *Detroit Free Press* quoted Bill Appleton, one of the three officials who judged the fight: "At this stage of his career, I'd say he's a better prospect than Joe Louis at a comparable point."

"Liston is handled by Frank Mitchell, a wise old ring hand," said the *Free Press*. "If he shows patience and understanding, if he has the luck and good connections of Roxborough and Black, then maybe Liston will fulfill the bright promise he now shows." (John Roxborough and Julian Black were the managers of Joe Louis from the outset of his career, in 1934, to 1949.)

"His backers," said the *Press*, "are prepared to move his headquarters from St. Louis, his home town, to Chicago."

Backers. Connections. Chicago. If only they knew.

Less than a month later, on September 7, fighting again at the Motor City Arena — not televised this time — Liston suffered the only loss in his rise to the top, when he was defeated by Marty Marshall, the light heavyweight champion of Michigan.

A story circulated that Liston, who had never seen anyone he prostrated spring so sprightly back to his feet, was so bewildered and bemused when Marshall rose from a first-round knockdown that his mouth hung open in disbelief, and Marshall caught him off guard with a punch that dislocated his jaw.

The truth is that the punch that allegedly fractured Liston's jaw came three rounds later, and Liston, busted jaw and all, lost only by a close decision after the full eight rounds. It is with the loss to

Marshall that the record entry for CHARLEY (SONNY) LISTON ends in *The Ring Record Book* of 1955. Regarding that sole and unlikely loss to a fighter twenty pounds lighter than Sonny, Frank Mitchell contended that "Marty Marshall is a clown," and that Sonny could have knocked him out if he had wanted to when he hit him in the second round. "But Sonny tells me he was told to carry the boy three or four rounds so the fans could get their money's worth. Sonny got to laughing, Marshall hit him, and broke his jaw."

Sonny himself told a somewhat similar story: "I was told to take it easy for a couple rounds. Marshall's a clown, they told me, who'd bounce around and flick punches from all sides.

"I was standing there, kinda wondering, when all of a sudden he lets out a yell, and with my mouth wide open, gaping, he slugged me right in the jaw. It didn't hurt, but I couldn't close my mouth. I had to fight the last six rounds with my mouth open. After a while it hurt bad."

Neither of these accounts makes much sense. The blow that busted Sonny's jaw came in the fourth round of an eight-round fight, and by then Sonny surely should have fulfilled his crowd-pleasing obligations. But that is not what intrigues. It is the casual, almost whimsical *"he was told to carry the boy three or four rounds,"* the casual, almost whimsical *"I was told to take it easy for a couple rounds."*

Who was doing the telling and who was concerned that the humble ticket buyer should get his money's worth? Who was so compelling and so powerful that he very likely decided the outcome of the fight?

Note that in Mitchell's version, he himself is innocent of knowing anything about anybody's being told anything until Sonny, after the fight, "tells me he was told." In fact, said Mitchell, he was not even with Sonny in Detroit. "I was busy with the newspaper," he said. "I sent Sonny up there alone." Mitchell said that Sonny was "very angry" with him for not going to Detroit with him, and for giving him the bill for having his jaw wired. But Mitchell expressed no anger at Sonny's listening to *them,* and Sonny expressed no anger at *them* for telling him to take it easy. "Marshall's a clown, they told me" — those were Sonny's words. "Marty Marshall is a clown" — those were the words of Mitchell.

As for Marshall's being a clown, of the fifteen fights of his four-year career, he had lost only twice and drawn only once.

One thing is certain. Nobody in the fight racket ever gave a fuck about the suckers in the seats, except maybe for the guys that were selling the peanuts.

And it wasn't like it was back in the ring in that penitentiary yard; it wasn't even like it was back in those alleys of dirt, fist, feet. It was a world of *they* and of *them.* And, just like back in those sandy-slough plantation fields, when the Man says move, you got to move.

With his decisive defeats, not once but twice, of the formidable favorite John Summerlin, Sonny's days as an underdog had come to an end. All that could be hoped for by those who bet on him was that short odds could be made longer. The more ineffectual a fighter appeared to be in one fight, the longer the odds against him in his next fight against a strong opponent. In this light, Sonny's loss to Marshall turned out better than hoped for. But Sonny ended up out of action for nearly six months on account of that jaw. And there would be no further humanitarian concerns for the crowd by *them,* for Sonny was too exceptionally fine and potentially valuable an animal, and that potential must be brought to golden fruit. Soon, odds or no odds, he must be allowed to do what he did best, which surely was not to carry unknown clowns for the sake of those odds, but rather to bring ruin to them. Besides, *they* — somebody — owed him for that loss; and they owed him, putatively, for that busted jaw as well.

In his return to the ring after the layoff following the first Marshall fight, Sonny beat Neil Welch of Toledo on March 1, 1955, at the Masonic Temple in St. Louis. This victory over Welch was as strangely lackluster as his loss to Marshall had been. If the Detroit loss — a big long-money payoff for those foolhardy or wise enough to bet against him — made Liston look bad and raised the odds against him, the Welch victory did little to dispel the effects of that loss.

In a story headlined "Sonny Liston Outpoints Toledo Boxer but Disappoints His Fans," W. J. McGoogan of the *Post-Dispatch* wrote:

> Despite the fact that Liston pounded Welch at will and the Toledo boxer's only defense was to wrap his arms around his head, Liston was unable to floor the visitor, let alone knock him out.
>
> And on occasion, Welch managed to land a punch which momentarily stopped Liston, too, although Sonny wasn't hurt at any time while Welch appeared to be on his way out several times. He always managed to evade the kayo punch or Liston didn't find the right way to land it.

No one knew Sonny Liston better as a man or as a fighter than the St. Louis light heavyweight Foneda Cox. On the June night in 1953 when Liston's amateur boxing career ended with his defeat of Herman Schreibauer, the twenty-three-year-old Cox shared the evening's glory, defeating a West German opponent in the match preceding the Liston-Schreibauer contest. On the night in Detroit when Liston beat Summerlin for the second time, Cox was again also a victor, winning a five-round decision in a preliminary match against Bill Hunter.

Tall, rangy Foneda Cox was a protégé of Frank Mitchell, and Tony Anderson was his trainer. After Liston's parole from prison the previous year, "they put Sonny in the same gymnasium with me, and I started boxing with Sonny. That's how we got together." The two men became more than sparring partners and fellow boxers: they became fast friends.

"Let me give it to you this way," Foneda said. "There was no fighter living that could put on a boxing glove and stand up against Sonny Liston." That, to Foneda, was the plain and simple truth. "Nobody," he said, "could whip Sonny Liston."

Foneda's words should be borne in mind when regarding the loss to Marshall, or the lackluster Welch fight. They should be borne in mind always.

As should money. Those seven dollars and seventy cents taken from a man beaten down and dragged into an alley. One roll of pennies, one roll of nickels, twenty-four loose nickels, ten dimes, and twelve quarters. That two-yard price, that taste of undreamt fortune, on the night of that first professional fight. In yellow shirt and bib overalls, in white trunks and leather gloves — the same blow, the same motive.

With that first, two-hundred-dollar payday, Sonny had entered a world in which money was the kind and loving god of the ruling few and the predestining subjugator of the many. At best, it was a matter of "workin' on halves," as E.B. Ward said of sharecropping. "If you had ten bales of cotton, the white man got five." It was not right. It was not wrong. It was simply and supremely the way it was.

The first rematch with Marty Marshall was held in St. Louis on April 21, 1955. Liston sent Marshall reeling to the canvas four times, and the fight ended as a six-round technical knockout for

Liston. Marshall remained forever in awe of Sonny's power. "He hit me like no man should be hit," he told the reporter George Puscas of the *Detroit Free Press*. "He's tough. That's one thing nobody can deny about that man. He hurts when he breathes on you."

Liston's only loss, to Marshall, may have been a grievous error that Liston was able to wave away. But in the fourth round of the second Liston-Marshall fight, Marshall did something to Liston that was so unthinkable, so impossible, that Liston, doing his best to erase it from history, denied that it ever happened: Marshall knocked him down.

"I'm sorry to this day about that," said Marshall. "Man, am I sorry. He hit me after that like — *nobody* should be hit like that. I think about it now and I hurt. He came out after me in the fifth round. He hit me with a right hand on my ear. It didn't knock me out and it didn't knock me down, but it hurt so much I just had to go down anyway. The next round, he knocked me down three times," Marshall recalled. "He hit me in the stomach with a left hand in the sixth. That wasn't a knockdown, either. It couldn't be: I was paralyzed. I just couldn't move. I couldn't move enough to fall down." Later that round, said Marshall, Liston "knocked me down three times, and that was it."

For all of that, Sonny would never admit to his having been momentarily felled while off guard. "I just don't know why he wouldn't remember that," Marshall would say. "Everybody remembers. It was in the papers."

But Sonny didn't read the papers. Later, in 1956, when the time came for their third and final match, Marshall knew that he never again in his life wanted a beating such as Liston had given him; and if losing was inevitable, he wanted at least to avoid the new dimensions in pain to which Liston had delivered him: "I just knew I couldn't let him touch me."

The Marshall TKO of April 1955 was the first of five consecutive knockouts in an ever-widening territory. Sonny knocked out Emil Brtko in Brtko's hometown of Pittsburgh on May 5. He knocked out Calvin Butler in St. Louis on May 25. It was the Cleveland fighter's third defeat, the others having been delivered by Marty Marshall and Emil Brtko. Sonny knocked out the Chicago fighter Johnny Gray in Indianapolis on September 13. Two months later, on December 13, in the first professional fight held in East St. Louis in a quarter of a century, he knocked out Larry Watson, an Omaha fighter who had beaten Wes Bascom, the only conqueror of John Summerlin prior to Liston.

Frank Mitchell, the publisher of the black weekly *Argus*, used the newspaper to champion his prodigy. The first publicity photo of Liston — poised in the corner of the ring, gloved fists raised to the breast, white T-shirt, white trunks — appeared in the *Argus* of December 9, 1955, in a story announcing the upcoming Watson fight. The next week's issue, under the headline "Liston Wins Number 13," celebrated the "flashing left and right combination" witnessed by "a crowd of 780." The publicity picture ran again in the *Argus* two weeks later, above an item noting Liston's "climb toward the heavyweight title row." In concluding, Mitchell's *Argus* declared that Liston "may be a champ in a very short time."

By the time Liston was fighting out of town, Frank Mitchell was his sole manager of record.

"I was committed to paying thirty-five dollars a week for Sonny's support," Monroe Harrison would later say, "and my wife got sick and I just couldn't afford it. I had to turn my share of the contract over to Mitchell." Harrison spoke these words at a time when Liston was the heavyweight champion of the world and he himself still a school custodian. "Let's face it," he added, "a poor, colored trainer just don't ever wind up with fifty percent of a heavyweight champion's contract."

When Harrison died, Bob Burnes, in eulogizing him, would

tell a different tale. "There came a time," Burnes would write, "when Monroe Harrison came into the office on a Tuesday afternoon." Harrison's lugubrious demeanor "surprised me because I knew that Sonny had won the night before in Chicago, but that's all I knew."

"They took Sonny from me," Harrison said, according to Burnes.

"Who did?"

"Two guys touched me on the shoulder during the sixth round," Burnes claimed Harrison told him. "They said, 'We're taking Sonny,' and I said, 'When?' and they said, 'Right now.'"

"That was the beginning," Burnes would write, "of the takeover of Sonny Liston by the mob."

But Liston never fought in Chicago on a Monday night, and he never fought in Chicago at all until 1958, four years after Harrison had sold out his interest in Liston. It was a good tale that Burnes told, and it would become a part of the Liston legend. But it was a lie. Liston's takeover by the Mob had begun long before, right under the unseeing eyes of Burnes and the rest of them, the moment that Liston drew the first breath of that dream of a golden new morning.

Frank Mitchell, pillar of the black community, was, in his management of Liston, a front man for the interests of another gentleman, named John J. Vitale.

In those days, professional boxing was largely the domain of the International Boxing Club, a corporation formed in 1949 by James Dougan Norris, a wealthy forty-two-year-old Chicago sportsman who, with his father, James Norris, and his partner, Arthur Wirtz, already owned the Chicago Stadium, the Detroit Olympia, the St. Louis Arena, and considerable stock in Madison Square Garden.

Though Norris bankrolled it and was its president, the IBC was conceived, midwifed, and masterminded by Truman K. Gibson, Jr., a distinguished Chicago attorney whose involvement in boxing came through his relationship with the heavyweight champion Joe Louis.

Born on an Alabama cotton plantation and raised in the bad parts of Detroit, Louis was the first black champion since Jack Johnson lost to Jess Willard in 1915. Defending his title a record twenty-five times in an unprecedented reign that spanned the years 1937 to 1949, Louis, described by one writer as a fighter "with murder in his heart and thunderbolts in his gloves," was perhaps the only hero that Sonny Liston ever had.

It was during World War II that Gibson and Louis met. Gibson, also a black Southerner, was two years older than Louis. Born in Atlanta in 1912, he attended the University of Chicago, was admitted to the Illinois bar in 1935, and to the bar of the Supreme Court in 1939. He met Louis when, serving as a civilian aide to Secretary of War Stimson, he arranged the fighter's exhibition tour of army bases in Europe and North Africa. Gibson subsequently received a Medal of Merit. Appointed to the Compton Commission for Universal Military Training and the President's Advisory Commission on Morals, Religion, and Education in the Armed Services, he became an instrumental agent in the desegregation of the military, a role he attributed to the Louis tour and his observation that the white soldiers always had the good seats.

Though Gibson had little interest in boxing, the two became friends. After the war, when Louis — who had served four years of his championship in the armed forces and who had donated the entire purses of his 1942 title defenses to the Army and Navy Relief Funds — was set upon by the government for back taxes, he turned to Gibson for help.

It was Gibson who set up Joe Louis Enterprises, Inc., to set aright the exploited champion's financial situation. It was Gibson who freed Louis from the contractual clutch of Mike Jacobs's 20th Century Sporting Club. It was Gibson who, in early 1949, cut the deal through which Louis's resignation as champion brought the IBC officially into being: the deal through which Norris and Wirtz purchased from Joe Louis Enterprises contracts binding the four leading contenders to the title Louis abdicated, contracts that thus gave the IBC exclusive promotional rights to the heavyweight championship.

Once in control of the heavyweight title — won by Ezzard Charles over Jersey Joe Walcott in the IBC's inaugural presentation — the organization set out to place under contract and deliver to its fold the leading contenders in every principal division. As it succeeded, the IBC of Illinois grew into a network of tentacle entities: the IBC of New York, the IBC of Missouri, the IBC of Michigan, and various other related companies. Norris and Wirtz gained control of the Madison Square Garden Corporation; Norris became its president, Wirtz its vice president and treasurer. Exclusive television contracts were negotiated with NBC for the weekly Friday-night fights, with CBS for the Wednesday-night fights.

Gibson, who became, with Norris and Wirtz, one of the triumvirate that was the IBC's board of directors, would later flatly tell the Senate Subcommittee on Antitrust and Monopoly: "During the period 1950 to 1959, practically all of the championships in the major weight categories were staged by one or the other of our organizations or in conjunction with our television presentations."

In 1949, after its auspicious beginning, the IBC faced a bleak future. Beset by the demands and resistance of suspicious and disgruntled managers, picketed and boycotted by the Boxing Guild that represented those managers, it seemed that the IBC's dream of imperium, and the IBC itself, might be short-lived. It was then that the board of its directors came to know what wise old-timers already knew: in the world of boxing, there was only one true and sovereign power and he lived in New York. Some called him Mr. Gray.

Or, more poetically, The Gray. He had other names. According to newspapers, he had more names than God: Frank Martin, Frankie Tucker, The Man Down South, That Party, That Man, Our Cousin, Our Friend, The Uncle, The Ambassador, and, back in the less politically correct thirties, Jimmie the Wop, Frankie the Wop, and Dago Frank (the latter relinquished by the *New York Times* for the cuddlier but otherwise unattested Pug). And although his name was commonly believed to be Frank Carbo, his real name was Paul John Carbo, and he was born on the Lower East Side of Manhattan on August 10, 1904.

Carbo was well mannered, well dressed, and deadly. He spoke few words, and most photographs of him show him warmly smiling — being taken into custody, being charged, being sentenced, entering or leaving court (the verdict, guilty or innocent, seemed not to matter) — warmly, kindly smiling. He was, as they say, a gentleman among gentlemen, and, in a phrase less often turned, a killer among killers.

His criminal record went back to 1915, when he was sent to the Catholic Protectory at the age of eleven. His first murder rap came in 1924, when he was indicted for killing a taxi driver in the Bronx. He copped a plea to manslaughter and was sentenced to Sing Sing in 1928. Three years later, in September 1931, while on parole, he was arrested as a fugitive and charged with the Atlantic City killing of the millionaire bootlegger Mickey Duffy. When they seized him, he was holed up at the Cambridge Hotel on West Sixty-Eighth Street with an eighteen-year-old showgirl who went by the name of Vivian Lee. The following account comes from the

New York Daily News, September 3, 1931, back in the days when journalists could wield a sentence:

"Trapped in a Manhattan hotel with a pretty red-headed night club dancer, Paul Carbo, gang leader and ex-convict, was held last night charged with being the hired assassin who murdered Phil Duffy, Philadelphia and New Jersey beer overlord, in the Ambassador Hotel in Atlantic City last Saturday."

The teenage showgirl, whose real name, somewhat sinister, was Vivian Malifatti, was charged with Carbo in the murder of Duffy, as were a couple of Philadelphia racket guys named Herman Cohen and Albert Hodkinson.

Carbo was released. His next arrest for homicide came in January 1936, when he was seized again as a fugitive — on Eighth Avenue and Fiftieth Street, as he was about to enter Madison Square Garden — under a standing indictment against him for the April 12, 1933, double murder, at the Elizabeth Cartaret Hotel, in Elizabeth, New Jersey, of Max Greenberg and Max Hassell, two former associates of Waxey Gordon who were believed to have fallen victim of the bootleg war between the forces of Gordon and Dutch Schultz. The John Doe indicted with Carbo in the double murder was believed to have been a Dutch Schultz henchman, Chink Sherman, whose body had since been discovered buried in quicklime in a farm stable in Monticello, New York. Once again, Carbo was released.

In 1940, Carbo and several others, including Bugsy Siegel and Louis (Lepke) Buchalter, the head of Murder, Inc., were indicted for the Hollywood killing, on the eve of Thanksgiving 1939, of Harry "Big Greenie" Greenburg, a Lepke defector who had fled west. Although another Murder, Inc., turncoat, Al Tannenbaum, ratted out Carbo as the shooter, and a witness identified Carbo as the man she had seen running down a Hollywood street puffing a cigar moments after she heard the shots that killed Greenburg, all charges were dismissed, and he was freed in March 1942.

By 1935, Carbo was the licensed manager of the middleweight champion Eddie "Babe" Risko — changed from Henry Pylkowski — and other boxers. "Fight Manager Is Held," read the headline of the *New York Times* report of his capture in the Greenburg case. "Prize Fight Manager Held in Gang Killing" ran the headline of the *New York Sun*'s report. By the summer of 1940, when the *Times* reported his indictment as the "trigger man" in the Greenburg murder, he was "a New York and Seattle fight promoter." By early 1942, when charges in the Greenburg case were dismissed, he was "Frank Carbo, former fight promoter."

In his retirement from the light of day of the world of boxing, Frankie Carbo became the leviathan of its unseen realm. Through his long and occult career, he had helped many men and killed enough to command fear in many more. Few were the managers, promoters, and fighters who were not in his debt, financially and otherwise, and fewer still who did not court his favor, for good things seemed to happen to those whom Carbo's smile graced. And wherever the dew of profit, no matter how meager or how plentiful, gathered, Frankie Carbo, as the guys from the other side used to say, wet his beak.

IBC founder James Norris had known Carbo casually for some years. They were both gamblers who lived the lush life, and, as Norris's partner Truman Gibson expressed it to me, "Jim was enamored of all the mob guys."

Norris himself recalled how the intercession of Frankie Carbo was the vital catalyst in the rise of the IBC. Encountering him in the street one day when Norris was visiting New York, Carbo asked Norris how things were going with his new venture.

"Oh, no good," Norris said. "If it isn't the managers, it's a lack of talent or some other problems nobody could anticipate."

These words, Norris said, were designed to elicit a helpful suggestion, if not a downright offer of help. "As I recall, he grumbled and said he had problems of his own. I asked him if there was anyone he knew we could use that might be helpful."

"No," Carbo told him.

Soon after this, despite this "no," the IBC placed Carbo's girlfriend and future wife, Viola Masters, on the payroll. Though she performed no known function, she received payments of $40,000 over a period of three years. Further considerations, tribute, and propitiations were to ensure a marriage of the interests of the IBC and those of Frank Carbo, a secret partnership in which both would prosper.

"And was that the policy you finally decided upon," the investigating committee would later ask Gibson, "to cooperate with these underworld elements?"

"No, not to cooperate, but to live with them."

Carbo's lieutenant was Frank Palermo, a man everybody knew as Blinky.

"Do you know a Frank Palermo?" Sonny Liston would one day be asked by one of those investigating committees.

"No," he would say, "I never heard of Frank Palermo."

The inquisitor pressed him, again and again.

"You mean Blinky," Sonny finally said. "Yeah, I know Blinky. Everybody knows him."

Carbo came to know Blinky in the thirties, when The Gray, in addition to his house in Maspeth, Queens, and various Manhattan hotel rooms, also kept a home at 5542 Walnut Street in Blinky's hometown of Philadelphia.

Operating from a sixth-floor office in the Shubert Building on South Broad Street in Philadelphia, Frank "Blinky" Palermo was a licensed manager through whom Carbo shared in the control of many fighters, such as Billy Fox. Blinky was a legend, especially in Philadelphia, where, as a bookmaker, in 1950, he staged a running gun battle through the city streets in pursuit of a numbers runner who pocketed the payoff on a seventy-five-cent bet. Through the years, Blinky would lose his licenses one after another — in Illinois in 1952, in his native Pennsylvania — as through those years, in his alliance with Carbo, his power as an undercover manager grew greater than that of any licensed manager.

It was by betting on Billy Fox in his 1947 fight against the overwhelming favorite Jake LaMotta that Carbo made one of his greatest scores, as no one but he and Blinky and Jake knew that LaMotta had agreed with Carbo to throw the fight to Fox in exchange for a shot at the middleweight title.

Another fix did not go so well. Early in his career, in December 1942, Sugar Ray Robinson was supposed to carry Al Nettlow for the full ten rounds of a fight in Philly. But in the third round, when Nettlow hit him with a nasty right, Ray lost his temper, hit him with a left hook, and Nettlow was counted out. That night, Ray went to the newsstand where Blinky hung out, and he tried to explain what had happened. "It was an accident," he told Blinky. "I just happened to catch him."

"It's all right," Blinky said. "Nothin' we can do about it now."

Everybody knew Blinky. Everybody liked Blinky.

But, contrary to popular belief, fixed fights were rare. When one had a piece of both fighters, it mattered little who won. Truman Gibson told me that of perhaps a thousand fights promoted by the IBC, he knew of only three that were fixed.

In a world of guys that have been around, Gibson has been around longer than any of them. Robust and serene and sharp, and still practicing law well into his eighties, he had about him the aura of a man who has captured a wisp of wisdom from every breath, bitter and beautiful alike; and there was a gleam in his eyes as we sat in a Chinese restaurant in the On Leong section of Chicago and he recalled those fixes.

The biggest of them was the dive Archie Moore took in his 1955 New York title bout with Rocky Marciano. It was Marciano's last fight, and the fix ensured that Marciano would retire undefeated. After the fight, Gibson went with Moore's manager, Jack Kearns, to see Moore in San Diego. "Archie was happy and took us to his offices, beautifully appointed. Then he said, 'I want you to meet my partners.' Brought two guys in, and Jack Kearns looked over and said, 'You dirty son of a bitch, why didn't you tell me?' The minute he saw those guys he knew what had happened."

The gleam became a beam as he told me of another fix. "The lamb was killing the butcher in this case. Frank Carbo was the victim because the guy he was betting on took a dive. Red Top Davis was the fighter. They took him out, they wanted to throw him in the Hudson River, they did everything to him." (Ted "Red Top" Davis was a New York lightweight also known as Murray "Sugar" Cain.)

As for the third fix, I doubt if history and the lawyers that stand between these words and my paycheck are ready for that one.

Blinky Palermo was Carbo's lieutenant, but there were other friends through whom Carbo controlled other fighters. One of these fighters was Virgil Akins, the welterweight champion of 1958.

Akins and Liston came up together in St. Louis. "I first met Sonny up at Johnny Tocco's gym, on the corner of Blair and Cass. Johnny had a lounge downstairs and the gym was upstairs. There wasn't no name on it. A lot of people didn't know the gym was up there." It was right after Sonny had got out of prison. One of his first victims had been a Tocco, now one of his first trainers was another. "It was like he was mad at the world," Akins said. "There wasn't a smile on his face." He remembered Sonny training under Tony Anderson. "He couldn't hardly get sparring partners. It wasn't no play thing. It was a war. Nobody wanted to fool with him." Tony would try to cajole other fighters into sparring with Sonny, saying that if they asked him to take it easy on them, he would. "And they'd say, 'No, you can't talk to Sonny.' "

Through friends of Carbo, Akins came to be managed jointly by Eddie Yawitz of St. Louis and Bernard Glickman of Chicago.

Yawitz was a well-to-do pharmacist in St. Louis. Monroe Harrison claimed that it was in Eddie Yawitz's drugstore, in February 1955, that he sold Yawitz his interest in Liston for six hundred dollars. According to Frank Mitchell, it was he who bought out Harrison's share and sold it in turn to Yawitz.

Frank Mitchell was a man whose past was a well kept secret. When he died at the age of sixty-five, in 1970, obituaries spoke of him reverently: as a publisher whose paper, the *Argus*, had "won wide recognition for its reporting and interpretation of racial problems; a charitable and civic-minded man who served the Annie Malone Children's Home and the American Cancer Society; a man "active in police-community work." Nothing was said of a well-hidden criminal record that included eighteen arrests for gambling, seduction, and counterfeiting.

From the government transcripts of Mitchell's testimony before the Senate Subcommittee on Antitrust and Monopoly:

> "Did you at one time manage a heavyweight contender named Charles 'Sonny' Liston?"
>
> "I take the fifth amendment."
>
> "Were you the on-the-record manager of Liston from 1952 until 1958?"

"I decline to answer."

"Do you know a person named John Vitale?"

"I decline to answer."

"During this period while you were the on-the-record manager, is it a fact that this person, John Vitale, was the undercover manager of boxer Sonny Liston?"

"I decline to answer."

"You are directed to answer."

"I take the fifth amendment."

"During the period from 1952 until 1958, did you give this man, John Vitale, the proceeds from Liston's purses?"

"I decline to answer that question."

"In March of 1958, did you go to Chicago with John Vitale and meet with a man known as Frank 'Blinky' Palermo?"

"I take the fifth amendment."

With a man named Anthony "Tony G" Giordano, who was not well liked, John Joseph Vitale, who was, ran what there was of the Mob in St. Louis. Though it was popularly believed that Giordano was the boss, law-enforcement officials suspected that the crude and boorish Giordano was merely the bulldog in Vitale's yard.

The cops in St. Louis divided the Italian population into two groups: the predominantly Sicilian "downtown dagos," from among whom emerged the majority of the city's rough-cut Italian mobsters, and the predominantly non-Sicilian "Hill dagos," pleasant, middle-class people, whose neighborhood, in the southwestern part of town, was one of safe streets and old-country gentility. According to one St. Louis police detective, residents of the Hill were "scared to death of the people downtown."

The borders of the downtown dago neighborhood were Sixth and Ninth Streets, Franklin and Cass Avenues. It was a part of the Fourth Ward, like the black neighborhood, Sonny's neighborhood, that adjoined it; and the hub of the mobsters' action lay in the pocket between Seventh and O'Fallon. The old neighborhoods were identified by their local churches; and for the downtown dagos their neighborhood was the neighborhood of Our Lady Help of Christians.

Born on May 17, 1909, to those downtown streets that were shared by the Mob and the Virgin Mary, John J. Vitale had a criminal record that stretched back to 1927. Ranging from suspected larceny and armed robbery to gambling, it included two busts for suspicion of murder, and three narcotics raps, the latter two of which, in 1941 and 1943, were incurred in prison, at Texarkana and Leavenworth, while he was serving his sentence for the first, in 1940. He was ostensibly in the jukebox, pinball, and vending machine business; and if the St. Louis Mob had ever been given a name, it should have been the Anthony Novelty Co., as Giordano and all of Vitale's lieutenants were members of that company.

St. Louis was never a Mob stronghold, but more of an outpost, a listening post, for Chicago. What power Vitale and his men had was equalled, if not surpassed, by that of the so-called Syrian Mob, the criminal element of the city's considerable Lebanese population, whose presence and pull in ward politics eclipsed that of Vitale and his kind.

From the government transcripts of Vitale's own testimony before the Senate Subcommittee on Antitrust and Monopoly:

> "Is it a fact, Mr. Vitale, that from 1952 until 1958, Frank Mitchell acted as front man for you in the management of Sonny Liston?"
>
> "I stand on the fifth amendment."
>
> "Do you know the present No. 1 heavyweight contender, Charles 'Sonny' Liston?"

"I decline to answer on the grounds that I may tend to incriminate myself."

"You are directed to answer the question."

"Fifth amendment."

"Is it a fact that in 1958 you divided up Sonny Liston with Frank Palermo and Frank Carbo and he is presently managed undercover by you, Frank Palermo, and Frankie Carbo?"

"I decline to answer on the grounds I may tend to incriminate myself."

"Would you care, on the basis of your general knowledge of boxing, to give the subcommittee some of your own thoughts as to how to eliminate underworld racketeering and monopoly in the field of boxing?"

"I take the fifth amendment." [Pause.] "What a question."

Vitale and his men shared the organized-labor racket with the Syrian Mob. Local 110, the most important of the city's labor unions, was controlled by the Syrians in alliance with Vitale's crew.

In 1952, not long before Liston was released from prison, Vitale took to feuding with Joe Gribler, the business agent and head of Local 110, and with Gribler's union aide George Meyers. Meyers was shot in the head that spring, Gribler that summer. A Vitale ally in the Syrian community, a thirty-one-year-old South Side gambler named Raymond Sarkis, was appointed to head the union. Vitale, who had been seen entering Gribler's car on the night of the slaying, was arrested on suspicion of murder but never tried. His girlfriend, Millie Allen, was given a job working for Sarkis.

When Sonny was paroled that fall, all his jobs were Local 110 jobs, including three months of summertime labor with Vitale

Cement Contractors, Inc. Thanks to Vitale, Sonny Liston held cards with both the cement-finishers' and the hod-carriers'-and-building-laborers' unions.

Claude E. Lyles, Jr., remembered working with Sonny at Building 101 of the government ordinance plant out on Goodfellow. It was the spring of 1953, toward the end of Sonny's amateur rise. Lyles, then in his mid-twenties, worked in the production-scheduling department. Sonny operated a machine that produced cartridges for .50-caliber arms.

"He didn't want to talk to anybody. He was always very, very quiet," Lyles said. "Whenever he went over to eat, he would sit by himself. He didn't want anybody to sit with him."

In the winter of 1953–1954, Sonny was a part of the Local 110 crew that renovated Sportsman's Park, which would become Busch Stadium. One Lebanese co-worker on that job remembered him as "a hard worker" who was "a terrific guy" with a "very good heart."

In the summer of 1954, Liston worked as a laborer at the Union Electric plant down in South County. Two fellow workers who came to know him, Larry Gazall and Terry Lynch, were high-school kids who had gotten summer work at the plant. Gazall got his job because he was Lebanese, Lynch got his because he had Lebanese friends and Sonny got the job through Ray Sarkis. Gazall and Lynch, like Sonny, were hod carriers. "We were unloading boxcars of fire-brick that they used for the chimney down there," Lynch recalled. "It was hard work, heavy work," Gazall said.

They remembered Sonny fondly. "He was quiet," said Lynch, but it was a quiet that led Lynch to feel "like he was more embarrassed about his being uneducated and things like that." Away from others, he spoke freely with the two teenagers. "He was open with us 'cause we were just kids," said Lynch, who thought that

Sonny was, "I don't know, maybe in his twenties, late twenties, something like that."

"He was a real nice guy," Gazall said, and Lynch agreed. "He was really a friendly guy."

It would always be said of Sonny that he liked kids, that they saw the best of him.

"Some days he wouldn't be there," said Terry Lynch, recalling Liston and the summer of the Union Electric job. The belief was that he worked, too, as "a kind of chauffeur, quasi-bodyguard," for Ray Sarkis. "You'd hear stories of what he did," said Lynch, "break people's legs and stuff like that. And these were, to a seventeen-year-old kid" — Lynch searched for a word — "romantic." It felt good to know him, privileged even, in the blossoming of his legendry as boxer and legbreaker: the toughest of tough guys, a bigger-than-life figure of unspeakable deeds and unspeakable romance, and a source to them of kindness.

That report from that gas-station job in 1950: #1 Unknown Negro, "black chauffeur cap." There was no hat now, just a long black shiny car. He worked for Sarkis for about a year and a half. "He was a good friend," Sonny said.

David Herleth, the cop who had busted him, recalled running into Liston, prosperous-looking and wad-flashing — "that sucker had two hundred dollars" — not long after his release from prison:

"I walked into another rib station up on Franklin Avenue, which is now Martin Luther King, and he was sitting there. That's all tore down now. I said, 'Hey, don't I know you?' He says, 'Get out of here, you know me, man. I'm Charles Sonny Liston.' I said, 'Uh oh. Keep your nose clean.' He didn't."

Sonny's prison trainer, Sam Eveland, recalled that, within six or seven months after Sonny got out of prison, Sam was walking toward a joint called Preacher's when "I seen him driving a Cadillac. He had a big black Cadillac and he was eating a hot dog. I brought him in, it's an all-white tavern, and I said, 'This is gonna be your next heavyweight champ of the world.' But at that time I didn't know." The rumor, said Sam, was that "Vitale had got ahold of him" and "gave him a job being a strong man."

Sonny's early trainer William Anderson knew Vitale — "J.V.," as he called him — and he said that "J.V. was really involved deeply with boxing. He had his hand in just about everything."

It has been said that Sonny worked as a legbreaker for the union, and Anderson believes this to be true. "He was kind of a heavy man for the union," he said, "him and a man named Big Barney Baker."

Barney Baker. I remembered IBC founder Truman Gibson, that gleam in his eye, saying of Sonny, "Barney Baker was his guy."

Robert Bernard Baker. He liked to tell a story about how he had fought on the U.S. boxing team at the 1936 Olympic Games in Berlin, how he had stood in the ring before Hitler with a Star of David emblazoned on his trunks. Then again, by his own account, he was rejected for army service during World War II "because of the obesity."

Big Barney Baker. Born in New York on the day after Christmas of 1912, he had spent the thirties on the West Side waterfront of Manhattan. The forties found him in Florida, working for Jake and Meyer Lansky at their newly opened Colonial Inn, and then in Washington, D.C., where he drove a produce truck, worked in a warehouse, and where, in 1950, he was elected president of Local 730.

Barney Baker. He had come to Lansky as a wanted man, a fugitive sought in the New York murder case of a man named Hintz. And when the heat followed him to Florida, he headed west to

Los Angeles, and then to Las Vegas, where he took a room at the Flamingo, which was not yet officially open, since Bugsy Siegel, whom he had met in Florida, had not yet quite finished building it.

He was, physically, a very big man, well over three hundred pounds, thrice wed, and, according to one union official, "a very gregarious man" and "very much fun." Though Baker was known as a labor organizer, and as "a feared enforcer" and "special assignment expert," Truman Gibson seemed to see him as one of the great mystery figures of our time. "He was ubiquitous," Gibson said. "Always appearing on the scene. In Detroit, in Washington, in Las Vegas." Gibson first met him at the Morrison Hotel in Chicago, where Baker was running a gift shop. Ubiquitous. The files of the Warren Commission show that he was one of the last people Jack Ruby called before the assassination of John Kennedy. Whoever, whatever, he really was, Barney Baker's secrets died with him, in March 1974.

From his position at Local 730 in Washington, D.C., Baker had risen in the Teamsters to serve both Harold Gibbons and Jimmy Hoffa and according to Gibson, Baker was very close to Paul Dorfman, the power behind the Teamsters. It was Gibbons who moved him to St. Louis in 1952, to straighten out some trouble at a taxicab company owned by Vitale's associate Joe Costello. The membership of Local 688, which Baker had been summoned to deal with, was black.

William Anderson recalled that, in the course of his union work, Liston also did some work for Costello. Sonny and Barney, said Anderson, "were muscle men for the union. And Barney was a great fight fan."

The rematch in which Sonny avenged his sole loss by beating Marty Marshall was a preliminary event in the gala Teamsters Benefit Boxing show at Kiel Auditorium in St. Louis on April 21, 1955 — a night of boxing matches organized and overseen by Barney Baker, whose mysterious and mercurial station in life was here described as "co-chairman of the Teamsters Boxing committee."

By then, Liston's fights were a part of the grand and arrased scheme of the IBC. This involvement dated at least to his second professional fight, when he beat Ponce de Leon, on September 17, 1953. De Leon was a heavyweight that the IBC had tried to develop several years earlier. Forsaking any hope that he had the makings of a contender, the IBC fed him to Liston for breakfast as a gesture of goodwill.

Barney Baker was in town for that fight.

Liston, interrogated by Senator Estes Kefauver:

"Do you know John Vitale?"

"Yes; I know him."

"Do you know a person named Barney Baker?"

"Yes; I know him."

"By the way, what does Mr. Baker do for a living?"

"I couldn't say. I'm not — I don't know."

"What does Mr. Vitale do for a living?"

"I wouldn't know either."

"How did you come to meet this fellow Barney Baker?"

"I have a very short memory."

"Do you believe that people like this ought to remain in the sport of boxing, Mr. Liston?"

"Well, I couldn't pass judgment on no one. I haven't been perfect myself."

"Since you left St. Louis in 1958, have you met Mr. Baker?"

"Yes, sir."

"Where did you meet him?"

"Chicago."

Chicago. For Sonny, the road there was not fast enough. St. Louis had become his hell. He was the only real heavyweight contender that ever came out of that town; and instead of treating him like a hero, like something and somebody to be proud of, or at least like a man trying to get by in this world, he was hounded down, reviled, and treated like dirt by all except those few who understood, those few who knew, those few he would never forget. Was that the deal, that some little man beats you when you are too small to beat him back, and then when you can beat them all, they still won't let you be? Shit, it got to where he believed in God but not in man, and even where God was concerned, he slept with one eye open.

Liston's rap sheet from 1953, when he got out of prison, to 1958, when he got out of St. Louis, shows a record of fourteen arrests.

In my journey through the chthonic regions of Sonny Liston's years in St. Louis, the deputy chief of police of that city, Lieutenant Colonel James J. Hackett, was to prove my Virgil and my Drummond. He was a man doing a job, the best he could with the best he had; and he spoke straight, even if at times it did involve shutting off the recorder. He gave me history that could be found in no book, led me to people and places and connections that only he was in a position to lead me.

When we met, he was counting down time to his retirement. I began to feel that, to Hackett, the mystery of Sonny Liston, with which I came to him, represented a new case, rekindled a sense of street detective excitement that had ebbed. If I am right — and I have never asked him about this — I can only be thankful that I came along when I did.

I asked Jim to study the rap sheet and, if he could, analyze it as if its subject were without name or identity. He studied it carefully for a few minutes.

"Most of these are just sausage pinches," he said matter-of-factly.

I hesitated a moment, then asked him what a sausage pinch was.

"A sausage pinch. You pick the guy up, put him on the steel for twenty hours, feed him a baloney sandwich, send him home."

Twenty hours on the steel: no way out unless a lawyer showed up with a habeas corpus.

Liston remembered those nights on the steel. He spoke to the subcommittee man who asked him if he recalled a certain arrest when, under questioning, he had stated that he had been introduced to Ray Sarkis by John Vitale:

> No; I don't. The way it is there — I mean I may have said anything because they just kept grabbing me, picking me up, holding me overnight. If nobody come down to make a squawk to get me out, they keep me; then they finally let me go. Next day, back in. So what am I supposed to do? I said what they wanted me to say, because who wanted to sleep on that cold steel all that night.

The more he drank, the more he got in trouble. And Sonny drank all right. "Canadian Club," Sam Eveland said. Truman Gibson named the same. "By the bottle," he added. "He loved the 1843 Bourbon," William Anderson said. Lowell Powell, another black cop who befriended Sonny in those days, told me, "He'd drink anything. He would drink white lightning."

This went against all natural law. Boozers made bad boxers. "The fighters in those days, they didn't drink," Truman said; but Sonny "was a heavy drinker. He might have been an alcoholic." He seems to have had a sense of shame about his drinking, a shame that compelled him to hide it from priests and certain others, who believed him to be a man of temperance, even abstinence. But booze was his mistress, the one true lover that shared with him and understood and could never betray the secrets of those places inside him.

The only entry on that rap sheet that Hackett saw as more than a sausage pinch was the incident of May 5, 1956. There are a lot of tales about the truth of that night. According to the story accepted by the police and the press, forty-one-year-old Patrolman Thomas Mellow of the Tenth District was making his rounds that night at about ten minutes to eleven, when he saw a Harris taxi parked in the alley east of Taylor, beside Liston's home at 4454 St. Louis Avenue. It was a pleasant balmy night of spring in full, a foretaste of sweet summer to come. Sitting out on the porch, drinking beer and talking with, or around, Sonny were a twenty-seven-year-old neighbor and fellow ex-con named Willie Patterson — who later told the cops that he and Sonny had been "going around together" for about two months — and two sisters who also lived there. The sisters were identified as Ada Chambers, age twenty-six, married, housewife, and Geraldine Clark, age thirty-one, single, factory worker. Ada, who was three years older than reported, lived there with her husband, Arthur Chambers, who was also twenty-nine.

Geraldine worked in the S&W food-canning factory. She had an eleven-year-old daughter named Arletha. She was a very pretty woman, and she was Sonny's fiancée.

The cab's parking lights were on, and Mellow asked aloud whose cab it was. Willie Patterson said it was his. Mellow told him he could get a ticket and suggested that he move the cab. "Then," as Mellow told it, "Liston came down. 'You can't give him no ticket,' he said, real tough like. 'The hell I can't,' I said. I took out my ticket book, flashlight, to get the city sticker number off the cab. As I started over, Liston came over and gave me a bear hug from the front, lifted me clear off the ground." In the alley, the three men struggled, and Liston took Mellow's Colt .38 service revolver. Patterson said, "Shoot the white son of a bitch." Liston put the gun to Mellow's head. Mellow hollered, "Don't shoot me." Liston then struck the cop over the left eye "with either the gun or his fist. It took seven stitches. My left leg was broken in the knee from the fall or somebody stomping me. Then they run up the alley." Liston "appeared to be drinking; the fellows that arrested him had a little trouble."

According to Liston:

> I called a cab to come pick me up. I saw the cab pull up into the alleyway, and I hurried out of the house. Meanwhile, a cop came up and told the cabbie he was going to give him a ticket. I said, "How come you going to give this cab a ticket? He's just doing his business." Then the cop turns to me and says, "You're a smart nigger," and when I say "I'm not smart," he reaches for his gun and tries to take it out his holster, but I take it away from him. Later the cop said I was drunk. Now how could a drunk handle a sober cop trained to make arrests and to pull a gun? I never drink any hard liquor anyway.

According to the police report based on Patterson's statement:

> About 10:30 o'clock P.M. (5-5-56) he went to the home of Charles Liston at 4454 St. Louis Avenue and parked his vehicle in the alley adjacent to the house and then he and the mentioned two women began drinking beer on the front porch, and shortly thereafter they were joined there by Charles Liston, and as the four of them were seated there drinking beer a uniformed police officer came to the front of the house and inquired about the taxi-cab parked in the alley and stated that he was going to give a ticket to the driver of same. Patterson adds that he told the Officer that he was the driver of the vehicle and offered to move same from the alley and about that time Liston joined in the conversation and began to argue with the Officer and shortly afterwards Liston and the Officer began to struggle with each other, and he (Patterson) tried to separate the two men. He further states that Liston and the Officer fought into the darkness of the alley and shortly thereafter

> Liston came back to the mouth of the alley and told him to drive around to the Maffit Avenue side of the alley which he complied with and a few minutes later Liston emerged from said alley and told him to take him downtown, during the ride he displayed a revolver which he stated was the Officer's gun. Patterson continued that he drove Liston to the home of his (Liston's) sister at 1438 (rear) N. Fifteenth Street, where he left the revolver, and rejoined him in the taxi-cab and he took Liston to 23rd and Franklin Avenue and left him.

Patterson was arrested almost immediately where he dropped Sonny off, at about half past two in the morning. Sonny was arrested about an hour later, a few blocks away, at Franklin and Elliot, in his old neighborhood; more specifically, in the vicinity of Cole and Carr, near that alley where Anthony Tocco had been taken down six years ago and more. It was as if one alley led to another, the first to this and this to that, in a world that was nothing but alleys. When beer was in the blood and blood was on the britches — and Liston and Patterson both had bloodstains on their britches, when they were taken in — when one felt like going home but had no true home to go to, when the night was dead and the morning uncome, it was like that.

According to the police report, Liston "refused to make any statement concerning the incident, stating that he did not know the Officer and had never seen him before, further refusing to answer any questions in this connection. The attitude of Liston at this time became very belligerent due to indications that he had been drinking."

The revolver was retrieved by police from the home of Sonny's sister Alcora Jones, "who stated that at about 11:30 P.M. (5-5-56) her brother came to her home and left a package in the bottom of a wooden clothes chest in her bedroom."

As for the report concerning Geraldine: "Officer Mellow began talking to Patterson regarding the violation during which time his conversation was interrupted by Charles Liston, who began to berate the Officer, as Patterson was observed to attempt to separate Officer Mellow and Liston." The three men then

> disappeared into the darkness of the alley, and shortly afterwards she heard an outcry from the Officer of "don't hurt me" and she could see Liston striking at someone apparently Officer Mellow, a short time later Liston and Patterson came out of the dark alley and Liston told Patterson to drive around to the other end of the alley, at this time Patterson drove west on St. Louis Avenue, and south on Taylor Avenue and disappeared, Liston walked south through the alley and apparently met Patterson at the Maffit Avenue side of same.

Ada, who had gone up to her room during the fight, corroborated her sister's version of what transpired before the fight, and stated "that she heard the outcry of 'don't hurt me' come from the alley while she was in the house from her raised window which is adjacent to the alley."

Liston pled guilty of assaulting a police officer, and was sentenced, on January 28, 1957, to nine months in the City Workhouse. Patterson drew thirty days in jail.

He had not had a fight since his third encounter with Marty Marshall, in March of 1956, two months before the Mellow incident. Almost immediately upon news of that assault, the St. Louis boxing commissioner, Charles Pian, had moved to suspend Liston's license to fight. Bob Burnes was one of the local sportswriters who successfully urged Pian to lift the suspension after Liston had served his term in the workhouse. In so doing, they joined with Captain John Doherty, the cop who ruled St. Louis with a thyrsus of lead-filled hardwood, and who in many ways was the nemesis and sworn enemy of the man to whose defense he came. While other cops supported Liston's suspension — "Every time he fights," one of them complained — "half the hoodlums in the country show up in St. Louis" — Doherty demanded of the commissioner, "What do you want to do, give him a license so he can get in a ring and fight, or a gun so he can go out and rob? Those are the only two things he knows how to do."

On August 28, four days after Sonny got out of the workhouse, he and Geraldine applied for a license. The Affidavit of Male bears Charles Liston's earliest known signature, faltering but proud. Above that signature, Sonny swore his date of birth to be May 8, 1932, and his place of birth to be Memphis, Tennessee.

Geraldine stated that she was a native of St. Louis. She stated her name to be Geraldine Chambers, her marital status as single, her date of birth as January 25, 1932 — if it was fine enough a year for Sonny, it was fine enough for her — and the license was issued three days later.

In the past fifteen months, Geraldine had grown six years younger; and, bearing the surname of her sister's husband, Arthur Chambers, she had now become Geraldine Chambers instead of Geraldine Clark. Later records would show the loss of another three years, with a date of birth of January 25, 1935. This would mean that she had been all of nine years old when she gave birth to her daughter, Arletha, on June 2, 1944, as opposed to the childbearing at age twelve postulated by the information on her marriage license application. If indeed she was thirty-one, as reported at the time of the Mellow incident, her year of birth thus would have been 1925, meaning that she was nineteen when her daughter was born.

On September 3, 1957, Sonny and Geraldine were married by the Reverend G.L. Hayden, Minister of the Gospel, of 4965 Cote Brilliante Avenue, six blocks south of that alley at Taylor and St.

Louis Avenue. As husband and wife, they lived at 4439 Farlin Avenue, to the north. It was to be Sonny's final St. Louis address.

Cops such as William Anderson and Lowell Powell had been his friends. "I was a policeman and he was something of a thug," Powell recalled, but none the less they had been friends. In the big picture, however, there was no love lost between Sonny and the cops.

"He has no finesse, tact whatsoever," Frank Mitchell said. "He doesn't realize that he has to keep his name out of the paper. He's kind of mean, too. He hates policemen; they hate him."

He hated them, they hated him. The assault on Mellow had made his situation dangerous. "At that time," Lowell Powell said, "the policemen were the real bosses around St. Louis, and fighting a policeman was unheard of really. We'd call them 'nixie fighters.' " (Etymology unknown, even to Jim Hackett.) Another black cop, Detective Sergeant James Reddick, made no secret of his feelings. "He's a bad man," Reddick declared. "If he ever crossed me, I'd baptize his ass. He'd be like a coffee sieve."

The harassment intensified. Between his assault on Mellow in May 1956, and his sentencing, in January 1957, he was popped five times: for suspicion of theft; speeding; failing to appear on a summons; suspicion of larceny; and careless driving. He was released on every charge: only the twenty-five-buck speeding ticket stuck. Sausage pinches, nights on the steel.

Four days after his wedding, he was busted again, for general peace disturbance and individual peace disturbance; both charges nolle-prossed. Two more pinches for suspected robbery followed on September 28 and September 29. His car was stopped again, another speeding ticket issued him, later that fall. His rap sheet was no longer the playsheet of St. Louis alone. He had what they called a "Hoover sheet" now, too: a centralized criminal record designated by an FBI record number — his was number 272 767 B —

copies of which were duly issued to the criminal identification bureaus of other law-enforcement agencies, such as the Missouri State Highway Patrol. In his record as circulated by the United States Department of Justice in October 1956, the charge for his encounter with Mellow is set forth as "aslt to kill."

Captain John Doherty, the boss, was a man with a penchant for running people out of town. He had gotten rid of Barney Baker. There was nothing that compared to the ire Sonny roused in Doherty. "Five coppers tried to lock Sonny. This ain't no bullshit story. They broke hickory nightsticks over his head. They couldn't get his hands cuffed. He was a monster."

The tale has been told that Doherty literally took Liston to the tracks at the outskirts of town, stuck a gun to his head, and told him to leave. Sonny's story, though less melodramatic, amounts to much the same: "Well, the captain, Captain Doherty, told me to my face, if I wanted to stay alive, to leave St. Louis." Doherty's words were: "If you don't, they're going to find you in an alley." The meaning was clear to Sonny: "He said that his men was going to put me in the alley."

Between trouble, suspension, and the workhouse, Sonny had fought only one fight in 1956, none in 1957. In late January 1958, he left St. Louis for his first professional match in Chicago, a fight against Billy Hunter, the boxer that Foneda Cox had beat the night Sonny vanquished Summerlin for the second time, back in 1953. The fight was to be held at the Chicago Stadium, which was owned by the Norris group and where all boxing was controlled by the IBC.

Frank Mitchell told a reporter for *Newsweek* that he met with Irv Schoenwald, a prominent Chicago insurance man and fight promoter, and that he signed over to Schoenwald half of his interest in Liston in return for Schoenwald's promise that he would get Liston bigger purses and break him into the lucrative market of the big-time television fights, which paid not in the hundreds but in the thousands. Mitchell said that his deal with Schoenwald was executed the week following the Hunter fight.

Thus, at this point, according to Mitchell, he and Schoenwald now shared a twenty-five percent interest in Liston. Eddie Yawitz and the half-interest he had supposedly bought for six hundred dollars in early 1955 were suddenly and inexplicably no longer a part of the picture.

Don Wake, who set down Mitchell's story in an unpublished 1963 background report for *Newsweek,* noted in parentheses: "The mention of Schoenwald certainly should be checked — I've never seen his name mentioned before as one of Liston's managers, and there may, some way or other, be libel involved. Bob Burnes, in his *Saturday Evening Post* article avoided using Schoenwald's name, describing him as a 'respected' Chicago insurance man." In his 1963 book, *Sonny Liston: The Champ Nobody Wanted,* A.S. "Doc" Young quotes Mitchell in the following manner: "*'I referred him to ——— ' — Mitchell mentioned the name of a Chicagoan.*"

Less then two months after the Liston-Hunter fight, Frank Mitchell traveled again to Chicago, ostensibly to attend the March 25 rematch between Sugar Ray Robinson and Carmen Basilio, who had taken the middleweight title from Robinson the previous September in New York. Although Mitchell never said so, he came to Chicago this time in the company of Liston, John Vitale, and Vitale's *cummari,* Millie Allen.

"When I was in town," Mitchell told *Newsweek*'s man, "I met Blinky Palermo in a hotel lobby. I told him, 'I've got the next heavyweight champion.' "

Blinky's response, according to Mitchell, was, "I can't manage him, but I can get somebody to help you."

Joseph "Pep" Barone, a close associate of Blinky Palermo, operated as a fight manager out of Allentown, Pennsylvania. His listing in the managerial directory of *The Ring Record Book* read: "JOE (PEP) BARONE — Fair Grounds and Allentown High School, 643 No. 6th St., Allentown, Pa. Phone Allentown 3-2513, 2-7229."

Mitchell recalled, "When I got back to St. Louis, I got a long-distance call from Pep Barone. He said, 'I understand you have a fighter you want some help with.' "

"Yes, I do," Mitchell said. He then apparently referred Barone to Irv Schoenwald and "told him I was going back to Chicago for a fight," and he and Barone could speak further at that time. As Mitchell told the story, it was then that Pep Barone told him that he was taking over Liston and moving him to Philadelphia. Mitchell said that he assumed "they'd" gotten in touch with Schoenwald to work out a deal, and that he, Mitchell, retained his twelve-and-a-half-percent interest in Liston's career. "Barone said when Sonny was made, I'd be in."

From that moment, Mitchell said, he never received a cent from that interest he claimed to have held. "Sonny has a moral obligation toward me and he knows it," he said after Liston had become champion. According to Mitchell, Liston had "visited with mother and me" soon after winning the championship. "He said, 'Frank, I know you've got somethin' comin', and I'll see that you get it.' Someday, I think Sonny will." Mitchell's homiletic tale, here drawn from several recorded variations, ended invariably with the insistence that he "didn't get a penny." Furthermore, "the income-tax people have checked and rechecked that twelve and a half percent of Sonny's contract that I discovered I don't have. They haven't found it either."

Why had no one ever seen these various "contracts": the one that Liston had with Harrison and Mitchell; the one that Yawitz bought from Harrison, directly or by way of Mitchell; the one by which Schoenwald and Mitchell became partners? Mitchell himself elsewhere dropped the fact that there was no contract, at least not in the formal or legal sense: "If I had to do it over," he said, "for one thing, I'd have something in writing."

Why, if the IBC had been involved to some extent in the course of Liston's career since at least his second professional fight, in 1953, would Mitchell need to apprise Blinky Palermo, the cohort of the power behind the throne of the IBC, of the existence and promise of Sonny Liston? Why, if his interests were so momentously at stake, would a man of Frank Mitchell's experience and wiles not have a written agreement, and why would he ever *assume* that Barone — or *they*, as he said — had negotiated a proper deal with Schoenwald in which those interests had been protected?

Why would Sonny tell Mitchell, "I know you've got somethin' comin', and I'll see that you get it" if Sonny himself was in no way party to or responsible for any transaction concerning that interest in himself that was not his own? "*He who is by nature not his own but another's man, is by nature a slave.*" Liston's alleged promise was the equivalent of a slave consoling a slave trader with a promise to make good for a default on payment by the new master to whom the trader had sold him.

Irving Schoenwald and his partner, Jack Begun, had indeed been powerful and important promoters in the old days, and their office at 127 Dearborn Street was one of the cathedral seats of Chicago boxing. Like many independent promoters, however, Schoenwald was laid low by the ascendance of the IBC. By 1958, when Mitchell allegedly entered into business with him, Schoenwald's importance in the boxing racket was a vestige of what it once had been, and he was nearing the end of his career as a promoter. While Jack Begun tried to persevere, opening an office of his own on South Wabash, Schoenwald faded from boxing by the end of the decade.

Why, then, would Mitchell, at that point in time, have sought

Schoenwald's help in furthering Liston's career and his own interest in it? Schoenwald by himself was in no better a position than Mitchell to fulfill the promises he allegedly made in exchange for half of Mitchell's interest in Liston; and Mitchell, who well knew both the fight racket and the powers behind it, must have known this as well.

Frank Mitchell, pimp and pillar of the community, lived a lie and was perhaps not above telling one. His tale of innocence and indignant righteousness is embroidered with all the right names and dates and places. But it was beneath that superficial embroidery, not in it, that the truth lay.

Eddie Yawitz, whom Mitchell never mentions in his account of the events of 1958, still held the half-interest in Liston that he had procured — through six hundred dollars, as both Harrison and Mitchell claimed, or otherwise — back in February 1955. When Mitchell transferred half of his own interest to Schoenwald, as recounted or otherwise, Yawitz became the majority holder.

In that presumed transfer, Schoenwald would have been acting on behalf of a man who actually could fulfill the promises that Mitchell alleged Schoenwald to have made and himself to have believed. That man was Schoenwald's friend and associate Bernie Glickman, a fight promoter and a friend of Chicago mob boss Tony Accardo.

Any contract agreed to by Mitchell in early February 1958, could have been nothing but confirmation of what had already gone down, known or unknown to Mitchell, through an unwritten and more binding contract.

For even before Sonny came to Chicago to fight Hunter in January, Bernie Glickman and Eddie Yawitz had taken charge of him through the benison of Frankie Carbo and the IBC, to whom John Vitale had delivered Sonny forth as he had delivered forth other St. Louis fighters, such as Virgil Akins and Jesse Bowdry.

Ben Bentley — he was born Ben Goldberg in 1921 — was the IBC matchmaker, publicist, and ringside announcer who was called upon to promote Liston's fights under the new management of Glickman's alliance with Yawitz. Ben was a friend of both Schoenwald and Glickman, and as Ben once told the story, it was Irv Schoenwald who called him about a heavyweight that was being brought up from St. Louis. Years later, Ben told me that it was Bernie Glickman who called him about handling Sonny's first Chicago fight.

Ben remembered that Sonny arrived forty-five minutes late for the weigh-in. The boxing commissioner told Ben to get another fighter, and Ben was about to scratch Liston from the card when Sonny appeared. He'd driven up with Foneda Cox, and they'd gotten lost, he said. Ben warned him that this wouldn't work in Chicago, and he told him to be at the stadium at seven o'clock. As they were walking out, Sonny said, "Can I get ten dollars' eating-money?" Ben gave him the ten.

That afternoon, Sonny, who was licensed to fight in Missouri, Michigan, and Pennsylvania, but not yet in Illinois, was examined under oath by Commissioner Frank Gilmore of the Illinois State Athletic Commission.

> "You are twenty-five years old and you are applying for a professional boxer's license. Have you ever been convicted of a felony? Have you ever been in prison?"
>
> "Once. City workhouse."
>
> "That is not prison. How long?"
>
> "Four months."
>
> "What was the reason?"
>
> "Resisting arrest."
>
> "Have you ever been penalized by any state or city athletic association?"

"No, sir."

"Was that the only trouble you have been in?"

"That's right."

"Have you been boxing since then?"

"Yes, sir."

"When did you get out?"

"August 24, 1957."

"Have you been in training since then?"

"Yes, sir."

License and eating-money in order, Sonny showed up on time at the Chicago Stadium that night, and he knocked out Billy Hunter one minute into the second round.

The tide had shifted for Mitchell before, not after, that first Chicago fight. One way or another — bought out, cut out, or conned out — Mitchell was already out of the picture when he entered Irv Schoenwald's office. For Sonny, the tide had merely risen. Since 1953, the shadow of the IBC had been a vague but increasing presence; for longer than that, he had been indentured to John Vitale and his kind. Now, instead of Vitale and his kind, there would be those who were to them as master to slave.

Harrison. Mitchell. Vitale. Yawitz. Glickman. The IBC Barone. Palermo. Sonny had lost track of who owned what pieces of him, and of through whose and how many grasping hands his money and his freedom passed, dwindling like slough-bottom sand through the clutching, sifting fingers of those hands until what remained reached his own. But he knew who called the shots. It was The Gray, Paul John Carbo.

Glickman, whose welterweight Virgil Akins was on the verge of becoming champion, saw in Liston an opportunity to work with a fighter possessed of the greatest possibility he had ever known. But it was not meant to be.

Chicago mob boss Tony Accardo was very fond of Bernie Glickman, and Glickman considered Accardo a friend. They got together almost every Sunday. Bernie would bring bagels and lox to Accardo's River Forest mansion, and the two men would while away the morning together. Accardo had told him, however, never to bring his fight business with him, for he wanted nothing to do with it. They could talk awnings, they could talk football, they could talk food, they could talk the ass on this one, the lungs on that one, they could talk the breeze through the trees and the meaning of fucking life itself. But no boxing business. There, Bernie was on his own.

But in the fight business, nobody was on his own. Glickman operated through the goodwill, and at the mercy of, the IBC and its sub rosa directors, Frankie Carbo and Blinky Palermo. Bernie's friend Accardo was a powerful and respected man; but lox and bagels were one thing, the tie between him and men such as Carbo was another. Virgil Akins, brought up from his scuffling days by Glickman and Yawitz, won the welterweight title on June 6, 1958, in his hometown, at the St. Louis Arena, which was owned by James Norris and Arthur M. Wirtz of the IBC. Upon that championship victory, Carbo and Palermo seized control of interest in Akins from Glickman and Yawitz. It was like the devil returning inevitably for his due; for in the IBC years, no fighter fought without Carbo's choosing the opponent or the arena, and in this way he controlled the destiny of every fighter. None got anywhere without him; and thus, though he and not nature had dictated and enforced this unwritten law, it followed to him that all of them — enfranchised managers as well as their fighters — owed him. As to when and how much they owed him, it was solely a matter of his own discretion. Like Accardo, Frankie Carbo and Blinky Palermo were fond of Glickman. But *la bisines* was *la bisines,* and things were what they were.

So impressive was Liston, now fully embraced by the forces of Chicago, that Carbo and Blinky did not wait long to claim him as their own.

Sam Giancana, after taking over from Accardo the previous year, returned from a meeting in Philadelphia, and called Glickman.

"He meets my father at the Armory Lounge," said Bernie's son Joel, who was in his early twenties when his father had Liston. "They go in the kitchen, and they're having dinner, just the two of them, and he tells my father that he had to give up Liston." Glickman was to receive a buyout price of fifty grand.

Liston's next fight, with Ben Wise, brought him again to Chicago in March 1958.

"Well," as Sonny would tell it, "I went up to fight this fight and Frank Mitchell told me when I left St. Louis that it would be a man by the name of 'Pep' Barone to come up with the contract and for you to sign it and he will get you East where you can get sparring partners and more fights, a better trainer."

The contract — a standard, supply-store Form 1-B — was signed and duly notarized in Chicago on the night of the fight: a fourth-round knockout of Ben Wise at the Midwest Athletic Club on March 11.

"Buck admission," Ben Bentley recalled.

The single-page, five-year contract with Joseph "Pep" Barone entitled Barone to fifty percent of Liston's income, in terms that rendered Liston the receiving party:

> The Manager agrees to pay the Athlete 50% per cent of all sums of money derived by him from any services that the said Athlete may render hereunder, before the deduction of all training expenses and railroad fares that may be incurred by the Athlete in the performance of his duties hereunder, and further agrees and guarantees

said Athlete that the said per cent of the monies to be paid to him as above provided shall in no year during the term of this contract be less than $1,500.00.

The unwritten clause, the Mephistophelean clause, the only clause that mattered, stipulated silently that Sonny now belonged, body and soul, to Frankie Carbo and Blinky Palermo. For a boxer in those days, there was no greater fate; because Carbo and, beneath him, Palermo were fate itself, divider of destinies and allotter of days.

Sonny returned to St. Louis to beat Bert Whitehurst on April 3. After that, he left St. Louis for good and moved to Philadelphia, where Barone, Blinky, and the big time awaited him. He moved into the Hamilton Court Apartments, a seven-story red-brick building at Thirty-ninth and Chestnut that was run by Blinky in association with his friend Sam Margolis and his son-in-law Carlo Musciano, who were also partners in the Sansom delicatessen, located on the Thirty-Ninth Street side of the building. In early 1960, with Blinky's help, Sonny would secure a mortgage and buy his first home, a two-story house of red and white brick at 5785 Dunlap Street, in the Overbrook section of West Philly, where he welcomed Geraldine's parents to live with them. His own mother still lived in Gary, Indiana, at this time. She would move to Forrest City, Arkansas, in December 1961, to live with the family of her eldest son, E.B. Ward.

The big time. Liston's first national television exposure came on May 14, when he knocked out Julio Mederos of Havana in the third round of a fight that was broadcast from the Chicago Stadium as part of the IBC's Wednesday night program on CBS. On August 6, in another nationally televised IBC Wednesday night fight from the Chicago Stadium, he knocked out Wayne Bethea in the first.

Whatever you might say about Blinky and The Gray, one thing was certain: they delivered.

There was no stopping Liston. By the end of 1961, his professional record, marred only by his sole, narrow-decision loss to Marshall, consisted of thirty-four wins, twenty-three of which were knockouts, including eleven of his last dozen. Only one man stood between him and the heavyweight championship of the world. And, still, he was in a bad place.

The IBC's Ben Bentley considered Blinky Palermo "a good friend," and one of the few men who seemed truly to care for Liston. When Bentley was close to Liston and traveled with the fighter constantly, Blinky would call him frequently when Liston was in training, instructing him always to call him back collect from a pay phone at such and such a number. "He'd wanna know how did he do in training, how is he doing in training, does he see this guy, does he see that guy, who's his sparring partners, is he behaving himself, is he runnin' around?" When they were together, Blinky would put his arm around Bentley. "Tell me, has he been drinking?"

And Blinky, in turn, seemed to be one of the few men that Liston trusted: intercessor, paternal protector, and, as Ben Bentley said, they represented the sort of tough guy that Sonny had always wanted to be. "They were class," Bentley said of Blinky and Carbo.

But Blinky and The Gray were about to fall. Back in St. Louis, on June 6, 1958, a few weeks after Sonny moved to Philadelphia, his friend Virgil Akins won the welterweight title by knocking out Vince Martinez in four rounds. Present at the fight was an investigative representative of a New York County grand jury inquiry into prizefight fixing.

The investigation had been under way for several months. Subpoenas had been handed out immediately following the previous

Akins fight, a welterweight championship elimination bout with the Cuban boxer Isaac Logart at Madison Square Garden on March 21. In that fight, Logart, the odds-on favorite, had dominated until the sixth round, when he seemed to fall under a spell, as did the referee, who began to count him out while he was still standing and then stopped the fight at the count of eight, only seven seconds before the bell would have saved him. Logart's cornermen seemed under the spell as well, for there was not even the show of a protest at the fight's outcome. It was then that agents of District Attorney Frank S. Hogan moved through the ringside crowd passing subpoenas to the unsuspecting assortment of characters whose names those subpoenas bore.

That spring, as the New York County grand jury gathered the testimony of those who had been summoned forth, the boxing community grew intensely more embroiled in anxiety, speculation, rumor, and suspicion of betrayal. On April 18, James Norris, fearing the worst, tendered his resignation as the president and director of the International Boxing Club, leaving behind Truman Gibson to face the increasing heat as his duly appointed successor.

On June 7, the day after Akins won the welterweight title, it was announced that "indictments involving alleged 'fixing' of some professional boxing matches are expected next month after the New York grand jury concludes the first phase of its boxing investigation."

Blinky Palermo, who was under subpoena in the grand jury investigation, was in St. Louis for the Akins title fight. Under the direction of Captain John Doherty, detective squad surveillance of the fight was heavy. Later that night, Doherty himself arrested Blinky and his companion, Abe Sands of Paterson, New Jersey, as the two men drove up to a house at 5822 Waterman Boulevard. It was the home of Millie Allen, the mistress of John Vitale, who a few minutes earlier had passed the house, but had continued on, apparently having sensed the presence of the detectives who lay in wait.

> On the ride to police headquarters, Palermo made an unsuccessful attempt to shove a bottle of pills and a box of capsules behind the seat cushion of a police car [reported the *St. Louis Post-Dispatch*]. On reaching headquarters, the prisoner was reluctant to be photographed or fingerprinted. Sgt. Frank J. Burns said in his report "armlocks" were applied to obtain the prisoner's co-operation. The report added that Palermo threatened to "have you cops fired."
>
> Sgt. Burns said Palermo threw himself to the floor and demanded to be taken to a hospital. Later he laughed and said: "All I want is to get out of town." He admitted knowing Vitale, whom he described as "a nice guy." He was suspected of gambling, although denying that he made any bets on the fight.
>
> Sands, who said he is a salesman, also denied betting on the fight.

Later, Abe Sands would be identified as a bagman for Carbo and Palermo, in which role he was often known only as "Mike."

Blinky was held overnight in lockup. A sausage pinch, a night on the steel. But it was for him the first of many dark nights to follow.

Among the items found on Blinky's person at the time of his arrest were "receipts for a hotel bill and telephone numbers indicating he is closely connected with Charles (Sonny) Liston, heavyweight boxer, who recently transferred headquarters from St. Louis to Philadelphia." The newspapers failed to mention that the telephone numbers indicated that he was closely connected to George Raft as well.

On the night of his arrest, Blinky denied any official connection with Sonny. As Sonny himself would later say regarding the hotel bill, Blinky explained that he had taken care of the boxer's bill simply because Sonny's manager "was ill in a hospital" in Allentown.

> Investigators in the boxing inquiry [concluded the *St. Louis Post-Dispatch*], have expressed interest in communications last March between Vitale, who attends most of the important fights, and Palermo. The communications included a long-distance telephone call from Vitale to Philadelphia in which the St. Louis hoodlum warned against any attempt "to gyp me." This was followed by arrangements for a meeting in Chicago.

It was on March 11 that Liston had signed his contract with Pep Barone; and it was also in March, two weeks later, that Vitale and Millie Allen had traveled to Chicago in the company of Frank Mitchell and Liston.

The New York grand jury investigation led to the formal indictment of Frank Carbo on July 24. With the kind of headlines he had been pulling down, or Hogan's press lackeys had been pulling down for him — "The Mystery of Frankie Carbo — Will New Hogan Probe Solve It?" — it was inevitable.

In the indictment against him, Carbo was charged with conspiracy, multiple counts of undercover management of prizefighters, and unlicensed matchmaking in fights whose official matchmaker was the International Boxing Club of New York.

Ever the fugitive, Carbo went south. This shit had been going on for over ten years. That's how long Hogan had been after him. The *New York Sun*, June 3, 1947:

> District Attorney Frank S. Hogan announced today that Frankie Carbo, former fight promoter, sought for questioning in the investigation here of alleged gangster influence in the boxing world, has

> been located in New Haven, Conn., and will be brought here for a Grand Jury examination set for June 10.
>
> According to the District Attorney, Carbo, who is said to be a secret power in the prizefight world and the undercover manager of several well-known fighters, was located after a two-week search in which detectives traced him from Maine to Maryland.
>
> Hogan said that Carbo disappeared around the end of January when the Grand Jury heard middleweight Rocky Graziano state that he had been offered a bribe of $100,000 to throw his championship fight with Tony Zale.

That was Hogan's first investigation into boxing, back in '47. Charged with no offense, but sought only as a witness, Carbo was brought to the Criminal Courts Building on November 20, the second day of the investigation. Six days earlier, twenty-six-year-old Jacob LaMotta, going down in the fourth, had thrown a fight to Billy Fox at Madison Square Garden in exchange for a shot at the middleweight title. Jake's performance was such that reporters had voiced suspicions of a fix. This, Hogan figured, was a godsend, a blessing: an instance of corruption, a controversy, fresh in the public eye and mind, upon which to center the inquiry anew. LaMotta was called by the grand jury to testify on the same day that Carbo testified. What Hogan failed to consider was the importance to LaMotta of that promise of a chance to win the title. If LaMotta was willing to go down in ignominy for that chance, why should he not be willing to prevaricate to protect that chance?

Speaking from Philadelphia on November 18, Blinky Palermo had said that he welcomed an investigation because Fox had won an honest fight on his own merits. Now, two days later, Jake said that he had fought his best, and that was that. Carbo said he could not comment because he had not seen the fight, and that was that.

The boxing shit came up again six days before Christmas 1952, during the New York State Crime Commission investigation into waterfront racketeering. The Italian-born overlord of the waterfront, deadly Umberto Anastasio, better known as Albert Anastasia, "the man generally considered the most feared figure in the underworld" (the *New York Times* of December 20, 1952), was a defiant and angry witness who refused to answer ninety-seven of the questions put to him in the hour of his time that he gave: "The witness' sinister reputation as the man who reputedly had given the orders for possibly sixty-three murders kept the hearing-room audience in New York County Courthouse spellbound. His demeanor on the stand had the deceptive languor of a jungle cat."

The hearing veered into an examination of Anastasia's ties to boxing and of the influence he was said to have in so-called Jacobs Beach, the area around Broadway and Forty-Ninth Street, which was the gathering place of fight managers both known and covert. In this context, Frank Carbo was called to the stand. Described by the commission as an associate of Anastasia, Carbo sat mute in a fine blue suit and tie through most of the questioning. His response to the opening request to state his name was, "I refuse to answer the question. I rely on my constitutional rights." Later he refused to answer one question as to whether he refused to answer.

The hearing was recessed until the new year. At two o'clock on the morning of January 17, 1953, two detectives of District Attorney Frank S. Hogan's squad arrested Carbo in the Jacobs Beach area above Times Square. After questioning at the district attorney's office, he was brought downtown to the Elizabeth Street station and booked on charges of violating the Executive Law, an obscure, thirty-year-old statute that rendered it a misdemeanor offense to refuse without reasonable cause to answer questions in a public inquiry.

He smiled once again his beautiful smile for the photographers — *che faccia, serena e molto vivace, come quella dello zio gentile e amato.* "His record," noted the *New York Times* of the next day, "shows a facility in beating murder charges."

Three Special Sessions justices acquitted him of all charges, agreeing that he did indeed have grounds for silence, as he "could have reasonably sensed the peril of prosecution" had he answered.

He seemed above the law, jurisprudence-proof as well as bullet-proof. His image, power, and sovereignty — and his mystery — were the stuff of headlines. "Boxing and the Mobs: Who Is Frankie Carbo?" asked the *New York Post* in bold white display set from black. "Paul John Carbo had a constant companion as a youth," the article began. "It was a gun." The second paragraph blossoms into dire metaphor in true *Post* fashion: "Today, some 30 years later, Carbo is still the man behind the firearms in the shot-gun marriage of underworld mobs and prize ring."

Winds changed and things turned bad for his friends from the good old days. Frank Costello got his retirement notice, a close-range scalp-grazing bullet, on May 2, 1957. Less than six months later, on the morning of October 25, Anastasia was assassinated while relaxing in a barber's chair. But Carbo continued to flourish. The bullets served on Costello and Anastasia were Genovese bullets; Carbo's old partner in the management of Babe Risko was Gabe Genovese, a cousin of Vito Genovese and now, according to Assistant District Attorney John G. Bonomi, "a chief lieutenant of Frankie Carbo."

After Anastasia's murder, while the police, to no avail, sought him for questioning, newspapers reported front-page warnings that "Frankie C." was next. The *World-Telegram* described him as "known far and wide as the underworld's commissioner of boxing"; the *Times* as "a man with wide but shadowy associations in the prizefight field."

After Carbo's flight from indictment in the summer of 1958,

District Attorney Hogan sent out a nationwide alarm for his arrest. "Warrant issued. Will extradite," declared the wanted notices that were broadcast to every police agency in America.

Despite all attempts to track him down, Carbo remained at large until late the following spring, when he was finally captured, living in a house in a quiet suburban township near Camden, New Jersey, directly across the Delaware River from Philadelphia and from his good man Blinky. Upon his seizure, a few minutes past midnight on May 30, 1959, he casually told his captors that he had been planning to surrender "in a couple of days" anyway. On June 5, he was sent to Camden County Jail, where he awaited the outcome of an application filed by his attorneys for a writ of habeas corpus to test the validity of extradition proceedings. In voicing opposition to any possibility of bail, Alfred J. Scotti, chief assistant district attorney for New York County and head of the Rackets Bureau, called Carbo "the most corrupt, corrosive and degrading influence in the sport of boxing."

Carbo's trial opened, in New York, before General Sessions Judge John A. Mullen, on October 5, 1959. Several weeks later, on October 30, after a conference among defense and prosecution attorneys, Carbo brought the trial to an unexpected close by withdrawing his plea of not guilty and entering a plea of guilty to three representative counts of the ten-count indictment: one each of conspiracy, undercover managing, and undercover matchmaking. These counts were taken to "cover the indictment," meaning that he could not be prosecuted for the other seven counts.

Carbo was sentenced on the last day of November. Chief Assistant District Attorney Alfred J. Scotti read from an eighteen-page prepared statement: "The evil influence of this man has for many years permeated virtually the entire professional sport of boxing," Scotti declaimed. "I believe it is fair to say that the name of Frank

Carbo today symbolizes the degeneration of professional boxing into a racket.

"This man is beyond redemption."

Judge Mullen spoke at less length and with less melodrama, addressing his words directly to Carbo: "In boxing, your wish was tantamount to a command performance. You had terrific, improper, and illegal influence in the fight game. You enriched yourself to a degree I can't contemplate."

Mullen observed that the medical reports he had seen on Carbo were not "happy." (The Gray was diabetic, had liver and kidney trouble, and also allegedly suffered from racket syndrome, the all-but-inevitable heart ailment of those prone to prosecution and sentencing.) It was only because of Carbo's poor health, said Mullen, that the maximum sentence of three years was being reduced to a term of two.

"Thank you, Judge," Carbo whispered to Mullen as he was led past the bench.

Carbo, gentleman and killer, had reason to be grateful. From the Prohibition days of bullets and teenage redheads to his present breath, he had led a chosen and charmed existence, getting away with murder, in every sense of that phrase, for more than thirty years.

From the New York State Crime Commission of 1952–1953 to Hogan's grand jury investigation of 1958; from his fugitive months underground in 1958–1959 to this magic moment before Judge Mullen in General Session Court, Carbo had operated with impunity and his dominion had been inviolable. He and his man Blinky had taken control of Sonny Liston beneath the approaching storm of Hogan's investigation; and neither that investigation nor Carbo's flight from it, neither law nor so-called justice itself shook that control, which was absolute and which Carbo exercised freely, in and beneath the light of day, in hiding or in the open.

Throughout 1958 and 1959, Sonny fought a dozen fights under that control. Eight of them were in 1958: Billy Hunter in January; Ben Wise in March; Bert Whitehurst in April; Julio Mederos in May; Wayne Bethea in August; Frankie Daniels and again Bert Whitehurst in October; Ernie Cab in November. All but the first two of these were fought while Carbo was in hiding.

Carbo was still at large for the first two fights of 1959, with Mike De John in February and with Cleveland Williams in April. Carbo was awaiting trial for the third, with Nino Valdez in August, and he was in Riker's Island Prison for the last, with Willi Besmanoff in December.

The Daniels fight in October and the Cab fight in November took place in Miami Beach, where Sonny had never before fought. The first fights of 1959, with De John in February and Williams in April, were also fought in Miami Beach, as was Sonny's first fight of 1960, an eight-round knockout of the Reno, Nevada, heavyweight Howard King.

Carbo, who kept a Manhattan residence at 400 East Fifty-Ninth Street, also kept a home in Hollywood, Florida, at 2637 Taft Street, less than twenty miles north of Miami Beach. His associate and "chief lieutenant" Gabriel Genovese lived at 1668 Alton Road in Miami Beach. James Norris, the former head of the IBC, had moved from Chicago to Coral Gables, which lay just south of Miami.

While the nationwide alarm for his arrest intensified, Carbo continued with business as usual, summoning Blinky and others to several secret meetings in Florida, at the Coral Gables home of James Norris and elsewhere. Later, in early 1959, after Carbo had moved in stealth from Florida to the quiet New Jersey community that lay just a few miles across the river from where Blinky and Liston lived, Blinky would deliver those summoned by Carbo to his new hideout at 357 Crystal Lake Terrace, Hayden Township.

One of the Miami meetings, on January 5, 1959, involved a forty-three-year-old Los Angeles promoter known as Jackie Leonard, an ex-fighter whose real name was Leonard Blakely but who retained the ring name under which he had fought. Leonard was an associate of Donald Paul Nesseth, a thirty-two-year-old used-car dealer who managed a promising Los Angeles welterweight named Don Jordan. Nesseth was unable to arrange nationally televised matches for Jordan; and Leonard, interceding, had called upon Truman Gibson. Three nationally televised bouts suddenly followed, and Don Jordan just as suddenly was a contender for the world welterweight title that Virgil Akins had held since the night before the grand jury indictments were announced.

Gibson met with Leonard and Nesseth in Los Angeles to discuss the upcoming title fight between Jordan and Akins. During that meeting, Gibson was called to the telephone. After exchanging a few words with the caller, Gibson passed the telephone to Leonard. The caller was Blinky Palermo.

"Do you know we're in for half?" he demanded of Leonard.

"Half of what? I don't know what you're talking about."

"We're in for half of the fighter, or there won't be any fight."

Nesseth absolutely refused to go along with any such arrangement, but Leonard was intent on the fight.

The fight was held in Los Angeles on December 5, 1958. It was a long and close fight, which Jordan won by a decision in fifteen rounds.

Exactly a month later, on the morning of January 5, 1959, Leonard was brought to Miami, where he was met at the airport by Blinky and his cohort Abe Sands, the guy everybody knew only by the name of Mike. At one point, Sands left Blinky and Leonard to have breakfast together in the coffee shop of the Château Resort Motel, where Blinky was registered under a false name and address. When Sands returned to the coffee shop, Carbo was with him. The men adjourned to Blinky's room, where Carbo confronted Leonard, demanding to know whether or not Leonard could set his partner straight:

"Can you or can't you?"

Blinky told Leonard that he was going to force Jordan to fight Garnet "Sugar" Hart, a formidable young Philadelphia fighter whose management Blinky now controlled, and who was now the foremost contender for the welterweight championship.

"Nesseth won't go for it," Leonard said. "He can make a lot more money fighting easier fights than Sugar Hart."

"He's got to," Blinky told him. "The only reason I got control of Hart is by telling the manager I would get a title for him. What the hell is the difference? A fighter wins the title, and Nesseth gets fifteen percent of Hart. That's the way it works."

Carbo said that he was little interested in money for himself. He gestured to Blinky, to the unseen that Blinky represented: "As long as these fellows are making money, I don't have to be doling out money to them."

Two other men then joined them: Gabe Genovese and Chris Dundee.

Dundee, an older brother of the trainer Angelo Dundee, was originally from Philadelphia, where he was born, as Cristofo Mirena, on February 25, 1907. His older brother Joe, a Philadelphia club fighter, had taken the name of Dundee from another, more celebrated fighter named Johnny Dundee. Chris had followed suit as a teenager, at the outset of his own career as a boxer; and he, like Leonard, kept his ring name after that career was finished. In the early years of the alliance between Carbo and the IBC, Chris Dundee operated as a boxing manager, with an office in the Capitol Hotel, close to Madison Square Garden. He had since moved to Miami, where he was now that city's most important boxing promoter, with an office at the Miami Beach Auditorium. Sonny Liston's four Miami fights in 1958–1959 were Dundee promotions, held while Carbo was a fugitive, whereabouts unknown except to a chosen few.

When Carbo and Dundee left the room to confer, Genovese told Leonard that it was good to see that he had joined the "family." Carbo, he told Leonard, was "a great guy."

Later that night, on the drive back to the airport, Blinky took Leonard to an apartment where Carbo was in the company of a woman. Blinky and Carbo stepped into the bedroom to talk, and when they came out, Carbo once again confronted Leonard: "Are you sure you can handle everything all right now?"

"I'll try," said Leonard.

At that, Carbo bared his teeth: "God damn it, don't *try*. You are going to do it, aren't you? You are the man we are looking for, and you are the man responsible out there. This is your baby; you're the one that is going to handle the thing."

The IBC was dissolved by law a week later, on January 12, by a Supreme Court affirmation of a judgment that found the IBC and its many-tentacled subsidiary and sister companies to have violated the Sherman Act by conspiring to control the promotion of boxing. But the broken bones of the IBC survived for a while as National Boxing Enterprises, administered by Truman Gibson as its director of record. It was Gibson who played the good-cop role in convincing Leonard, as he was drawn in ever more deeply, that it was all just a matter of placating Blinky.

Carbo reportedly threatened Leonard's life in a telephone call of January 27. "You son-of-a-bitching double-crosser," Carbo intoned. "You are no good. Your word is no good. Nothing is good about you. Just because you are two thousand miles away, that is no sign I can't have you taken care of. I have got plenty of friends out there to take care of punks like you. The money had better be in." Another, more ominous call came from Carbo on April 28, about a month before Carbo was captured. "We are going to meet at the crossroads," he told Leonard. Gibson had tried to calm Leonard, to reassure him. "They wouldn't resort to violence or anything like that, so severe."

Leonard still could not get Nesseth to go along with him; and on May 1, while Carbo was hiding out in Jersey, Blinky traveled to Los Angeles. After a dinner meeting with a local gangster named Louis Dragna, he called and commanded Leonard to the lobby of the Beverly Hilton, where Blinky awaited him in the company of another local gangster, Jack Sica. The three men took the elevator to Blinky's room, where Palermo turned angrily on Leonard. After much yelling and threatening by Palermo, Sica told Leonard that he, Sica, had been a friend of The Gray for many years, and that Leonard was in grave trouble and liable to get hurt.

"Look, Jackie, you made a choice. It is a question of either you or Don Nesseth is going to get hurt. Wouldn't you rather go grab him by the neck and straighten him out, than for me to go back and tell The Gray? You try it, you're all right, but it is Nesseth that's no good. The way it is now, you and Blinky have both got your necks in a sling. Something has to be straightened out. If you have to, go and beat hell out of Nesseth. If you need help, we will go with you and help you drag him out of bed."

Leonard demurred at the proposed violence against his partner, and he promised once again to try to work things out with him.

"Try, hell," Palermo said. "You are going to straighten it out. I can't go home like this. I am in a hell of a jam with The Gray."

A few days later, Palermo and Sica met with Leonard at his office in the Hollywood Legion Stadium. This time, Nesseth joined them. Sica reviewed the situation. Leonard, he said, had sought and accepted help from certain people, "and by dealing with these people, there were certain commitments made." He concluded, talking directly to Leonard and Nesseth, "Now, when you fellows

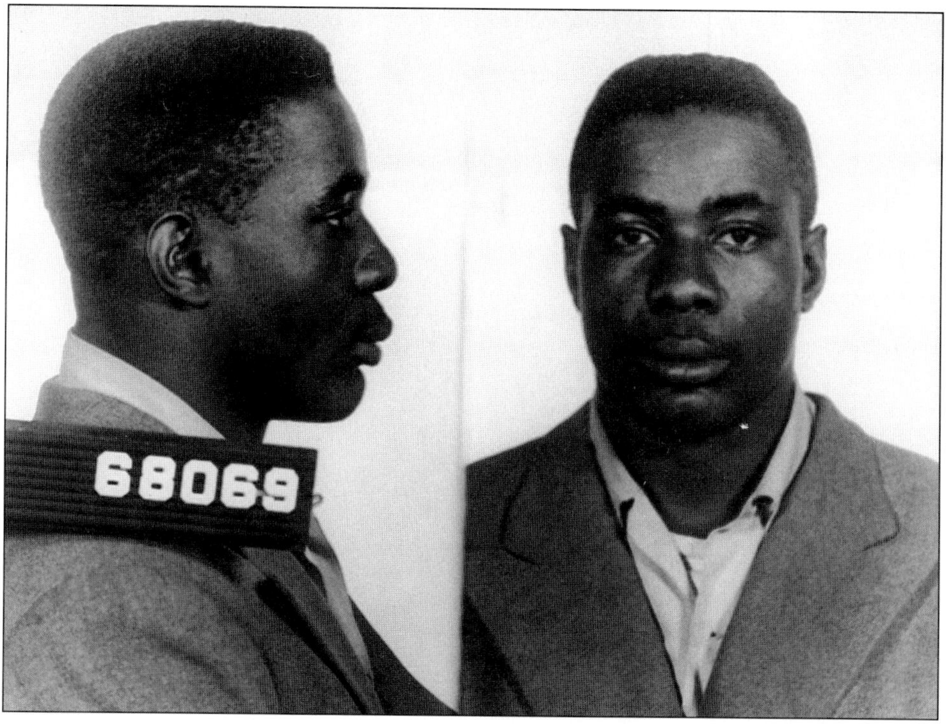

(COURTESY OF JAMES HACKETT)

Charles "Sonny" Liston. St. Louis, May 1956.

(AP/WIDE WORLD PHOTOS)

Another day, another pain-in-the-ass, two-bit motherfucking cop, another endearing smile: Paul John Carbo, alias Frankie Carbo, alias The Gray, being booked, Elizabeth Street station, New York City, January 1953, while far away and unknown to him, Charles Liston, himself barely ten weeks out of the Missouri State Penitentiary, prepared for his first Golden Gloves fight.

(UPI/CORBIS-BETTMANN)

Irving "Ash" Resnick, dressed resplendently for blind justice, gets a good-luck kiss from his new bride, Marilyn, as he prepares to testify before a federal grand jury investigating a Midwestern gambling syndicate. Indianapolis, August 18, 1958.

(UPI/CORBIS-BETTMANN)

Big Barney Baker, waiting to be interrogated by Bobby Kennedy, Senate labor rackets committee. Washington, D.C., August 19, 1958.

(*opposite*) Frankie Carbo (*left*) and Blinky Palermo leave federal court after sentencing. Los Angeles, December 1962.

(AP/WIDE WORLD PHOTOS)

The new heavyweight champion of the world. Chicago, September 25, 1962.

(UPI/CORBIS-BETTMANN)

Helen Liston with a picture of her boy, two days after his victory over Floyd Patterson in Chicago.

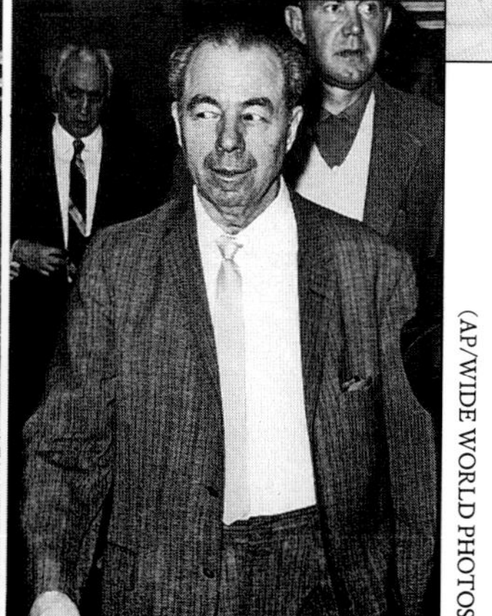

(AP/WIDE WORLD PHOTOS)

(AP/WIDE WORLD PHOTOS)

With his wife, Geraldine, celebrating her birthday at a Chicago nightclub, January 25, 1963.

With manicure, gentry-man's walking-stick, diamond pinky ring, and his friend and only idol, the former heavyweight champion Joe Louis. Denver, November 1963.

(UPI/CORBIS-BETTMANN)

(UPI/CORBIS-BETTMANN)

With Vice President Lyndon Johnson, Washington, D.C., March 29, 1963, hours before his alleged assault of Pearl Grayson.

(UPI/CORBIS-BETTMANN)

Jack Nilon, before the Senate Subcommittee on Antitrust and Monopoly, Washington, D.C., March 25, 1964, a month after Liston's title was passed to Cassius Clay.

Christmas Day 1964, in a Denver patrol wagon.

(UPI/CORBIS-BETTMANN)

At the station, after refusing a Breathalyzer test, Christmas 1964: another day, another pain-in-the-ass two-bit motherfucking cop.

In court. Denver, January 1965.

(UPI/CORBIS-BETTMANN)

At the weigh-in for the Liston-Clay rematch. Lewiston, Maine, May 1965. Note stingy-brim hat.

(UPI/CORBIS-BETTMANN)

A none-too-convincing pose. Lewiston, Maine, May 1965.

Returning home to Denver, May 1965.

(COURTESY OF CHUCK WEPNER)

The last fight, with Chuck Wepner. Jersey City, June 29, 1970.

Vegas, near the end.

got lucky and won the title, there were certain things that were supposed to be fulfilled."

Nesseth objected that he was a free man and that Jordan's fights were not to be dictated by Carbo or Palermo.

Sica and Palermo rose. As they left the room, Sica whispered into Leonard's ear, "Jackie, you're it."

The conversation was bugged. Driven by fear and desperation, Leonard had gone to the police the previous day, and Sica's words, like everything else said at this meeting, were recorded.

Before boarding his flight to return to Philadelphia, Blinky stopped at an airport newsstand. He picked up a couple of sporting magazines and a couple of packs of gum. On his way to the cashier, he picked up a pack of peanut butter crackers; and when he got to the cashier, he paid only for the crackers. A plainclothes cop had been watching him, and Blinky was arrested as a petty thief of eighty cents' worth of cheap magazines and chewing gum.

He was taken in and booked. Bail was set at five hundred dollars pending trial by jury. Blinky made bail, then split town. Before he left, however, he was questioned by Police Captain James D. Hamilton. The captain asked Blinky what had brought him to Los Angeles. Blinky told him that it was a social visit. When the captain asked him about Louis Dragna and Jack Sica, Blinky said that he had never heard of them.

A few weeks later, on May 30, Carbo was captured in New Jersey.

In his sentencing by Judge Mullen several months later, Carbo got off easy. But just as Carbo was unto others a fate in himself, so the fate which was his own lay beyond the powers that were his own.

In May, after his bugged meeting with Palermo and Sica, Jackie Leonard had told his story to an investigation board of the California State Athletic Commission. His fear had ebbed, as Captain

Hamilton had assigned him police protection. But two weeks later, on June 3, as he was about to draw up the garage door at his Los Angeles home, Leonard was struck in the base of his skull by a concussive blow that drove him to his knees, whereupon his two assailants commenced to kick him.

While awaiting trial in New York, Carbo had been allowed to travel to Johns Hopkins Hospital in Baltimore for kidney treatment. In Baltimore, at about half-past nine on the night of September 22, as he lay in his hospital bed, he was arrested under an indictment charging him with attempting to extort control of Don Jordan. At the same moment, under the same indictment, Truman Gibson was arrested in Chicago, Blinky Palermo in Philadelphia. In Los Angeles, Dragna and Sica were already in custody for close to half an hour.

Appended to the December 1, 1959, *New York Times* report of Carbo's sentencing, there was a small item datelined Los Angeles, November 30:

> Five men charged with attempting to cut in on the earnings of Don Jordan, welterweight champion, had their trials continued to March 29 by Federal Judge Ernest A. Tolin today.
>
> Both the Government and attorneys for defendants agreed additional time would be necessary to secure witnesses.
>
> The defendants include Frankie Carbo, Frank (Blinky) Palermo, Philadelphia fight promoter, Truman Gibson Jr., president of National Boxing Enterprises, of Chicago, and Joe Sica and Louis Tom Dragna, both of Los Angeles. The trial had been set for Dec. 8.
>
> Carbo will be flown here tomorrow to face arraignment in Federal District Court, the United States Attorney's office said.

After his arraignment in Los Angeles, Carbo was returned to New York to serve his two-year sentence at Riker's Island Prison. He could not have been too worried about the Jordan case: more of the same old conspiracy shit, another few flies to swat away, another few cockroaches to crush underfoot.

Christmas came and went: turkey with the fellas. The new year came, then spring, then summer, then fall. One year down. It was an easy bill, and he slept away the better part of it in the prison hospital. The rest of the time, he did what he always did: controlled the fight racket, by way of Blinky.

Under their thralldom, Sonny flourished. For just as they had rendered him not his own but another's man, so in the ring they had freed him to prevail and to conquer. There was no more of carrying opponents, no more of holding back. In the witnessing of his victory upon victory over all whom he was set against, they had come to realize that he was one of a kind, and they knew there would not be another like him again. He was invincible: a sure thing. And in that, he must not be fucked with, but ridden wild to the sea of golden glory that raged and awaited him; and when the time came that they sold the scrap metal of that glory to the junkman, they would make more money than anybody in the fight racket ever dreamt of making, as would Sonny, for he was the best and he was their boy.

In October 1958, when he beat Whitehurst for the second time, he knocked him with fury clear through the ropes and out of the ring.

In February 1959, when he knocked out Mike De John in Miami Beach, the *Miami Herald* described it as "one of the most brutal outpourings of punishment in recent heavyweight history." The odds that night were with Liston, at eight to five.

In April, when he knocked out Cleveland Williams in the third round, it was the third of what would be a run of nine straight knockouts of ever more formidable opponents. (And, to be sure, although he was a two-to-one underdog against Sonny, Williams himself was quite a formidable character. A strange motherfucker, yes; a strange motherfucker from Georgia who heard voices, but who none the less had lost only three of forty-seven fights and was on an eleven-fight winning streak, with eight of them knockouts, when he came into the ring against Sonny.) The *Miami Herald* declared that Liston, in defeating Williams, had now evinced his "credentials for a shot at Floyd Patterson's seldom-defended heavyweight championship."

"That was the night I really found out about myself," Liston would say some years later.

> If I had one weak spot anywhere, in my body, my chin, or my heart, it would've showed up with all the whuppin' he put on me in the first round. But I was never really hurt bad, no matter how it looked. I knew what was goin' on. Even before I sat down, I was thinkin' to myself, "This cat's gotta put it to me like that for nine more rounds to win this fight, and I don't think he can do it."

Sonny would dispose of Williams again, and more quickly, in a return match the following spring. That rematch, he said, "was no sweat, because I knew his ticket number goin' in."

He was now one of the ranking heavyweight contenders. His August 1959, Chicago defeat of Nino Valdes was covered in *Time* magazine. ("The massive-shouldered Negro looked like just another pug until he stung the man with a left to the belly in the third round.")

Following the Valdes fight, Sonny returned to St. Louis for a visit. On August 12, while visiting St. Louis, a week after the Valdes fight, Sonny was picked up and charged on suspicion of gambling.

In April 1960, when he fought the Texas state heavyweight champion Roy Harris at the Houston Coliseum, the referee halted the fight after only two minutes and thirty-five seconds, in which time Harris had been collapsed three times by three left jabs. He had been beaten only once before, by Floyd Patterson in a heavyweight title match in the summer of 1958, and Patterson had taken twelve rounds to do the job. The *New York Times* published coverage of the fight under the headline "Referee Steps in to Protect Texan."

The Whitehurst fight of October 1958, drew an arena crowd of 1,442, grossed a gate of $2,830.50, and was a nationally televised Friday night fight.

The De John fight drew 5,000; but De John, who was considered to have been the bigger draw, got the better part of the gate.

By the time of the Williams fight, Sonny was ranked sixth among the world's heavyweight boxers, and he was the favorite over Williams at three to one. The fight drew a crowd of 2,842 and a gross of $5,984.

The Harris fight drew a crowd of more than 12,000 and a gate estimated at $70,000. In addition, it was broadcast as a closed-circuit main event on live cards in Dallas, San Antonio, Odessa, New Orleans, Mobile, Atlanta, Miami Beach, Baltimore, Milwaukee, and Minneapolis. Liston was guaranteed the greater of $10,000 or twenty-five percent of the gate, and twenty-five percent of the closed-circuit revenue.

In eighteen months: from a head-count of 1,442 and an underdog's taste of $2,830.50 to a crowd of 12,000 and a twenty-five-percent share of seventy grand; from television to closed-circuit main event; from an eight-to-five favorite against De John to a five-to-one favorite against Valdes; from small-town notices to *Time* magazine and the *New York Times*.

That piece of him that remained to him, what money was his after it passed through the shifting clutches of others, was beginning to be something, as he himself was beginning to be something.

"I ain't complaining," he would say, later in 1960. He spoke as one who knew in his blood what few others admitted: that no man — neither he nor they who had claimed him; neither prisoner nor he who sat in judgement; neither he in the gutter nor he who ruled from the Big House; neither he who knelt before God nor he who knelt before the indwelling darkness of himself — was ever his own man. No one in this world was free; and all, slave and master, victor and vanquished alike, were one, as chaff from the threshing of man against man, the threshing not only of man's will to enslave, but of will itself, and of willfulness itself. It was not true that some men were by nature free and others slaves. Such was the folly of those who refused to, or could not, see themselves for what they were, or the world for what it was. That, and that alone, was nature; and to be aware of this, in thought and in blood, or in blood alone, was to possess something of wisdom, and therein lay the only manumission, the only, elusive windblown cornsilk strand of freedom that was real amid the illusive and delusive freedom that all professed and praised.

"They treat me good," he would say. "I got money in the bank, I'm fighting regular. I like fighting. It's the only thing I know how to do. As long as I'm fighting and making money and driving a good car and eating regular, nothing much is bothering me."

Back in 1947, Jake LaMotta had lied when he told the grand jury investigating committee that he had not taken a dive to Billy Fox in exchange for a shot at the title. As a stand-up character, LaMotta had indeed been rewarded with that shot as promised; and he had seized it, beating the French Algerian fighter Marcel Cerdan for the middleweight championship of the world in the spring of 1949. He held the title for almost two years: Ray Robinson took it from him in 1951. LaMotta quit fighting the following year, tried but failed to make a comeback two years later, then quit again, for good. When he was called in 1960 to testify before a new investigating committee, Jake, having had the shot they had promised him, having won and lost the title, and having nothing left to show for it, was now ready to rat out those who had given him that shot, ready to tell the truth, the whole truth, or something like it.

Jake was a terrific opening act for the new subcommittee of the moral crusader and frustrated presidential aspirant Estes Kefauver, the well-intentioned but naïve Tennessee Democrat whose chairmanship of the 1950–1951 Special Committee to Investigate Organized Crime in Interstate Commerce — which became known among the populace as the Kefauver Committee — was the beginning of an enduring and renowned career built on righteous persecution and the publicity value thereof. Through the new medium of television, Kefauver used the sideshow of his hearings to grasp the vice-presidential nomination from John F. Kennedy, himself the brat offspring of a criminal fortune. By September 1951, Kefauver's investigator Rudolph Halley was hosting *Crime Syndicated* on CBS, and by November of that year, Kefauver himself had a Hollywood stage act. Humphrey Bogart introduced him at the Los Angeles Philharmonic, where his presentation "Crime in America" was advertised as "ENOUGH EXCITING MATERIAL FOR 100 MOVIES."

Kefauver's chief examiner and assistant counsel in the new Senate Antitrust and Monopoly subcommittee hearings was young John G. Bonomi, the former New York assistant district attorney who had been out to get Carbo for years.

LaMotta testified that the offer of $100,000 to throw the Fox fight had come through his brother, Joey, who had often served Jake as a manager of sorts, and who now distributed pinball and vending machines. An earlier offer to throw another fight, against Tony Janiro at the Garden, had also come through his brother, said Jake. He insisted, however, that he didn't know the names or identities of those who had delivered these offers, even though in a signed deposition the previous month, he had named Billy Fox's then-licensed manager, Blinky Palermo, as one of them. An investigator testified that a "terrific amount of Philadelphia money flowed into the city and all of it bet on Fox."

On the following day, June 15, 1960, as the hearings in Washington progressed, a New York detective testified that he believed Frankie Carbo had "controlled the boxing racket by himself" for the past thirty years, that Carbo still controlled boxing from within Riker's Island, and that this control was exercised through a "legman" he identified as Palermo.

Blinky himself was subpoenaed in October to appear before the Senate subcommittee in early December. Two weeks after that subpoena was issued, Federal Judge Ernest A. Tolin ordered Blinky and his four co-defendants — Carbo, Gibson, Dragna, and Sica — to stand trial in Los Angeles on December 8 for their attempt to control Don Jordan. This date was later postponed to February 14, 1961.

December 9, Washington, D.C., as reported in the *New York Times:*

> In open testimony today, John Vitale and Frank Mitchell of St. Louis pleaded the Fifth Amendment in refusing to answer questions about the management of Sonny Liston, the No. 1 heavyweight contender.
>
> The questions were designed to show that Vitale — who is familiar here from previous appearances before the Senate Rackets Committee — was the undercover manager of Liston, along with Carbo and Frank (Blinky) Palermo, while Mitchell had served as manager of record.

A St. Louis police lieutenant, Joseph Kuda, also called to appear that day, testified that Carbo owned fifty-two percent of the contractual interest in Liston, that Palermo owned twelve percent, that Vitale also owned twelve percent, and that the remaining twenty-four percent was owned by others. It should be thought that at least part of what remained went to Sonny's manager of record, Pep Barone, who by contract was the only one entitled to anything. Barone was also under subpoena to testify, but was reported to be ill in an Allentown hospital.

December 12, Washington, D.C.: The former lightweight champion Ike Williams testified that while Palermo managed his career, offers of four big-money bribes had been relayed to him by Palermo. Two of the bribes were for title fights, and the biggest was one of $100,000 to go down in his title fight against Kid Gavilan in 1949. He said that Palermo in each case had advised him not to accept, and that he rejected them all. None the less, he had lost two of those four fights on the square, including the Gavilan title fight.

"I should have taken the money," he mused.

Senator Kefauver suggested that Williams probably "felt better" for having withstood temptation and having kept himself clean.

"I do not!" declared Williams bitterly. "Believe me, I do not."

Sonny had been under subpoena since before Labor Day, and his appearance before the subcommittee came on December 13, as did Blinky's.

Blinky's lawyer read a prepared petition, which began: "I appear before you as counsel for Frank Palermo, a witness who has been subpoenaed to appear before your honorable body." The petition asked that Blinky be excused from appearing at this time because he was presently under indictment and scheduled to be tried in the U.S. District Court for the Southern District of California on charges that "arise from matters pertaining to professional boxing." As any "attendant publicity of Frank Palermo's appearance before your committee today will be widespread," it could "prevent him from receiving such a fair and impartial trial as he is entitled under the American system of justice."

"I would think, sir, that he has already gotten considerable unfavorable publicity," said Senator Kefauver, "so that he might welcome the opportunity of stating his side."

Blinky's lawyer thanked Kefauver for "the wide latitude you gave me in my address."

KEFAUVER: I will ask Mr. Palermo, where do you live, sir?
PALERMO: Eight hundred North Sixty-Fourth Street, Philadelphia.
KEFAUVER: How old are you, sir?
PALERMO: Fifty-five.
KEFAUVER: You have a family?
PALERMO: Yes, sir. Five children.
KEFAUVER: Outside of your connection with boxing, do you have any other businesses?
PALERMO: I respectfully refuse to answer the question. It may tend to incriminate me under a federal offense.
KEFAUVER: I am not asking you about any alleged improper business. I just asked you if you had any —
PALERMO: I respectfully refuse to answer for the reason that the answer —
KEFAUVER: The chairman directs you to answer the question.
PALERMO: — may tend to incriminate me under a federal offense.

Blinky would say nothing more than this in response to every further question, and in the end Kefauver announced that he would seek a contempt citation against him.

Sonny showed up in a suit and tie that shone. He looked good. He looked better than good. He looked like Charles L. Liston, the mightiest of men and the sharpest of dressers. He was too cool to be real, too real to be cool. He just was what he fucking was: Charles L. Liston, mightiest of men, sharpest of dressers. Had more pasts then most people had socks. Go on, pick a past, any past. They were all the same to him: sand slough and alleys, barrooms and prison cells, fancy ass big bad gangster men and bent-down cotton pickers. All the same. Working for halves here, Boss, working for halves: you and me, we're working for halves. Sing it loud, sister: "Oh, what a friend we have in Blinky. Oh, what a friend we have in Mr. Gray." Can't barely hear you, sister; why don't you slide up on in here. Gonna be the world champeen. Good Lord told me so. Told me buy this damn suit, too. Had him a whole flock of suits, one for every motherfucker he knocked out. No, not that many; nobody had that many, not even Mr. Frankie C. Gray, not even him. No, maybe one for every past, one for every day of the week. Yeah, had a gal for every day in the week, too. A lot of tail lately, yeah, a good amount of tail. No crime in that, is there, Your Honor, or Your Holiness, or Your Let's-Get-Blinkiness, or whatever the fuck you are? Yeah, he'd heard that one: *"Your Honorable Body."* Shit, whip this dick out from these guinea britches, show you some honorable fucking body. He was the baddest man with the biggest dick that ever was. That's what those women said. All of them, the free ones and the store-bought, too. That old sign-casting hoodoo-Jesus lady, midwifed him way back when: he knew, all right, he knew where that "L" came from. Yeah, that's what he told those chicks, but, no, he didn't know. He wondered on it, but he didn't know. Charles Lost Liston. Yeah, that would've been a good one: *"and in this corner . . . Lost Charles Liston."* Charles Loverboy Liston. Knock the men out with one hand, squeeze the women with other, drink whiskey and shoot dice all at the same damn time. Charles L. Liston. Maybe it didn't stand for nothing. Maybe it was some other man's name that mama and that woman couldn't say outright. Maybe that was it. Maybe that's why Tobe had all the mean in the world coming out of those eyes when he looked at him. That wouldn't be half bad, no. Least that way it would halfwise make sense. No use in asking. Mama can't tell you where or when her boys were born or where her eyeglasses at, but sure can tell you a Mississippi flood time mouthful about what ain't never been no way nohow at all.

Fuck this shit — adjournment for dick in the midst of this ever more precipitous and perplexing narrative. Let's talk cock. Let's talk all sorts of shit.

Sonny Liston knew that he had what those lying niggers bragged about and those white motherfuckers feared they did.

"Did you ever see him in the dressing room?" howled the famous St. Louis character Dean Shendal, extending his open palms outward as if in sacerdotal orans. "He had a prick this big. Holy Christ, he could scare a horse."

"He was huge in his size," said Foneda Cox, his friend and sparring partner. "That was the biggest man I have ever seen, and I've been through the service, in gymnasiums all across the country, and I have never seen a man as big as that man was."

That attracted the women, all right, said Foneda, who not only ate, drank, and traveled with Sonny, but fucked with him, too, in the hotel suites they shared.

"When he wasn't training, his big sport was women. He used to get the hotel rooms and pick up women left and right. We would meet girls, and I think this is one of the reasons Sonny wanted me, because I would attract a lot of girls for him. So, this was what we would do. We would go into a new town, and we would have girls in there. When Sonny would have sex with women, I would have sex with them, too. And it's amazing the things that they would do."

Foneda was a handsome, charming man, but he knew he was

merely the procurer, the sidekick, the bait for Sonny's line. In the hotel suites, once Sonny had his britches down, "he was the main target for the women."

It was a part of their routine. "We'd pick up a girl and keep her all night, and then, the next morning, that's when they would leave. So then we'd have some more the next night."

When they couldn't get free women, they went with store-bought; and these were usually the women that Sonny let loose on.

"He put some of the prostitutes in the hospital. Yeah, because he would jam up on the inside, see. It would just be terrible the way he would be banging on some of them. You wouldn't believe the prostitutes he sent to the hospital."

Sometimes they shared one woman, sometimes they shared a brace of women. Sometimes each man took a woman for himself, sometimes each took a brace for himself. Sonny liked that, going to bed with two ladies. It befitted him.

I had heard a story about somebody who once called on Sonny at a hotel. There was a woman with Sonny, and the room was littered with bottles and crumpled paper sandwich wrappings. When the caller arrived, Sonny slipped something into the woman's hand and bade her adieu. She looked at what he had put in her hand.

"Damn it, Sonny," she remonstrated. "Here I am with you all last night and half of today, all these hours, and this is all you give me?"

Sonny looked at her and said, "What about that tunafish sandwich I bought you?"

It was this story that prompted me to ask Foneda if Sonny was cheap with prostitutes.

"No, 'cause, see, he would give me the money, and then I would give the girls a hundred dollars apiece. I didn't let him worry about that."

When morning came, Sonny and Foneda usually took breakfast together. "We never took 'em to breakfast too often," he said of the prostitutes. "They would be on their way. Once they got their money, they were ready to go."

Foneda seemed at times wistful for those bygone days. As he spoke, phrases such as "It's amazing the things that they would do," "You'd be surprised at the things that they would do," and "They did everything" seemed in their utterance to be not so much a commentary or a part of his narrative, but rather recurrent, passing inner reflections of nostalgia stirred by the raised memories of that narrative.

Both he and Sonny were blowjob men. Sure, Sonny liked to "jam up on the inside, see"; but a good piece of tail and a good blowjob were unto each other like penitentiary gruel and prime steak, or a dreary but winning decision after the full twelve rounds and a knockout through the ropes in the first. It was all the medicine, all the religion, that any man needed at times; and it was likely, polio vaccine and such notwithstanding, the greatest invention of the white man.

Foneda remembered being around "maybe once or twice" when Black Muslim proselytes hovered near Liston, trying to get his ear.

"He just didn't think too much of their expression on separating races. Sonny liked white women as much as he did black women. Sonny just didn't like the expression that they would greet the women with, call them 'white devils' and stuff. That wasn't his make at all."

Actually, Sonny's loathing of the Black Muslims dated to his earliest exposure to them, at the Missouri State Penitentiary in Jefferson City. Some say it was fear as well as loathing, as Sonny generally was apprehensive of people who were, or were seen by him as, crazy, and in his suspicious and unspeaking eyes the Black Muslims were just that — crazy. He did not like them, and he did not like their ways, and he did not trust them.

The so-called Freedom Riders were in the forefront of the news in those days. Organized by CORE in 1961, Freedom Riders traveled through the South in buses to test the effectiveness of a 1960 Supreme Court decision declaring that segregation was illegal in bus stations that were open to interstate travel. The beatings and trouble the riders endured, which made crackerjack news, were a powerful demonstration of the gravity of commitment within the civil rights movement.

"I think those Freedom Riders is stupid," said Sonny in that year of 1961. "That ain't no way to do things. You have to fight for what you get. It's like boxing. No use being in there if you just catch punches."

Later, a writer from *Ebony* magazine asked if he regarded white opponents with particular severity.

"Yes," he answered.

What did he think of when the round one bell sounded and the man in the other corner was white?

"Kill him," Sonny said, sullenly, matter-of-factly. "I always say kill him when I'm in the ring with a white boy. You got to knock 'em out to win. You won't get the decision. I try to knock 'em all out, white or black."

This was the way of his life, and the way of his heart, and the way of his soul. Sonny Liston did not give a fuck what color you were when he knocked you down and dragged you in that alley. He did not give a fuck what color you were when he embraced you. He was — in good and in bad, if such distinction can or should even be made — *pure*. There were few friends in his life, as there are few real friends in any life; but for every Foneda Cox that he loved and trusted, there was some white gangster — and, yes, he did trust in thieves, as only a thief can — or some old Jewish cat that was writ just as deep in the lines of his palm.

The writer Mark Kram encountered Sonny some years later. It was in the early hours before dawn in a Las Vegas casino. Sonny told him a story, which I here pass on. The story takes place in Houston in 1960, on the night Sonny beat Roy Harris. Sitting in a chair in the deserted lobby of the hotel where he was staying, Sonny had fallen into a tired, boozy nod and was almost asleep when he heard something — the creak of leather bootsteps, then the click of a gun — behind his ear:

"Don't turn aroun', nigger."

"What you want, man? I got a couple hundred. That what you want?"

"You made a fool out of Roy in there tonight. Oh, you're a bad nigger, aren't you?"

"Just a fight, man. Me or him. No more 'n that."

"I got one bullet in this here Colt. I'm gonna pull this trigger till you tell me to stop."

"I ain't done nothin'. You crazy."

"I stop when you tell me you're a no-good, yeller nigger."

"Shee-it, git lost. You ain't got no bullet in there."

From behind, came the quite loud sound in silence of revolving chambers and their load.

"Now, just say you're a no-good, yeller nigger."

"Fuck you."

There was that sound again.

"You scared, nigger? Let's — "

"Wait. I'm a no-good nigger."

"A yeller nigger. Say it."

"Yeah, a yeller one."

"Don't turn aroun'."

He could hear the gun being uncocked, the creaking leather footsteps receding from him.

And when Sonny told Mark Kram this little tale, he kept on telling. "I've heard that creak ever since," he said. "Folks are violent. It got to be torture for me, bein' public. Like bein' the only chicken in a bag full of cats."

I don't think that Mark made up this story, but I wonder if Sonny did. I wonder if it filled some need to create a sense of himself as a victim of blind hatred. Those white cops in St. Louis, hell, man, that was no good a tale; wasn't just setting in no easy chair when they took to sweating him. Yeah, they were white, all right. But that other son-of-a-bitch cop, that one that wanted to baptize his ass with lead, well, hell, he was black. Maybe that creaking-up-behind-him that he made up was not so much made up as the man that went with it. Maybe that creaking-up-behind-him was a creeping-up-inside-him from those places he did not want to look, and maybe he could only express fear in terms of something for which he had no fear, that is to say another man. Or maybe it just happened. Or maybe he was just drunk and running in it.

Sonny's niece Ezraline, the daughter of his half-brother E.B. Ward, remembered Uncle Sonny coming down to visit his kin in Forrest City when she was a teenager. He had a fine big Cadillac convertible and a fine big white woman.

"He came down here with that white woman, and they was telling him that he had to leave, they didn't allow that down here." It was in 1961, "before King did the Civil Rights March." Ezraline never forgot her Uncle Sonny's "sharp car" or that "nice-looking white lady." She could still picture it, still recall the scent of it, many years later. "Convertible, honey. Yeah. He was lookin' good, smellin' good. A *whole* lotta money. Mmm. Givin' everybody money. White lady friend." But Ezraline was not sure about what they said: that the white woman "was supposed to have been in love with him." Uncle Sonny, she said, was getting famous and "really making that money" at that time. "You know how womens be all over you then."

In their travels with Sonny's dick, Geraldine Liston was not a part of the picture. "Sonny respected his wife," said Foneda, who was a bachelor in those days. "And he did not abuse Geraldine." But he rarely took her with him when he traveled.

"We talked about a lot of things, me and Geri," said Foneda. "Geri was a sweet person. She knew within her heart that Sonny was going out and messing around with other women. But I would try to tone it down. I would never tell her the straight truth of what was happening. And Sonny wouldn't. I would be trying to build him up in her eyesight. I told her, I said, you know, a lot of times Sonny just wants to be around different girls, different people. I said he wouldn't do anything, they don't mean nothing to him; he just wants to be seen with pretty girls. She would say, 'Well, I'm gonna leave judgment up to you.' And I would not tell her the whole picture at no time. I never told her once that Sonny had a relationship with any woman." Yes, he concluded, "Geraldine was all right."

Sonny loved children. They brought out the best in him, which is what he saw in them: the spirit of the loving child in himself, which had been extracted from him and butchered in the throes of his own miserable and stillborn childhood. If Sonny pretended to be good in the company of priests, he sincerely was good in the company of children, especially those in whom he discerned an echo of the loneliness and loss that had haunted his own boyhood. He wanted to give them something of friendship, goodness, and kindness — those same things that yet eluded him — and in giving them these things, in wanting to give them these things, he came closest to feeling and to having them himself. His compassion and the pangs of his own soul were one.

Yet Sonny's marriage to Geraldine was childless, and, while he was a paternal provider for Geraldine's daughter, Arletha, who was thirteen when Sonny and Geraldine married, he neither acknowledged nor knew the whereabouts of a daughter that he himself had fathered in the lost days before his penitentiary time. Her name was Eleanor, and only years later would he seek her out.

Yeah, that "L." How could a woman remember a goddamn "L" and not the goddamn name that went with it? A woman who had even less truck with the goddamn alphabet than him? How could she remember the "L" and not the goddamn day that she bore the child that got stuck to that "L"? And, knowing her, why in hell wouldn't she just make up something to go with that "L" instead of it leaving it by like some holy privy thing that came out the sky on a pentecostal tongue? It was a goddamn wonder she recalled that the other "L" stood for Liston. *"And in this corner . . . Lonesome Charles Liston."* Yeah. That had a chime to it, sure enough. And what was that other one he had a mind of that time, before that prison tattoo of a nickname stuck. Yeah, that was it: *"and in this corner —"*

"Where were you born, Mr. Liston?"
"Little Rock."
"Would you mind telling us how old you are?"
"Twenty-seven."
"How much education did you get?"
"I didn't get any."
"Do you know Frank Palermo?"
"Yes, sir, I know him."
"Do you know John Vitale?"
"Yes, I know him."

Senator Everett Dirksen stepped in to share questioning with Senator Kefauver.

"You have a family?"

"I have a wife."

"Children?"

"No, sir."

Subcommittee counsel John G. Bonomi stepped in to share questioning with Dirksen and Kefauver. He asked Liston if he remembered being arrested in St. Louis on August 12, 1959.

On that date, a week after the Valdes fight in Chicago, Sonny had been picked up and nominally booked on suspicion of gambling. Such had been his visitor's welcome as a hometown hero — one more sausage pinch. When the cops searched him, they found in his possession slips of paper bearing names and numbers — for John Vitale, Blinky Palermo, Barney Baker — that subsequently had been passed on to the investigators of the Kefauver Committee.

"I couldn't recall the date," Sonny told him. "I don't carry around a pencil to see how many times I was picked up."

"At the time that you were arrested in St. Louis in 1959, you apparently had in your possession a slip reading 'J.V. CO-1-4972.' Do you recall having a slip in your possession?"

"No, sir, I didn't have no such slip."

He was shown a photostatic copy of the slip in question, asked again if he recalled it.

"Maybe yes or maybe no. I don't remember. I can't remember now."

"What would 'J.V.' stand for?"

"'J.V.?'"

"John Vitale, is that correct? You know that John Vitale's home number is Colfax 1-4972, do you not?"

"That's right."

Dirksen wanted to know why he had been arrested in the first place.

"Why?" Liston said. "That's the question I would like to know."

"That is what I would like to know also," Dirksen said.

"Well," said Sonny, "I imagine he got the records — why did they arrest me?"

"We will go into that next, Mr. Liston," Bonomi said.

"Because they never told me anything. They just picked me up and put me in the can and questioned me."

"That is a form of arrest, of course," Bonomi said.

"Yes," Liston sighed.

"Do you know whether or not Frank Palermo has been your undercover manager in the period of March of 1958 to the present, or one of your undercover managers?"

"I only know what I got on paper."

The investigating committee had something on paper too — something besides those slips. It was a letter that Sonny had "written," through Geraldine's hand, to Ike Williams, the former lightweight champ who had testified here before the subcommittee only yesterday. The letter had been written seven months ago, in mid-May.

"'*Dear Ike,*'" Bonomi read aloud:

> *"I received your letter and I was happy to hear from you. I had not seen you in a long time. I was wondering what had become of you. Thanks for writing me. It give you a happy feeling to know that people are thinking of you. I hope I can get a chance at the title, and if I win, I hope I can be a good champ, as Joe was. He was a great guy. Frank and Pep are —"*

Here Bonomi stopped, and Liston was asked if he remembered dictating the letter.

"No, I don't remember dictating it."

"Is that your wife's handwriting?" Kefauver asked.

"I couldn't say."

"Do you read at all?" Dirksen asked.

"No, sir, I don't."

"He says he has no memory of dictating such a letter," interjected Sonny's counsel, Jacob Kossman, as if operating on a slight time delay. (Later Sonny would explain how he had chosen his attorney: "Well," as he put it, "I was downtown and I see him with Blinky.")

"Nothing whatsoever?"

"He can't read," Kossman spoke again.

Bonomi resumed reading aloud from the letter:

"— *are great fellows and I hope they will do all they can to get me a shot at the title. Well, I will close. Hope to hear from you soon. Oh, yes, I have moved out of the hotel. My wife and mother said hello.*"

Bonomi asked, "Weren't you referring there to Frank 'Blinky' Palermo?"

"If I was referring to him, I would have said him."

"Do you know of any other Franks that are interested in your management outside of perhaps Frank 'Blinky' Palermo?"

"Besides what?"

"What is that?"

"Besides what? There is a whole lots of people interested."

"Who else named Frank, in April or May of 1960, could get you a crack at the title?"

"Frank Kerr. I know a million Franks."

"Who is Frank Kerr?"

"Some guy in Philadelphia."

"Was he a manager?"

"Not that I recall."

"What is his occupation?"

"I couldn't say. I don't know."

"How could he get you a crack at the title?"

"Through friends."

"Through friends. What friends did this man have?"

"I don't know what friends do he have."

"What other Franks do you know, outside of this man Frank Kerr, who can supposedly get you a crack at the title?"

"Patterson," Liston said dryly.

"Frank Patterson? What is his occupation?" Bonomi demanded, as if swept by a strange, sudden belief that all men named Frank were guilty until proven innocent.

"You said what other man."

Finally Kefauver interrupted: "It could be Frank Carbo?"

"Yes," Sonny said, "it could be Frank Carbo."

"Did you mean Frank Carbo?" Bonomi pursued.

"I didn't write that, and I couldn't tell," said Liston.

"Who were you referring to?" Kefauver implored. "Do you know?"

"No, I don't know."

"Do you want to tell us," Bonomi said, "in light of that letter, whether or not Frank Palermo acts as an undercover manager for you?"

"Not that I know of."

Sonny was asked if he had seen Pep Barone lately. Two or three weeks ago, Sonny said.

"Did he say anything about coming down here?" Kefauver asked, referring to Barone's subpoena.

"Well, he said he had to come down."

"He didn't come."

"Yes."

"Did you see him in the hospital since he has been there?"

"He is getting badder and badder."

"He is getting bad?"

"He is getting badder and badder."

"I don't believe Mr. Barone is licensed in Pennsylvania anymore, is he?"

"No, sir, he isn't."

"So you don't have any licensed manager now?"

"It don't look like it."

"Who is making your fights for you now?"

"No one."

No one. Οὖτις. The baddest motherfucker of them all. Badder than a million Frankies.

And that was just about the truth of it — no one.

Carbo himself was hauled down from Riker's to appear before the Senate subcommittee the day after Blinky and Sonny appeared. "This is not a trial, this is not a court," Kefauver entreated. "Do you understand what I have said, Mr. Carbo?"

"Yes, sir."

"What is your occupation?"

"I respectfully decline to answer the question on the grounds that I cannot be compelled to be a witness against myself."

"The Chair directs you to answer the question."

"I respectfully decline to answer the question on the grounds that I cannot be compelled to be a witness against myself."

"Were you associated with, or have an interest in a contract with, John Vitale of St. Louis, Frank Palermo of —"

"I respectfully —"

"Wait, Mr. Carbo. Wait until I finish the question. You do not know what I am going to ask you."

But there was really no need for Carbo to wait, for he was willing to say nothing but the words that he held before him, written big on a little paper card.

"He really thinks you're a great fellow," Carbo's attorney, Abraham Brodsky, told Kefauver as they left.

Two months later, Carbo, Blinky, along with Truman Gibson, Sica, and Dragna, were on trial in Los Angeles. After all that Carbo and Palermo had been through, this seemed like little more than another dose of the same. The promoter Jackie Leonard, with whom this trouble had started, was a leading witness for the government. Under cross-examination by one of Carbo's lawyers, Leonard confessed in court on March 7 that he had offered to testify in behalf of Carbo's defense in exchange for $25,000. This alone, it seemed, should have been enough to blow Leonard's credibility, and the government's case, straight to hell. Furthermore, there was the courtroom appearance of Don Jordan himself, the fighter whose career Carbo and Blinky were charged with conspiring to control through the extortion of Jackie Leonard and of Jordan's manager, Don Nesseth. That career was now on the skids; and Jordan likely would have been far better off, certainly no worse off, if Carbo and Blinky had taken control of it. Not only had Don Jordan lost his title the previous spring, to Benny (Kid) Paret, but he also had lost his share of the purse from that title fight, having signed over in advance his $85,000 guarantee to Don Nesseth in order to free himself from Nesseth's management.

The trial lasted more than three months. On May 30, 1961, after deliberating for three days, the jury of ten men and two women found all defendants guilty. Robert F. Kennedy, the kid brother of John F. Kennedy, was now, under his elder brother's presidency, the attorney general of the United States. Upon Carbo's conviction, he issued a statement:

> Frank Carbo has been a sinister figure behind the scenes in boxing for more than twenty years. This verdict will be a great aid and assistance to the Department of Justice and local authorities in taking further action against the attempts of racketeers to control boxing and other sports.

After a delay of more than six months — Judge Tolin died in early June, before hearing motions or sentencing; the government designated and brought in a judge from the Western District of Washington, George H. Boldt, to close out the case; all defendants petitioned for new trials and were refused them — Carbo and the others were sentenced on the second day of December.

Carbo got twenty-five years. Palermo got fifteen. Sica got twenty. Dragna got five. Truman Gibson got five years, suspended. Each man was also fined ten grand.

Carbo was removed to Alcatraz.

Two nights later, in Philadelphia, Sonny fought Albert Westphal of Hamburg.

He had now fought and conquered every major heavyweight contender in the world, with the exception of Ingemar Johansson, the Swedish fighter who took the title from Floyd Patterson in 1959 and lost it back to him in 1960. Sonny considered Cleveland Williams, whom he fought in 1959 and 1960, to have been his toughest opponent. But others he vanquished were among the finest and most formidable of fighters: Nino Valdes, Zora Folley, Eddie Machen. On July 18, 1960, while the Kefauver hearings were underway, Sonny had knocked out Zora Folley in three. Little more than seven weeks later, on September 7, after Sonny had been served his subpoena and had before him the unsettling prospect of testifying in Washington, he beat Eddie Machen.

Folley, a twenty-eight-year-old Texan, was a fighter who had been knocked out only once before, back in 1955, and since then he had lost only one other fight. The brilliance of his technique and skill were such, and his prowess so threatening, that Floyd Patterson, the reigning heavyweight champion of the world, would not grant him a title fight.

The California heavyweight Eddie Machen, who was also twenty-eight when he fought Liston, had fought ten of the men Liston had beaten: Cleveland Williams, Howard King, and Benny Wise in 1955; Julio Mederos, Nino Valdes, and Johnny Summerlin in 1956; Zora Folley in 1958; Willi Besmanoff and Cleveland Williams, again, in 1959; Billy Hunter, Wayne Bethea, and Zora Folley, again, in 1960. Machen, like Liston, had fought and won twice against Williams. He had also fought Zora Folley twice. The first fight had ended in a draw; the subsequent fight had ended in the second loss of Machen's career. Like Folley — and, too, like Nino Valdes — Machen was also denied a shot at the title.

Liston was disappointed by his fight with Eddie Machen, for Machen spent much of the twelve rounds running and backpedaling from Sonny. "It takes two to make a fight," Sonny said afterward. "Machen wouldn't." But Sonny's victory over Machen rendered him the world's number-one heavyweight contender as of September 7, 1960.

On March 8, 1961, while Carbo and Palermo were on trial in Los Angeles, he beat Howard King for the second time: a technical knockout after three.

This second King fight, like the first, was held in Miami. In his account of the fight, Johnny Underwood of the *Miami Herald* wrote: "The small train wreck which is Sonny Liston's legendary left jab was the softening agent. It brought blood to King's nose in the first round. The setup was a left hook, the finisher a short right cross." Unlike Machen, King did not run from Liston in the ring, though he later regretted his bravery. "It was a terrible mistake," he said. "I've got to face reality. He's stronger than me, and any man I've ever fought."

Sonny did not fight again until after the two Frankies had been sentenced, and, with his victory over Westphal in Philadelphia that December, there was no contender of stature left for him to fight. Furthermore, he had beaten the three contenders whom the champion refused to fight; and the first-ranked among them had run from him in fear.

Floyd Patterson, under the guidance of his wily manager, Cus D'Amato, had avoided facing Valdes, Folley, and Machen under various pretexts of circumstance or business. "What would Machen draw?" D'Amato said. "Floyd and I regard ourselves as professionals. We are interested in the biggest gate." In the case of Sonny, the evasion of a title fight with him was quite simple: the man was a criminal who represented all that was unsavory and evil, and Patterson must not allow either himself, the championship, or boxing itself to be degraded by condescending to acknowledge Liston as a morally acceptable challenger.

Between the two fights Sonny fought in 1961, the King fight in March and the Westphal fight in December, there were eight months of trouble that coincided with the period of trouble that Carbo and Palermo were experiencing in a federal courtroom in Los Angeles.

On March 30, 1961, in Sacramento, the chairman of the California State Athletic Commission, Dr. Dan Kilroy, announced that Sonny Liston, the top contender for Floyd Patterson's heavyweight title, would not be permitted to fight in California under present conditions. In explaining the decision to bar Liston, the chairman mentioned the Kefauver hearings, the current trial in California of Carbo and Palermo, and the proven, ongoing control of Liston by Palermo. The commissioner said that Liston would have to change managers before he would ever be allowed to fight in California.

On April 8, Sonny declared his intention of buying back his contract from Pep Barone. He declared that he would pay Barone $75,000 over the next two years in exchange for the contract, which still had almost two years to run. Sonny followed this declaration by publicly daring Patterson to face him in a title fight.

"That bum Patterson don't want to fight me," Liston complained on April 10, 1961, in one of the letters he "wrote" through the hand of another.

A few days later, on April 15, Liston formally asked Barone to surrender the contract. While sportswriters and others wondered why anyone would relinquish for $75,000 a contract worth considerably more on the open market, Liston stated bluntly and not without an edge of weary disgust, "I want to get me a new manager that's O.K. with Patterson and Kefauver and the rest of the world."

Four days later, on April 19, the deal was done and Sonny Liston was a free agent.

Patterson and D'Amato were unmoved by Sonny's contractual break with Barone, remarking that the mere fact that Sonny "ostensibly" had purchased his contract did not mean that he no longer was affiliated with the dark forces that Barone represented. Sonny, said Patterson, "will still have to prove that he is free of all outside harmful influences" before he would be considered to qualify for a title fight.

Liston strode one day into D'Amato's office, catching him unawares and frightening him by his sudden huge presence. D'Amato gasped and put his hand to his chest.

"Is you is or is you ain't giving me a shot at the title?"

D'Amato composed himself and suggested that Sonny send him a list of proposed managers. D'Amato would choose one whose character he approved.

"Ain't that nice. What you mean is that you want to control me."

Sonny made a gesture of appealing to Senator Kefauver himself to choose a new manager for him, but the senator declined. Kefauver did, however, ask the attorney Alfred Klein, a member of the Pennsylvania State Athletic Commission and formerly a member of Kefauver's investigating committee, to guide Liston in his quest for probity.

Sonny announced the selection of a new manager, and introduced him, at a Philadelphia press conference on May 10. He was George Katz.

Born in 1904 and raised in South Philly, Katz had a background in local politics and boxing. He had done his share of politicking as a secretary for both Republican and Democratic officials, and he had been a boxing manager since 1928. His most notable boxer had been a welterweight contender named Gil Turner.

Sonny stated at the press conference that, with Katz as his manager, he now had broken with, and was free of, what the Senate committee and Floyd Patterson had described as undesirable elements in his management. Klein stated that his office at the state athletic commission had conducted a thorough investigation of Katz and found no valid reason not to approve him as Liston's manager.

The contract with Katz was for a term of two and a half years, and it entitled Katz to ten percent of Sonny's net earnings.

At about half past five on May 17, Sonny was hanging out on the corner of Fortieth and Market streets, when a patrolman named James Best came by and told him to move along.

"Why don't you arrest me?" Sonny said to the cop.

And that is exactly what the cop did. Sonny was brought in on disorderly conduct and resisting arrest. At the station, these charges were reduced to loitering — corner lounging, they called it here — and he was kept for four hours before he was freed.

On June 12, in the dark before dawn, twenty-nine-year-old Dolores Ellis was driving through Fairmount Park in the Philadelphia suburb of Lansdowne. Two men in another vehicle came abreast of her car, directed a spotlight toward her, announced that they were police officers, and motioned her to stop. One of the men ordered Dolores out of her car, and she complied. When a park guard, John Warburton, happened by, the two men quickly turned off the car lights and sped away. The guard, in pursuit at eighty miles an hour, fired a warning shot and caught them after a half-mile chase. There, sitting behind the wheel, was Sonny Liston. With his companion, a twenty-six-year-old man named Isaac Cooper, Sonny was booked on an array of charges, including impersonating a police officer.

His new manager came to his defense: "Sonny is a fun-loving person who likes to play pranks."

Although Dolores Ellis would subsequently file a damage suit against Liston, alleging more than five grand worth of mental stress and anguish, all charges against Liston and Cooper relating to the Fairmount Park incident were dismissed in Magistrate's Court on the first of July, when Magistrate E. David Keiser said that the whole unfortunate matter had been an "error in judgment."

None the less, five days later, Sonny was ordered to appear at a hearing of the Pennsylvania State Athletic Commission to offer cause why his license to fight "should not be suspended or revoked." At that hearing, on July 14, the unanimous decision of the three-man commission was delivered aloud by Alfred Klein: the license of Charles (Sonny) Liston was hereby suspended indefinitely for actions detrimental to boxing and the public. In addressing Liston, Klein said that the fighter would be allowed to appeal for reinstatement at "such time as you have rehabilitated yourself and shown that you have respect for the law."

Since Pennsylvania was a member of the National Boxing Association, the suspension of Sonny would be honored throughout the NBA's forty-eight-state jurisdiction.

"You are at the final crossroads of your career," Klein told Liston. "What you do after today will determine the course of the rest of your life."

A year earlier, during his first and only fight in the town of Denver, Liston had made the acquaintance of Father Edward P. Murphy, a kindly Jesuit priest whose flock of parishioners was predominantly black. Now, days after his suspension, he turned to the good Father Murphy to help bail his ass out.

That phrase they had used: *"such time as you have rehabilitated yourself . . ."*

"Liston Begins Educational Rehabilitation Program," read the *New York Times* headline of an Associated Press story datelined Denver, July 20. The story reported that Sonny was now under the tutelage of Father Murphy, who had taken him in to live at the rectory of the St. Ignatius Loyola Church.

Geraldine joined Sonny in Denver, and they rented a house near the church. There was talk of Sonny's converting to Catholicism, as Floyd Patterson had done five years earlier. As a young girl, Geraldine had taken instruction in the Catholic Church, and now, with the Reverend Murphy, her interest was renewed.

Sonny's friend and sparring partner, Foneda Cox, whom Sonny had summoned to move from St. Louis and join him in Philadelphia, now came to live with Sonny in Denver. He said that "Father Murphy was a great guy. He just tried to keep Sonny straight"; and

"Sonny thought a lot of Father Murphy, and when Sonny thought something of you, he tried to do what you would advise him to do." Foneda thought a while, or anyway was silent. "If Sonny had been able to spend more time with Father Murphy, he might still be living."

But, as for Sonny having religion, the closest he and Sonny got to church in the old days in St. Louis, was to work out at the Roch A.C., a boxing club that was a part of St. Roch's Church. "Sonny, to be truthful," said Foneda, "wasn't very much a Christian at all."

Father Murphy, who preferred the term *reorientation* to *rehabilitation,* had faith in Sonny. Whatever it was, it worked. After three months in Denver, the suspension of Sonny's license was lifted; and it was announced, on October 24, that Sonny would fight Albert Westphal at Convention Hall in Philadelphia on December 4, as the opening bout of the first doubleheader in closed-circuit boxing. Floyd Patterson's championship fight that same night in Toronto against Tom McNeeley would be the broadcast's main event.

The broadcast rights to both of the December 4 bouts had been awarded to TelePrompTer Corporation. In telegraphic prose, a TelePrompTer press release described the upcoming Westphal fight as — no definite article, no indefinite article — "first step in personal 'rehabilitation' program that he hopes will lead to shot at Floyd Patterson and heavyweight title." Sonny, stated the release, was born in Pine Bluff, Arkansas, on May 8, 1934.

According to Tom Bolan, an associate of Roy M. Cohn whose company, Championship Sports, Inc., promoted both fights, Sonny's guarantee for the fight would be $75,000; Westphal's, $15,000.

On the afternoon of the fight, Sonny had a party at his home on Dunlap Street. There was champagne for everybody but him. He played records.

"Where Dave Brubeck at?" he wondered aloud as he searched

through his collection until he found what he was looking for: Brubeck's "Take Five" on the 1960 album *Time Out*.

"Hey, get this," he said, pulling out a recent album on the Chess label, "*Pigmeat Markham at the Party*. This guy's the best."

Sonny was the first rock 'n' roll champ. Foneda remembered those tapes blaring fine and loud as they drove through the night. Sonny liked Ray Charles, Bo Diddley, Little Milton. "We had records going back to all the great artists. The black artists," Foneda said. "This is what Sonny loved to listen to."

Back in February '61, James Brown and his Famous Flames had recorded a version of "Night Train": same night, same train, but with a rhythm like a nasty automatic instead of Jimmy Forrest's big bad long revolver. "Sonny was crazy about that record," said Foneda.

"Sonny," one guy asked him as the records played and Sonny danced the Twist with Geraldine at that party before the Westphal fight, "don't you like to talk about boxing?"

"When I met my wife," Sonny answered, "I didn't talk too much. So why should I talk to a man?"

After a dinner of steak and peas, Sonny excused himself and took a nap.

The crowd at Convention Hall numbered 3,227, with gross receipts figured to be $19,020. The money was in the closed-circuit action.

Sonny disposed of Westphal in one minute and fifty-eight seconds, which was less time than it took to do the Twist with Geraldine.

The West German boxer was asked how he felt. "My body feels good, but my soul not so," he said. He declared Liston to be the "best fighter I saw ever."

Would he like to fight Liston again?

"No."

Westphal at the time was ranked fourth among heavyweights. When Liston was asked how he himself would rank Westphal, he hesitated, then smiled. "He's all right," he said. "He's a nice fighter."

In the next day's *New York Herald-Tribune*, Jerry Izenberg would write: "Westphal, a blond master baker from Hamburg, said yesterday that he has never been knocked off his feet. For a while last night it looked like it would be a long time before he was on them again."

Having barely broken a sweat, Sonny walked with a quiet pulse to the press room under the stands. He sat there on a wooden chair in his white robe, sipping orange juice and watching Patterson beat McNeeley on a closed-circuit monitor.

"If he were here, I'd go back and fight without even takin' a shower."

The guys in the press room started asking him questions. How had he taken care of Westphal with such devastating haste?

Sonny shrugged distractedly: "Left jab, right hand."

That right had knocked Westphal unconscious for almost two minutes, almost as long as the fight itself. "How did it feel looking down there at Westphal? I mean, with his eyeballs rolling around and his tongue sticking out like that," a reporter asked.

Sonny looked at the reporter with an expression that said nothing. "It felt good," he said.

Sonny leaned forward in his chair during the postfight interview with Patterson, who was asked if Sonny Liston was among his future plans. Patterson would say only that he had "the greatest respect for Sonny Liston — in the ring."

Upon his return from Denver, he had been asked by a reporter in New York what he had learned in his rehabilitation.

"I've been learning to be around different kinds of people," Sonny said.

"What kind?"

"The right kind."

The reporter wished him to elucidate.

"There are only two kinds of people. Good and bad, right?"

A wire from the Religious News Service, datelined Philadelphia, December 5, 1961: "Re-established in boxing's big time after taking only 118 seconds to knock out his first opponent in nine months, Sonny Liston is heading back to Denver to continue the 'rehabilitation' and '3R's' course conducted by Father Edward P. Murphy, S.J."

He had been after Floyd Patterson and the title for a long, long time. Patterson was the first heavyweight in history to regain the title; but from the time he regained it, from Ingemar Johansson, in June of 1959, until the December 1961 closed-circuit doubleheader he had fought only one other fight, and that had been yet another rematch with Johansson.

In December 1960, when Sonny appeared before the Kefauver Committee, Patterson and his manager Cus D'Amato had accepted no challengers for almost a year and a half.

> SENATOR DIRKSEN: I would think after seven years of hard experience, you would have some recommendations to make to improve boxing if it is to survive. Have you any suggestions?
>
> LISTON: Well, the onliest thing that would bring it back to life is a guy that would fight like Louis, who would fight anybody and everybody, and just fight.

D'Amato wanted to see a big gate? Sonny offered to fight Patterson *and* Johansson on the same night.

Patterson was not alone in his resolution that he must not fight Liston. Black champions had ruled heavyweight boxing from 1937, when Joe Louis won the title from James J. Braddock, to

1952, when Rocky Marciano took it from Jersey Joe Walcott. Patterson brought it back in 1956, after Marciano had retired undefeated. Floyd, so unlike Joe Louis in many ways, was like Louis in that he was a champion beloved both by blacks and by whites. In the eyes of black leaders, such a champion was among the greatest of ambassadors in the cause of acceptance by, and advancement in, white society. He was also among the greatest sources of pride for black people to draw upon. Patterson was a soft-spoken, erudite, and mannerly champion. He was, as they said in those days, a credit to his race. In those days, bad niggers were not the darling middle-class iconic commodities and consumers of a white-ruled conglomerate culture. In those days, bad niggers were bad news. And the bad made it hard for the good. Black leaders and their followers feared the prospect of Sonny Liston as a champion as much as Patterson feared fighting him. A champion such as Liston, it was believed, would bring disgrace and trouble; would impugn and abrogate black respectability; and would be like gasoline to bring white hatred flaring forth anew. His infamy would become theirs. He was anathema.

The National Association for the Advancement of Colored People was against the idea of a Patterson-Liston fight. Its president, Percy Sutton, came right out and said it: Patterson "represents us better than Liston ever could or would." Liston was seen, by black as well as white, as the Bad Nigger. Of course, if the NAACP had any faith that the Good Nigger had a shot in hell at vanquishing the Bad Nigger, they would have supported the fight. This lack of confidence, shown him by the very ones who laid upon his shoulders the responsibility of protecting his race from dishonor, placed Patterson under pressure that was difficult to bear. And it was not the black community alone that burdened him. White political leaders who made a show of supporting civil rights invested Patterson with the same duty, as if the course and furtherance of those rights would be endangered should Patterson allow Liston to represent his race.

The writer Peter Heller interviewed Patterson in 1970 for his book *"In This Corner . . . !" 42 World Champions Tell Their Stories*. In that interview, Patterson recalled what was then not yet a decade past.

> "The president of the United States, Ralph Bunche, all the big celebrities, all the big leaders of the country," he said, "they made Liston a bad guy, and I was a good guy. I don't ever want to endure that kind of pressure again. To me, fighting is fighting. It's a sport. I met the president of the United States, and he even said to me, 'Make sure you keep that championship.' His brother Bobby Kennedy said I was good for the youth. In fact, he gave me a trophy that night for the youth of America and all that, 'keep your example up.' It was nice but I would have much preferred to have went up in the mountains somewhere, seclude myself away until I fought, and then come out and let everyone tell me this after it's done if I was successful. I don't think anyone should be compared, 'This guy's better than him because he's a nice guy. This guy's been in jail, this guy's no good.' "

Patterson said that all the kind words he increasingly put forth regarding Liston were in part a subterfuge designed to free himself from onus.

> "I constantly went on TV and made interviews and said, 'Liston is all right. Give him a break.' I tried to yell for him, but actually this was to save me, so to speak, because I figured if I could get people to see him the way I was saying you should see him, then they wouldn't look to me so much."

How had boxing become psychomachia? How had it come to be charged with such meaning and such moment and such madness? How could one man, in all human weakness and vulnerability and insignificance, come to bear the fate of others? Was there no subcommittee to probe and to ponder this sort of underground control, this sort of hidden interest? Were the Suttons and the Kennedys any less constraining and demanding and imposing than the Carbos and Palermos of this world? Had the Carbos and Palermos ever in their grasping exerted such pressure on any fighter?

Sonny may not have been able to read, and he may not have been able to write, but in his way, beneath that taciturn and deathward brooding, he was brilliant. Jose Torres, the writer and former light heavyweight champion, has said, "I have never met an athlete in baseball, basketball, or football who is smarter, more intelligent than Sonny Liston." And Sonny knew that beneath the anxiety that Patterson felt, deep in that quiet, complicated, and insecure man, there was, as in most men, a shackled and secreted child whose greatest fear was to have his fear exposed. Fear stops men, as Homer said. It also impels them. And so Sonny's ceaseless and rising implications of that fear within Patterson, his taunts that Patterson was afraid of him, were the lashes that provoked his prey and commanded the attention, excitement, and expectations of the masses.

"Patterson says it's the Mob that keeps him from fighting me," Sonny said; "but I'm the only Mob he's worried about."

Patterson, beloved and beset, was nearing his judgment day. It was inevitable. That other, greater mob, those roused masses, the vast and thirsty populace of bread and circuses, demanded it.

Blinky was back in Philly, out on bail appealing his case, looking at those fifteen years that lay ahead.

Sonny was looking to dump his new, clean manager, George Katz.

The previous summer, a Chester, Pennsylvania, food concessionaire named Bob Nilon had made Katz and Liston an offer for the rights to promote a proposed Liston-Johansson match. Now, in the first days of 1962, Bob's younger brother and partner, forty-three-year-old Jack Nilon, applied to the state athletic commission for a manager's license. On January 10, it was announced that Jack Nilon was to take over the management of Sonny Liston from George Katz. He would be referred to not as Liston's manager, but as his "adviser." The Irish Catholic Nilon would say that he came to Sonny by way of a recommendation by Father Murphy. Sonny entered into a contract with Jack Nilon more than eighteen months before his contract with Katz was due to expire. Their memorandum of agreement, executed on March 1, 1962, stated that "I, Charles 'Sonny' Liston, do hereby appoint Jack Nilon of Ridley Park, Pa., as my sole and exclusive manager." The agreement, which entitled Nilon to a third of "all purses," was stipulated to remain in effect until April 27, 1965.

By the end of January, a deal for a Patterson-Liston fight was on the table. After negotiations with Patterson's manager Cus D'Amato, Tom Bolan of Championship Sports offered Liston a guarantee of $200,000 against twelve and a half percent of both the gate and the ancillary rights. Sonny balked. He wanted twenty percent. Even Joe Louis's many challengers had gotten that much.

Irving B. Kahn, the president of TelePrompTer, said the fight could gross seven and a half million dollars in ancillary rights. (As usual, the promotional ballyhoo exceeded the eventual actuality, which was a total gross of some four million dollars in stadium and theater ticket sales combined.)

Sonny sought a fair-price ruling from the National Boxing Association. A compromise was reached. Sonny would take the twelve and a half percent this time around, but he would get twenty-five percent of the rematch money.

At the contract-signing ceremony on March 16, Sonny and Patterson — both in dark conservative suits, white silk shirts, and hyperbolical cufflinks — faced the press with Tom Bolan, Roy Cohn, and other principals. Sonny was asked if he was now happy with the terms of the agreement.

"No," he said.

In a report of the signing and press conference, *Time* magazine quoted Liston: "A boxing match is like a cowboy movie. There's got to be good guys, and there's got to be bad guys."

Later, he put it another way: "I'm the bad guy — O.K., people want to think that, let them." As in the cowboy movies, the "bad guys are supposed to lose. I change that. I win."

Arrangements were pursued for the fight to be held in New York, where, at a place such as Yankee Stadium and a top ticket price of a hundred bucks, a gate of two and a half million dollars was not unthinkable.

But Benny Paret had recently died following injuries inflicted in the ring at Madison Square Garden on March 24 — he died in a coma on April 3, the same day newspapers reported that Liston's driving license had been suspended after he had been pulled over for doing more than seventy miles an hour on the New Jersey Turnpike — and the state was wary of any further controversy surrounding boxing. On April 27, under the direction of Governor Nelson Rockefeller, the New York State Athletic Commission denied Sonny a license to fight in New York, on the grounds that his past "provided a pattern of suspicion" that could be "detrimental to the best interests of professional boxing and to the public interest as well."

On that same day, Gay Talese interviewed Patterson for the *New York Times*. "One night in bed, I made up my mind," Patterson said. "I knew if I'd want to sleep comfortably, I'd have to take on Liston even though the N.A.A.C.P. and the Kefauver committee didn't want me to take on the fight. Some people said: 'What if you lose and he wins? Then the colored people will suffer.'"

By the end of the month, Al Bolan, the vice president of Championship Sports under the presidency of his brother Tom and the untitled steering of Roy Cohn, announced that eight cities had come forth with offers to host the fight that New York had banned.

As he went about the business of promoting his newly published autobiography, *Victory over Myself,* Patterson tried to speak kindly of Liston, but the press seemed intent on countering his words as he spoke them. A *New York Times* writer, Arthur Daley, quoted him as saying, "Liston is a nice guy." Daley then immediately followed that quotation with the terse editorial statement, "He isn't at all."

The fight was set for Chicago, in September. On May 2, Sonny left for training camp at the Pines Hotel in South Fallsburg, in the New York Catskills.

> Preparing for the biggest fight of his life [reported *Newsweek*], Liston fortifies himself with two meals a day (five strips of bacon, three soft-boiled eggs, two glasses of fruit juice, and two cups of tea for breakfast; 2 pounds of steak for dinner), walks 7 miles in 7-pound shoes, shadow boxes four rounds, and skips rope nine minutes to a jazz recording of "The Night Train." For diversion, he watches television, pitches nickels with members of his entourage, or stands on his head. Sometimes he rides a red bicycle.

In late August, after Sonny had moved camp to the site of an abandoned racetrack in Aurora, Illinois, he was asked by a reporter what his fight plans would be if he won the title.

"If I win, I might fight Johansson. But first he must fight Cleveland Williams. There is a one-year return match in the Patterson fight, but my plan is to make him not want a return fight.

"I hear Johansson say I'm slow. I saw him fight Patterson twice. He was lucky. He should be locked up for impersonating a fighter.

"I went the full eight rounds with Eddie Machen. It's the longest I ever went. It takes two to tango, and Machen wasn't in the mood to. I don't think Patterson will run. I caught Machen, and I don't think anybody can run as fast as him.

"As for Archie Moore, I don't think I would fight him. If I could hold the title for as many months as he has years, I would retire.

"As for Cassius Clay, I'll probably fight him, but he would have to fight Williams first.

"Williams was the hardest puncher I've fought. No one wants to fight him. He can punch as hard as I can, but he can't take it like I can."

A week later, he told reporters that Patterson "will be the first fighter I have ever met that I actually have been mad at"; that "never before have I had such a feeling against any fighter I have ever met."

He revealed that he had foreseen the fight in a dream a week or so ago. "The dream told me just how the fight would end; but I'm not going to say anything about it." He would say only that he was "certain that the fight won't last long and I'll be the winner."

On September 16, Patterson spoke from his training camp in Elgin, Illinois: "I have met Sonny Liston several times and I believe there is much good in him. Should he be fortunate enough to win the heavyweight championship, I ask that you give him a chance to bring out the good that is in him."

"If Liston should be lucky enough to win," he said on another occasion, "I hope you'll accept him the way you've accepted me. You know, there's a little bit of good in everybody."

Sonny would have none of it. There were no kind words. "I'll kill him," he said. "I'd like to run over him in a car."

"Liston is as ill-mannered and insolent as a chain gang boss. Hatred seems to ooze out of his every pore," wrote Dan Parker, a columnist with a pencil-thin moustache, on the eve of the fight.

A week before the fight, Liston had been an eight-to-five favorite in Las Vegas. In Chicago, the odds narrowed to seven and a half to five.

The boys at the Missouri State Penitentiary at Jefferson City were gathered round radios, hoping that their most celebrated alumnus would do them proud. As William P. Steinhauser, the deputy warden, put it, he was their kind of guy. "He don't box," Steinhauser said, "he fights."

The night of the fight, September 25, 1962, was a chill one, and the cold of Chicago cut through the dark and glare of Comiskey Park, the ballpark where Sonny's hero Joe Louis had won the title back in '37.

In boxing, nothing is better for business than a fight between a black man and a white, such is humanity shorn of hypocrisy. Short of that, nothing is better than a fight between good and evil. Here, in Comiskey Park, on this chill gray night, there was such a fight, perhaps the most dramatic of them all; and barely had breath been drawn by the more than eighteen thousand gathered there, and by the half a million gathered before the closed-circuit screens of America, when an astounded silence overtook them, and then a loud and roaring anger.

It lasted two minutes and six seconds. Liston struck with a left hook, and in the next breath moved to follow that blow with a right uppercut. But there was no one there to take that uppercut, for Patterson was down, unconscious, and deposed.

The loud and roaring anger grew into a howl of execration that was greater than the wind. But it was over; and there was no fucking with the dream-book of Charles L. Liston.

James Baldwin mourned the moment. He had left the fight sadly, he said, and gone "off to a bar, to mourn the very possible death of boxing, and to have a drink, with love, for Floyd."

It was the fastest heavyweight title drop since Joe Louis took Max Schmeling in two minutes and four seconds in June of 1938.

"I definitely wasn't afraid," said Patterson after the fight. "I wish to emphasize that. I was definitely not afraid."

He left the stadium disguised in a theatrical beard that he had brought with him. His reckoned share of the take was $1,185,253, which surpassed by almost two hundred grand the thirty-five-year-old record for the largest individual purse that had been set by Gene Tunney in his 1927 Chicago fight against Jack Dempsey. Sonny's take was $282,000.

In a quiet moment during the flight back to Philly, Liston saw it somewhat differently and with more compassion for Patterson than he had allowed himself before the fight. Fear was sometimes a good thing, Sonny said of that force of many colors, that force that could stop men, or impel them, or save them, or destroy them. "Patterson had fear in him, but he wasn't no coward."

Sonny seemed sincerely inspired to be a champion who would do good and make people proud. He had brought in Father Stevens and Father Murphy for the fight, and he posed smiling broadly with them for photographers at his late-night victory celebration at the Regency Room of the Sahara Inn, northwest of Chicago. He did not share in the champagne, but sat abstemious, even though Geraldine suggested that he truly deserved a taste on a night such as this. As the good priests present knew and said, Sonny did not drink.

"I have reached my goal as heavyweight champion," Sonny said to the press. "When you reach your goal, you have to be proud and dignified. You represent something and you have a responsibility to live up to it." As a champion, he said, "I can do something good for somebody else. As champion, I have the opportunity to do things that would not be possible otherwise." He said that he would model himself on Joe Louis, "who I think was the greatest champion of all and my idol. He did everything I want to do. I intend to follow the example he set and would like to go down as a great champion, too." He went so far as to make a rare allusion to his childhood: "I had nothing when I was a kid but a lot of brothers and sisters, a helpless mother, and a father who didn't care about any of us." He seemed to speak from a newly found cove of placidity within the lake of his heart when he said, "I promise everyone that I will be a decent, respectable champion."

Acting to satisfy tax claims against Championship Sports, Inc., the federal government placed liens on the promotional proceeds of the fight, delaying due payment to the fighters. After further difficulty in getting the money owed them, Liston and Jack Nilon swore that they were through with CSI. Where was one to turn in this new inchoate day when one was forced to wear the cloak of legitimacy? Men such as Carbo put their arms around your shoulders and reached into their pockets and paid you. The dice in every deal may have been loaded against you, but you went in knowing that. It was man to man, and there was no secret about those house dice. But how was one to survive when men were not men, when they had been replaced by such hideous changelings of legitimacy as Roy Cohn, sportsman.

As Jack Nilon would say, "Lawyers have come into boxing and run it into the ground."

Back in Philadelphia, at about half past eight on October 5, Sonny took another pinch, again in Fairmount Park, where he was stopped for driving his 1962 Cadillac at the unusually slow speed of fifteen miles an hour. As it turned out, he had just sideswiped a car on Girard Avenue.

Park guard Aaron Smith said that Sonny "became very nasty, and he said that I was prejudiced because he was colored." When Sonny stepped from his Cadillac, Smith said, "he swaggered and swayed," and "he had the smell of alcohol on his breath." He refused to enter the patrol wagon because a "white man" was driving. Finally, he agreed to go to the guard house in a car driven by a sergeant of color.

Alfred Klein, who as a member of the state athletic commission had suspended Liston's license for less, this time came to Sonny's support, describing the incident as nothing more than "harassment."

Sonny's attorney, Morton Witkin, stated that it was incredible that liquor could have been smelled on his breath. "He never touches a drop," Witkin said. "Somebody must be picking on him."

Foneda Cox said, "Sonny loved to drink, and he loved to drive while he was drinking. So this was one of the things that they kind of relied on me for, was to drive him around to try to keep him out of trouble. But then I couldn't stay with him twenty-four hours a day."

Sonny, he said, "was a good guy. I really hated to see things happen to him like they did because he would get drunk and then he would get outrageous, see. And when he'd go into his little rages — he's a big guy, anyway; you'd be scared just looking at him." When Sonny got upset, "he would blow off," Foneda said. "He didn't care who it was. But he would blow off, tell 'em off, and all this stuff, especially when he'd drink."

As Foneda recalled, Sonny went for that J&B Scotch. But he "would shut off his drinking when we would go into training. I mean, just like you turn off a faucet, this is the way he would turn it off."

"He never touches a drop. Somebody must be picking on him."

Morton Witkin was a distinguished Philadelphia attorney with an office in the Finance Building. Born in 1895, he had been practicing law for over forty years, and had served as majority and minority leader of the Pennsylvania House of Representatives.

Blinky Palermo was still free on bail. Morton Witkin was his lawyer. He had become Sonny's lawyer too around the time that Sonny bought back his contract from Pep Barone, in a show of severing his ties to the Mob.

George Katz, who had bought that contract, was still getting ten percent of Sonny. "I could choke him," Sonny said of Katz. "I don't have no manager. Katz is my manager of record. My contract with him runs until October 1963. There's nobody going to be my manager until my contract with Katz runs out." As he said, "I don't need no manager." Though Jack Nilon would often be described in the press as Sonny's manager, and though he performed the functions of a manager, his appointed role, according to Sonny and others, was that of "adviser."

"Actually Sonny didn't have a manager," as Foneda Cox expressed it. "What he had was Jack Nilon."

Nilon, said Foneda, "was a pretty nice guy," and he "did his duty for Sonny as a manager." He was "the guy that was around us mostly." He was "the main guy. He was the guy that went with us, and he was the one that brought orders."

Orders?

"Jack Nilon handled the situation between Sonny and the Mafia," Foneda said offhandedly. "He would do things, he would tell Sonny what he wanted done. This is what Sonny did, this is what we did. We relied on him for doing different stuff."

As Sonny's friend Lowell Powell said, Sonny both loved and feared Blinky, and he minded him. "But Jack Nilon and them, shit, they was just boys, so to speak, with Sonny. Sonny would sass 'em. He cursed Jack Nilon out. As a matter of fact, he called Jack Nilon up and said, 'I've got some friends here and I'm trying to show them a nice time. You get on that plane and bring me some money.' Shit, when that plane rolled in, about five or six o'clock, we met at O'Hare Field and he had one of them grocery sacks, one of them sixteen-pound bags full of money, hundred-dollar bills. Sonny gave it to me and said, 'You hold the bag.' "

Six days after Sonny's slow-driving pinch, at a Washington, D.C., meeting of ten U.S. Attorneys called by United States Attorney General Robert Kennedy, U.S. Attorney Drew J.T. O'Keefe of Philadelphia requested that a new investigation be conducted by the Department of Justice into the background and associations of Sonny Liston. This request, he said, was made after receiving "varied reports" that Liston might still be tied to the underworld.

In late November, Sonny took a trip to Chicago, where he let it be known that he was sick of Philadelphia. It was another fucking St. Louis. "I'd say I have been treated like a champion everywhere, except in my hometown of Philadelphia, where I'm treated like a bum." On November 30, he and Geraldine left Philadelphia for good.

Encountered in a Chicago hotel lobby, he was asked, "Is Chicago your official residence now, and are you going to stay here permanently?"

"Yeah."

"Where are you living?"

"Apartment."

Liston moved into his new home on December 4, a three-story, twenty-one-room mansion enclosed by a wrought-iron fence in an area of Chicago that thirty-five years ago had been the South Side's millionaire row. The mansion had belonged to the jazz pianist Ahmad Jamal, who had moved out a few days before. There was a twenty-by-forty-foot living room carpeted in pale blue; oak and walnut paneling, library cases, and a grand old fireplace. The Listons moved in their purple-upholstered chairs and their gold-colored chairs upholstered in pink and white. Moving into the house with Sonny and Geraldine were Geraldine's mother, a niece named Marjorie Wilheit, and Sonny's friends Foneda Cox and Ted King, the latter of whom served as Sonny's valet.

As he showed a few friendly newsmen around the house, someone asked him what the future held, and he paused unsurely before speaking.

"I would rather fight Cassius Clay than anyone. He's a young boy, and if I wait too long, age might catch up to me like it did Archie." (In mid-November, forty-eight-year-old Archie Moore, a light heavyweight champion of many years, had been knocked out by Clay in four.)

"But I'm going to keep fighting about ten more years and can wait for Cassius. I'll let him keep talking, but not too long, though. Maybe it would be better for me to fight Ingemar Johansson before giving Clay a chance. Or maybe Clay should fight Patterson. I think Patterson would win. I don't think Clay can hit hard enough to break an egg."

While the Listons were moving in, four squad cars pulled up outside, lingered, then were gone.

Before the first drumbeat comes down, the voice of James Brown:
All aboard! Night Train!

The Patterson rematch was set for Miami Beach, April 10, 1963. In February, while training in Miami for the rematch, Sonny befriended an eleven-year-old boy named Mike Zwerner. They met one morning at the Normandy Shores Golf Course, where Sonny did his roadwork, and close to where the boy lived. Sonny's newfound little pal called him, "the best friend I've ever had." It was while fooling around with the boy, chucking golf balls at the landscaped trees of the Normandy Shores course, that Sonny was said to have suffered an injury to his left knee. The injury was said to have worsened. Daily cortisone shots and deep-sound treatments were said to have healed the inflamed ligaments of his left patella, but there was said to remain a piece of torn cartilage that could be treated only by surgery, to which Liston would not submit himself.

The rematch, which was the final commitment of Liston and Nilon to Championship Sports, was put off until the summer, and the venue was changed from Miami Beach to Las Vegas.

According to Foneda Cox, there was no injury. "What I'm telling you," Foneda said, "they didn't get it together to make the agreements on the fight. They really had not decided whether they was going to let Sonny win the fight or not." It was clear that Foneda was talking not about the Patterson rematch, but of the machinations involved in the fight that was to follow the rematch. His claim that there was no injury would, if true, explain the troublingly casual reference to Sonny's undergoing cortisone treatment. As everyone close to him knew, Sonny had a fear of needles that was pathological in the extreme. It may also be not without meaning that a shift to Las Vegas came at a time when these alleged machinations were said to be unresolved.

Sonny's basic entourage at this time consisted of six men: Jack Nilon, who no longer was an advisory nonmanager, but a manager in full; Willie Reddish, his trainer; Joe Polino, his assistant trainer and cornerman; Foneda Cox, his friend and sparring partner; Teddy King, his friend and valet; and John Grayson, his bodyguard.

Grayson, the newest member of the troupe, was known as Moose. He was a black ex-cop who had been working as a detective in the Illinois attorney general's office when he was assigned, at Sonny's request, to provide licensed-gun protection during the Aurora training period before the first Patterson fight. Since then, Sonny had made Moose Grayson his full-time bodyguard.

Ben Bentley, the veteran Chicago public-relations man who had first met Liston during the last days of the IBC, had been brought aboard and charged with remaking the champion's image. Others had failed in their sporadic attempts to fulfill this imposing task. *Time* magazine in the summer of 1959 had bought a taste of the Horatio Alger story, which presented a young, imprisoned Liston who for inspiration "studied Joe Louis' *My Life Story* by the hour" in the meager light of his cell. But it proved a hard tale to sell about a man who could not read.

"All right," Bentley had shouted to the awaiting press the night Sonny won the crown in Chicago, "he'll be right out. Everything has to be done right, or else he'll clear you all out of here. You've seen presidential press conferences. That's how you do it."

The April 1963, *Ebony* featured Sonny as a happy homebody in its "Date with a Dish." A photograph showed a smiling Liston seated in suit and tie at a dinner table of wholesome plenty, a dainty glass of orange juice raised in his immense and manicured hand: "The Champ enjoys a glass of orange juice before he consumes his favorite menu. He feels that orange juice is the best cocktail and appetizer before dinner." The article made further revelations: "His favorite menu consists of orange juice, crabmeat salad, filet mignon, broiled medium and rare, Brussels sprouts, baked potato with butter, tossed green salad with thousand island dressing, tea, and ice cream." Several recipes followed, all of them "tested in EBONY's test kitchen."

Ben Bentley served as Liston's publicity director from 1962 to 1964. Liston hated the press, and the press hated him; and for Bentley, who was an easygoing man, it was not an easygoing time.

One of Bentley's greatest coups was to have Sonny invited as a guest of honor at the Big Brothers banquet hosted by the columnist and Big Brothers president Drew Pearson. The banquet was held in Washington, D.C., on March 29, 1963.

Director J. Edgar Hoover of the FBI had taken an increasing interest in the Liston file, personally reviewing and adding his scrawled and initialed comments to various of the Liston-related documents that crossed his desk. At the bottom of a United Press International report that "Liston was here tonight for a 'Big Brothers' dinner for which he and the vice president were the headline attractions," the Director wrote: "Just how naive can some of our VIPs get?" Later, in his column "The Washington Merry-Go-Round," Pearson recounted what Liston had said in addressing those assembled: "I feel that mothers and fathers should know where the child is at all times. And should have a deadline to get home at night." As for his own youth, well, "I would find stuff before it got lost." To a copy of the column, Hoover added, "It is nauseating the way Pearson tries to present Liston as a 'clean' person."

While in Washington for the Big Brothers dinner, Sonny visited Junior Village, a public home for abandoned and orphaned children, where he remained so long among the children that he was late to arrive at the Big Brothers affair.

In an unpublished letter to *Newsweek*, dated July 22, 1963, the institutional administrator of Junior Village, Joseph S. Kosisky, Jr., wrote to defend Liston amid ongoing bad press, describing Liston's visit, which had gone unnoticed: "He won the admiration of the youngsters, from the babies to teenagers, who seemed to sense that this man, this tower of strength, had a genuine liking for them. He awed the children and staff alike with his kindness and consideration." Kosisky said, "There is no doubt in my mind but that in the eyes of the 800 children living at Junior Village, he appeared as a real champ" and "an idol to look up to." He ended his letter by noting "that apparently this visit was not a publicity stunt, since there was no press coverage during his visit with the children."

It was true: children loved Sonny as he loved them. In Philadelphia, while the cops and the newspapers hunted him down, the kids in the neighborhood would run to gather around the man they all called Uncle Sonny.

The secretarial diary of Vice President Lyndon B. Johnson shows that Johnson met with Liston and Pearson at ten o'clock that morning in Senate Room S212, and that he led them on a tour of the Senate floor. Afterwards, Sonny and Ben visited with Johnson privately in the vice president's office.

Of course, an audience with President Kennedy could not be arranged, because of his brother's ongoing crusade against the element whence Sonny, like the Kennedy fortune itself, had come.

But Bentley viewed the opportunity to be accepted into the vice president's graces not only as an honor, but as a godsend for Sonny's image.

In Johnson's office, amid various decorative objects and mementos, there was "an alligator or something," Bentley recalled, "made out of leather or something."

"I know where that comes from," Sonny said. "That's what we made in prison."

After a few minutes in the vice president's company, Sonny grew restless, leaned toward Bentley, spoke low into his ear: "Let's blow this bum off."

As they flew back to Chicago, Sonny withdrew into an increasingly foul mood, and he got to drinking, and he went off by himself.

When Sonny had quit training in Miami following his knee injury, he had left Foneda Cox and Moose Grayson to close down camp and haul the training equipment back to Chicago in a trailer hitched to a car. They were traveling together toward Chicago, equipment in tow, on that night of March 29, as Sonny was flying back to Chicago from Washington, D.C.

Late that night, Ben Bentley got a call. It was Moose Grayson's wife, Pearl, and she was very distraught. Sonny, she said, had sexually assaulted her.

As I write this, I remember a pleasant dinner I had not long ago with the casting director Vickie Thomas. Sonny Liston, she said, struck her as a man who in the eyes of the world was so big and so bad and so black, and yet inside so gentle. Would that it were so, I now think, if only for the sake of storytelling, if only for the sake of what we might want to believe, if only for the sake of the dignity of tragedy itself; if only for the sake of understanding.

Liston's private acts of charity and kindness — to prisoners, the disabled, the poor — were many; his love of children was well-known; and he was a man without racism in him.

"We were riding down Fremont Street downtown, and I was driving his car," remembered his Las Vegas friend Davey Pearl. "Bumper-to-bumper traffic. And he says to me, 'Stop the car.' I said, 'I can't stop the car here.' He said, 'Stop the goddamn car.' I stopped the car, and he runs out, and there's a little woman sitting on a little dolly selling pencils. He emptied out both pockets and gave it to her, just dropped it on her tray," Pearl said. "And it was a white woman, so there was no racial thing."

If it is true that we feel compassion most for those in whom we see ourselves, these emanations of the heart say much.

But, as Lowell Powell said, "Sonny had a lot of gangsterism in him."

I asked Truman Gibson if Sonny had a sense of right or wrong. Truman thought awhile, smiled somewhat, gently shook his head, and softly answered: "None."

It was Sonny's first known sexual assault. Few would ever learn of it. Matt Rodriguez, the superintendent of police in Chicago, was one of those few. He told me he had encountered Grayson some years after the incident, and that Grayson told him that there had been a "settlement."

Sonny left town. His flight from Chicago was sudden, stealthful, and unquestioned by — for the most part unknown to — a press that remained unaware.

He and Foneda left Chicago together, with the idea of going to

California. They would drive southwest, because Sonny wanted to pass through Denver to visit Father Murphy.

They never made it to California, but only as far as Denver. Father Murphy "convinced Sonny that he should stay here. So we stayed here. And for a while we lived in that motel on East Colfax. We stayed together. Then, after a while, Sonny bought a house on Monaco. Thirty-fifth and Monaco. And then I rented an apartment over on Twenty-first and Race."

Sonny paid $28,500 for the brick house at 3633 Monaco Drive, on May 10, 1963. It was set on a corner lot with a lawn in an attractive black neighborhood in the parish of St. Ignatius Loyola Church.

The *New York Post* columnist Milton Gross, in his column of April 17, painted the sort of picture that Ben Bentley had wanted, but which in its falsity made Bentley feel somewhat uneasy and somewhat unclean. "Sonny," wrote Gross, "has been making the rounds since the April 10 bout was postponed. Instead of undergoing an operation, he hob-nobbed with Vice President Lyndon Johnson in Washington, visited his old cell mates at Jefferson State Prison in Missouri and is now at the home of Rev. Edward Murphy."

Sonny started roadwork in Denver on April 12. His trainer, Willie Reddish, soon joined him, and they began training at Lowery Air Force Base. Arrangements for the rematch were made in Las Vegas on April 12, with the fight set to be held at the Las Vegas Convention Center on June 27. Then, three weeks later, the fight was postponed yet again, to July, when surgery was required to remove a callus from Floyd Patterson's right hand.

Sonny arrived in Las Vegas in a gleaming black Fleetwood Cadillac with a white leather top and his initials on the driver's door. Inside, there was air-conditioning; there were two telephones, a television set. An engraved metal plate was inscribed, "This car was specially made for Sonny Liston." There was a crucifix on the dashboard, a pair of miniature boxing gloves dangling from the rearview mirror.

It was initially planned that Sonny's training quarters would be at the Dunes. But three previous champions — Ray Robinson, Benny Paret, and Gene Fullmer — had become ex-champions after training at the Dunes; and Sonny, who may not have had much religion, had a hell of a lot of superstition. So it came to be that the Liston camp set up at the Thunderbird, in a four-bedroom cottage behind the hotel, the same ninety-dollar-a-night cottage where Attorney General Robert Kennedy had stayed on his last visit to Vegas. In addition to Foneda Cox, there were two other sparring partners: the Nevada heavyweight Howard King, who had fought two professional matches with Sonny, in 1960 and 1961, and Leotis Martin, a light heavyweight who had begun his professional career the year before. As Willie Reddish explained, Foneda was there because he was the best puncher, King because he was good at attacking the torso, and Martin because he was "the nearest thing to Floyd Patterson with his shifty, peek-a-boo style."

Sparring matches between Sonny and the massive and heavily pomaded Howard King were presented as stage shows hosted by Ben Bentley. The sparring show was followed by the rope-skipping show, in which Sonny sometimes varied his moves but never the music — "Night Train" — to which those moves were performed. When he wasn't working out, he played blackjack and shot craps, often with his hero who now was his friend, Joe Louis.

Las Vegas, as a Vegas lawyer once said to me with the straightest of faces, was "a friendly environment for the right people."

It was at the Thunderbird that Sonny grew close to a character known as Ash Resnick.

His real name was Irving. He had been born in New York on

March 6, 1916. As a New Utrecht High School and New York University basketball star in the thirties, Ash had perfected the art of dumping and shaving points. It was said that he spent hours at a stretch in a playground on Bay Parkway in Brooklyn practicing foul shots that would bounce off the rim. In Vegas, he worked for several casinos and became, with Dean Shendal, one of the owners of Caesar's Palace.

He would be convicted of tax evasion for failing to report more than $300,000 he had skimmed from Caesar's. The same year, eight sticks of dynamite were found under his car. According to Dean, Ash put them there himself, and they were "nothing but Texas sawdust." Two years later, he was shot at, or seemed to be, while leaving Caesar's.

Everybody loved Ash, and everybody expressed that love with reservation. "Ash had balls as big as a canary," Dean said. "But I happened to like him. He was one of my best friends." But "he was no tough guy."

Though Resnick was often considered to have been mobbed down, those who knew him well saw this was a myth that he himself cherished. His real connection, according to the comedian Shecky Greene, was "a New York man called Abe Margolis in the jewelry business. Every time he needed money or something, he'd get it from Abe. I think Abe is even the one who gave him money to go into Caesar's."

Ash and Sonny were very, very tight, although no one could quite figure out why. "Ash had him hypnotized," Dean said, and "I don't know how." Later he would say, "Sonny Liston was the hardest guy in the world to get to know. Ash knew him."

Foneda Cox said that Ash "loved every minute of it. He wanted Sonny with him everywhere he went." And Ash took care of Foneda, too, throwing him a few yards every time he blew his stash at the tables. "I thought Ash was a nice guy. I honestly did." At the same time, he felt Ash to be more than a mobster manqué. As Foneda saw him in no uncertain terms, he was "a representative of the Mafia."

It was in 1955 that James R. Hoffa, the vice president of the International Brotherhood of Teamsters, consolidated scores of pension funds in twenty-two states into the Central States, Southeast and Southwest Areas Pension Fund. Hoffa became the president of the Teamsters, and the Fund became the Mob's chest of gold in Vegas, the bankroll through which the Mob's desert dream grew into the great and neon many-armed Moloch of a full-blown Mafia dreamland. Central to this relationship between the Teamsters and the Mob in Vegas was Moe Dalitz, an old-time figure of Mob majesty who was a friend of Hoffa's from the days when Hoffa was nothing, and who was instrumental in Hoffa's rise to power.

Truman Gibson told me a story, in that way he has of delicately spinning out a web that can be plainly seen only from a distance, the gossamer of a tale that seems to have no meaning in itself, but which, when the moon of understanding waxes, shines softly with the light of meaning that was there all along.

> After we organized the International Boxing Club, we promoted in several cities, including Detroit, and in Detroit, the Detroit Olympia Stadium. During the course of the boxing season, the Teamsters, which had a contract with the Detroit Olympia, would move the chairs, seats, about once or twice a month. So, after we started, the guy that worked for us in Detroit, Nick Londos, fell out with two Italians who had decided that *they* would become the matchmakers and have all the dealings with the fighters in Detroit. So, I was in New York when word came that the Teamsters were calling a strike on the Detroit Olympia because of problems

with Nick Londos. I hired a lawyer in Detroit to get an injunction. So, we went ahead with the fight as planned.

Then, in an unusual situation, we had a fight the next week there, and I went in and the two gentlemen who attempted to muscle in on us approached me in the offices of the Michigan State Athletic Commission, twelve o'clock in the day. One was about five feet three inches tall and about six feet wide, and the other was his companion. He said, "Come here, we wanna talk." So, we went in the office and the companion started picking his fingers with a knife, and the short one said, "You know, you think you're goddamn smart." I said, "No" — a very long *o* — "I don't think I'm smart, but I know you're stupid because it is twelve o'clock, there are a hundred people in the offices of the Michigan State Athletic Commission, and you think you're gonna blow me away." So I said we're not going to have any more fights in Detroit.

The next day, Paul Dorfman, whom I had known around the fights — Red Dorfman — came in. He was Jimmy Hoffa's right-hand man. Paul was very, very close to Jimmy. So, he came in and said there was trouble in Detroit. I said, yeah, we had trouble in Detroit, but, I said, we're not going to have any more trouble because we're not going to Detroit. He said, "No, no, let's take a hop over to Detroit tomorrow." So we went over, and Paul had the two guys in the office and said, "You know, Jimmy don't want this shit that you're pulling, and if you continue, you'll be in the bottom of the Detroit River with chains, you understand?" Understood. Had a victory dinner and no more problems in Detroit. I said to Paul, "What's the grief?" He said, "No, no, I'll call you, there'll come a time."

So, about a year later, Paul Dorfman called me in New York and said, "Pay-off time." I said, "What do you mean, Paul?" And he said, "Well, Jimmy's on trial in Washington, and the jury's all black, and we want Joe [Louis] to come in as a character witness."

I said, "No." He said, "What do you mean, 'No'?" I said, "Paul, character witnesses don't mean anything." "Well, have him come in and he'll stay a week and every time that the jury comes out, Joe will have his arms around Jimmy, talking to him and giving him advice." And we had Joe's wife hired as one of the counsel, sitting at the counsel table.

That was the case where Bobby Kennedy said, "If I don't get a conviction on this case, I'm going to jump off the top of the Washington Monument." So, Jimmy got a not-guilty and characteristically said, "When's the jump gonna take place? I wouldn't miss it for the world."

In the meantime, I had told Paul, "Don't give Joe any money, don't pay his hotel bill."

So, on the way to the airport — Joe was being driven by a chap by the name of Barney Baker, who is going to be an important connection with Sonny Liston — Joe says, "Goddamnit, I forgot to pay my" — "No, no, we took care of it" — "Oh, shit, oh, no, no, no." He said, "Truman's gonna kick the shit out of me." I had paid the hotel bill.

So we proceeded on our merry way, and about a month later, I got a call from the manager of the Justice Department's business affairs. He said, "I've got an affidavit for you to sign." "For what?" I looked at it and saw that Joe got thirty-five thousand dollars for going to Washington. I said, "I'll prepare an affidavit for you." So I prepared an affidavit indicating the facts: how I knew that Jimmy had insisted that his union not be used for purposes for which it was attempted to be used; which put me on Bobby Kennedy's shit-list forever. In any event, during the time that we operated, I went to Vegas several times. We started out with Jack Kearns a great deal, who was Jack Dempsey's manager, who knew all the players and others there. I met the owner of the Dunes Hotel. Morris [Shanker]. He had been a very prominent defense lawyer in St.

Louis. His wife was a judge. But he is the one that sponsored, maybe indirectly, Sonny as a former St. Louisan in his fight business. He's the one that was responsible for Sonny going to Vegas.

That, incidentally, was a Teamster-financed hotel, the Dunes. The Dunes was Teamster through and through.

But, yes, Barney Baker, a name familiar from Sonny's leg-breaking St. Louis days. "Always appearing on the scene. In Detroit, in Washington, in Las Vegas. Never in front." He was, as Truman Gibson said, "ubiquitous." And when Gibson alluded to those that "controlled Sonny's destiny in Vegas," the name of Barney Baker fell nearby.

Barney Baker, a friend of the Teamsters and a friend of boxing.

Ash Resnick worked a lot of places during his forty years in that Mob-controlled Teamster paradise: the Dunes, the Thunderbird, the Aladdin, Caesar's Palace, and more. He was, you might say, ubiquitous.

And Ash was a friend of boxers, too. He had put Joe Louis on the public relations staff at the Thunderbird, and he did the same for him when he moved to Caesar's Palace. Wherever he went, he took care of Joe the best he could.

Ash and Joe. Joe and Sonny. Sonny and Ash.

When Sonny moved his training camp to Las Vegas, twenty-one-year-old Cassius Marcellus Clay followed him. Clay had not fought Cleveland Williams, as Liston had said he must. He had, on March 13, fought Doug Jones, a New York light heavyweight who had lost to Eddie Machen in 1961; and he had, on June 10, fought Henry Cooper, the British heavyweight champion whom Zora Folley had knocked out in two rounds, also in 1961. The Jones fight was a ten-round performance so lackluster that even

Arthur Daley, the Clay-supporting columnist of the *New York Times*, was critical of "his miserable showing against Doug Jones." Jack Nilon claimed that he had offered Clay $75,000 to forgo the Jones fight, as it would be damaging to the potential value of the inevitable Liston-Clay fight. "I would have given Cassius anything not to fight Jones," Nilon said. "It was a dumb match. Did those Louisville millionaires need money that much?" He referred to the Louisville Group, the consortium of businessmen that were the backers and handlers of Clay's career. "When Jones was rapping Clay in the first round, I thought, 'Uh-oh, here it all goes out the window.'"

Clay rode Sonny's back for all the publicity it was worth. Cus D'Amato, before the Patterson fight, had likened Liston to a bear, and Clay now had taken Cus's phrase and in his amateur-theatrical mockery elaborated it into a ceaseless taunting of Liston as "the big ugly bear."

In July, as the fight approached, a reporter asked Sonny what he thought of Patterson personally.

"I think he's a nice guy."

And Cassius Clay?

"I think he's the nicest thing to come along since Christmas."

Nat Fleischer of *The Ring* magazine presented Sonny with his championship belt at a ceremony in Las Vegas on July 18. Sonny, who seemed moved, said nothing. Nearby Cassius Clay taunted him with whining cries of "Why don't you say something?" Sonny looked at him, waited for silence, then simply and sincerely expressed his thanks to Fleischer. This shut Clay's mouth, and when it did, Sonny gestured to the belt and looked at him again. "Cassius," he said, "there's something you will never get."

•

On July 22, the night of the fight, Patterson showed up with no false beard or moustache. "Those things are gone for me now," he said.

As Sonny entered the ring, the crowd greeted him with vicious cries and booing.

It lasted two minutes and twenty-three seconds. This time, Sonny knocked him down twice before knocking him down for good — a left to the body, a right to the head. As dictated by Nevada rules, there was a count of eight for each knockdown. Without these eight-count pauses, it was, in fighting time, a faster knockout than the first fight.

At the press conference afterward, he was asked what he thought when the crowd had booed him.

"The main thing that went through my mind was, 'I'll fix them.'"

He felt it, and he said it: "The public is not with me. I know it. But they'll have to swing along until somebody comes to beat me."

When the fight ended, Cassius Clay ran in from his fifth-row seat and vaulted into the ring. Three members of the Nevada sheriff's guard grappled him down in a corner of the ring, but he managed to slither free and rush to a closed-circuit microphone in another corner of the ring.

That rush to the microphone — and Clay's career was becoming one big rush to the microphone — said much about the youthful Clay.

And, hell, man, fuck youthful: he was twenty-one years old, a grown man, and it was not so much youth that he was full of but childishness.

A photograph taken before the fight that night shows Clay in a checkered sport jacket, eyes bulging, mouth open and as wide as the Holland Tunnel, screaming his praise for himself, while entertained white onlookers smile.

He was, at this point in his career, seen as an audacious but enamouring child, a frivolity of the noble white man, who perceived in Clay's persona none of the visceral, deep-rooted threat of a Liston, none of the implacable and troubling earnest of a Martin Luther King, or the incendiary aggression of a Malcolm X.

In his frenzy to self-aggrandize and to endear through his antics, his sense of humor, so central to those designs, was not much developed beyond the playground realm. Beloved, or tolerated, as he was by the great white middle class — and by many blacks, who found in this time of repression something fine and freeing about the rare black man who spouted off, seemingly without care or restraint or fear, in the very midst of white America — he was not a funny man, and his act was trite. Neither an Amos nor an Andy was he. Certainly Liston possessed a far more cutting and subtle sense of humor, as when he told the Big Brothers gathering that "I would find stuff before it got lost"; as when on his way to court one day in Philadelphia, he asked his lawyer, in the event that he should ever be sentenced to the electric chair, to please try to arrange it so that George Katz got "ten percent of the juice." He wasn't as funny as Pigmeat Markham or Moms Mabley or Dick Gregory or none of them. But he was benign.

That image of Clay rushing for the microphone on that night of another man's victory, so ravenous to hurl himself down the gullet and into the immense maw of mediocrity: it was an image to be reckoned with.

The best actors are often the most vapid. This is simply because, almost without exception, they have been in show business since childhood and have been playacting rather than living ever since. I remember Christopher Walken being asked if there was a role that he felt he could not play. Yeah, he said, he couldn't play a human being, because he'd never been one, as he'd been on the stage since childhood.

Clay had not been a child actor. He had been something more bizarre: a child boxer, whose life had been given over to the game at the age of twelve. Since then, from the Golden Gloves to the Olympics to that night in Vegas, he had boxed rather than lived, and his intelligence and involvement with life were as atrophied as any actor's.

His tiresome and trying wit, his harmless and drably colorful shows of playfulness, and his affected audacity were perfectly suited for the media of the day. *Mediocrity* and *media,* it should be remembered, are cognates of the same Latin root.

With his dangerous ways and his dangerous airs and his love of that rhythm and blues that the white man held to be dangerous, too, Sonny was to become the new hero of a different, younger minority, that minority of black street punks, and white street punks, who could not afford the ticket price to have their own voices heard at the fights when Sonny was booed and execrated. If Sonny is to be regarded as the first rock 'n' roll champ, Clay should be regarded as the first made-for-TV boxing idol. As he danced and cavorted in acceptable and inoffensive outrageousness before the masses and the cameras and the microphones of mediocrity, so mediocrity embraced him.

"Cassius," said the *New York Times,* "is a delightful young man."

White sentiment would later change when Clay allied himself with the Black Muslims and refused to enter the service. But in the summer of 1963, he was a child of the light who seemed to be all that Sonny Liston was not: a good, clean middle-class boy who instead of bringing shame and hostility to America had brought her a gold medal from the 1960 Rome Olympics. And, even as his image changed and the maw of mass mediocrity vomited him forth, he became the darling of a more elite mediocrity, a white intelligentsia who sought meaning and metaphor in boxing. Unlike

Sonny, who ignored or sneered at writers, Clay knew their value, and he accommodated them. Many of these writers, who could write no better than they could fight, found in him a willing and suitable accomplice in their conceits of the intellect and their deceit of themselves and others. It was through Clay, and with his implicit approval, that they were enabled to play out the marked deck — the dream cards of manliness, racial understanding, provocative sensibility, and bond between writer and warrior — that in reality were less of the soul than of fancy.

But in that summer of 1963, as Clay ran about proclaiming his self-greatness, the estimation of him as a fighter was otherwise among writers and observers who knew what they were talking about. "At this stage of his fistic development," wrote Nat Fleischer, "Clay must be regarded as no more formidable an antagonist for Liston than was Patterson.

"In fact, were Clay to fight Patterson I would pick Floyd to knock him out in six rounds, or less. Nothing that Clay did against Henry Cooper in London or Doug Jones in New York's Garden justifies throwing him to the Wolf."

Fleischer said "the widely advertised Lip" was no match for the Wolf. "Liston," he wrote, "should dispose of Cassius in a couple of heats, and then what?" There were no credible challengers in sight.

Said Joe Louis, "Nobody's gonna beat Liston 'cept old age."

Returning to Denver after the fight, Sonny received what Philadelphia had not given: a champion's welcome.

"He's happier than he's ever been," said Father Murphy. "When he flew back to Denver Wednesday night, there were several thousand people waiting for him at the airport, including the mayor."

Murphy said of Liston, "Now, this is a man who won't make any more mistakes."

Sonny made a homecoming visit to the Missouri State Penitentiary. He had his picture taken, smiling as he shook the hand of Warden E.V. Nash. He was greeted wildly by former cell-mates in the old A Hall, gave five-dollar tips to prison barbers, and ate in the general population dining hall instead of with the officials. It was the biggest story ever to run in the prison newspaper, *The Jefftown Journal.*

Jim Hackett had been studying a Liston fight film and was transfixed by a fleeting glimpse of a figure in Liston's corner, a presence he had not seen before. The figure seemed strangely familiar. "This guy had a straw hat on," he said. Then it hit him. He knew the guy. The guy in the straw hat had been a cop years ago in St. Louis. If he was alive, and if we could find him, Hackett was sure, he could unlock a door that no one else could. Hackett put the word out. With the help of his friend William Anderson, the guy in the straw hat was found. Hackett called him a number of times. Anderson called, and went to his home as well. But he was not forthcoming. Among the three of us, we had left many messages on an answering machine we were not sure was his. Then I dialed one morning, and he picked up.

"Wasn't no straw hat. Was a little old stingy-brim, porkpie."

I was talking to Lowell Powell, who was born in 1923, and who, like William Anderson, was a black cop who had known and befriended Sonny in the early days. Lowell was not in the best of shape. Like Frankie Carbo, like me, like a lot of people, he had diabetes, and the complications were getting the better of him. He had already lost a leg and a lot of his sight. But he was a hell of a guy and not past flirting with the pretty lady from the *St. Louis Post-Dispatch,* Chris Dickinson, who was doing legwork for me. Lowell died in 1998.

I came to him, he told me, through good people; and he would talk to me. I went to see him the next day, the first of several visits.

He told me that he had known Sonny in the old days; that it was in 1963, when he retired from the force that Sonny hired him as a bodyguard and right-hand man, to replace Moose Grayson.

Though Sonny and Geraldine had a childless marriage, Geraldine had a daughter from a previous union, and Sonny, though no one knew it, had fathered a daughter of his own before going to prison. Now, after moving to Denver, he asked his new right-hand man to bring him to her.

"He hadn't seen her in life," Lowell said, but he knew who the mother was.

> I found her and presented her to him, and, boy, you could look at her and tell she was Sonny's daughter. She looked like he spit her out.
>
> So, we were sitting at the dinner table, and she had done some things that he didn't like. She had taken some money off him or something, and he said, "Here's this police detective, and he's gonna get you"; and I said, "No, baby, I'm not gonna bother you." So he didn't know how to admonish me. He said, "You know, you're not nothing, you just ain't nothing," and blah-blah-blah.
>
> The J&B was talking. I introduced him to J&B and he started drinking J&B all the time he was champion. So I said, "Well, I'm sorry you feel that way." He said, "You know, I'm tired of you," and this, that, and the other, blah-blah-blah. I thought about all the guys that he had hit, you know, that worked at our stable, and I said, "Well, Sonny, let me say this in front of Geraldine." I said, "Geraldine, I'm talking with Sonny, and we're doing some arguing, and I'm no match for Sonny in a fight. I know that he's the heavyweight champion of the world, and I'll admit that I'm no

match for him, so he doesn't have to prove anything." I could see at first he had balled his fists up. "All I want you to do is stand out of my way and let me out of here." He stepped to the side and I shot out the door. The next day, he was crying and telling me he was sorry and all that. I said, "What you wanted was to pop me in the jaw and then apologize. But if you hit me in the jaw, it's not gonna be like that. There won't be no apologizing. It's gonna be some time drawn, and in all probability it'll be me, because if you miss and you don't knock me out, I'm gonna have to kill you. I'm gonna have to shoot you."

So we made up and we got even closer after that. He understood me, and I understood him.

The girl's name was Eleanor. They called her Choo Choo. She did not stay too long in Denver.

Years after Sonny's death, an aspiring prizefighter from North Carolina would claim to be the offspring of a St. Louis tryst between his mother and Sonny. Fighting as Sonny Liston, Jr., he made his professional debut at the Tropicana in Atlantic City in 1985. "Let's just say he got absolutely creamed," said the publicist for the fight. "No, let's say he was the worst fighter I've ever seen."

"When the J&B started working, that's when his personality changed. He was Dr. Jekyll as long as he was sober, and when that whiskey took over, he was Mr. Hyde."

As far as is known, Sonny's sexual assaults occurred during his championship reign. Lowell Powell recalled one incident involving a motel chambermaid.

The girl's crying and everything and getting ready to call the police. She said, "I'm gonna call my husband." I said, "It's all right to call your husband. You tell your husband but don't get the police right now." I allowed her to get her husband. I talked with him and I told him what the deal was, and I got about two or three thousand dollars in tens and twenties and fifties, and I laid 'em on the table. I said, "She said he did, and he said he didn't. I'm not trying to buy him out of it, but money beats nothing." That guy picked up that money and didn't look back.

A few days after the second Patterson fight, Jack Nilon announced the formation of Inter-Continental Promotions, Inc., of which Sonny Liston was to be the president, and of which Jack and Bob and a third Nilon brother, James, were to be the principal officers. A lawyer named Garland Cherry, known as Bill, was to be the attorney for the corporation, which henceforth would promote all of Sonny's fights, and in which Sonny would hold forty-seven and a half percent of the stock; the Nilon brothers, the same amount; and Cherry, five percent.

Dan Parker, in his *New York Mirror* column, implied that the corporation had secret associates. "It would seem that there's room for a lot of explaining from Liston and his errand boys before this piece of business is permitted to get out of hand. Sic him, Estes."

On July 28, Estes Kefauver announced that he would open an investigation into Inter-Continental Promotions.

Three days later, the Pennsylvania State Athletic Commission refused to grant a promoter's license to the new corporation, in accord with an opinion by state attorney general Walter E. Allesandroni, who said that Liston could not own substantial stock in a corporation that was promoting his own fight.

Jack Nilon was eager to arrange the Clay fight, and eager to have it take place in Philadelphia, as soon as four weeks later. An alternate plan was proposed whereby Bob and James Nilon would promote the fight. Jack said that he was willing to withdraw as Sonny's adviser, "in order that there shall be no confusion about interests." No mention was made of the 1962 contract that had appointed Nilon as Sonny's manager.

By mid-August, the fight had been postponed to the following year, and they had given up on Philadelphia. Sonny had tax problems, and was avoiding a subpoena from the Joint Legislative Committee on Sports and Physical Fitness, formerly the State Legislative Committee on Boxing.

"Mainly," said one of the committee's legislators, Hayward Plumadore, "I want to know what relations, if any, he has had with Blinky Palermo since he has testified before the Kefauver Committee."

And, yes, Blinky was still out on the outside.

On the last day of August, Sonny arrived in London with Jack Nilon, Foneda Cox, Ben Bentley, Willie Reddish, and Ted King for an exhibition tour of Great Britain and Europe. The tour began well. Introduced from the ring at a Shoreditch Town Hall welterweight match, he was given a standing ovation by the crowd of over two thousand. He fought a three-round exhibition with Foneda at Wembley Indoor Stadium, where he gave the British a taste of his "Night Train" skipping. He was photographed barechested and grinning, awaiting the stroke of branches in a Norwegian sauna; he rode in a suit and fedora through Newcastle-on-Tyne astride a white horse; he strode through Glasgow blowing bagpipes in a highland kilt and tam-o'-shanter. The Scots remarked that he was not the cold and gloomy man they had expected.

"I am warm here because I am among warm people, and I feel

that and react to it," he told them. "When I return to the United States, I will be cold again, for the people there are cold to me now and have treated me badly." He was presented with a blackthorn shillelagh by a local teenage beauty queen, was guided around town by a new little pal, Peter Keenan, Jr., the eleven-year-old son of Peter Keenan, a former British and Empire flyweight champion. Later, Sonny would have the boy flown to Denver to spend Christmas with him.

In the midst of the tour, abruptly, on September 18, Liston gathered his entourage and stormed to the London airport. Reporters sought an explanation. "All I know is that we are on the run from London," said Foneda Cox, as they stopped in Chicago en route to Denver. "I've never seen him in such an angry mood," said Bentley. At Stapleton Field in Denver, he swept past reporters, brandishing his shillelagh. "Boy, you can't get no word from me," he growled to the first newsman that approached, and he continued to growl as he moved through the reporters: "You ain't going to get no words from me. I don't have to answer your questions." He was said to have growled, too, in a lower voice, "I'm ashamed to be an American."

Foneda Cox told newsmen what Ben Bentley had told them in Chicago: that the anger and shame that Sonny expressed had to do with his reaction to the recent bombing of a black Baptist church in Birmingham, in which four young girls were killed.

The headline in the *New York Journal-American* read, "Liston: 'I'm Ashamed to Be An American.'" A day later, Dan Parker headlined his *Mirror* column, "Hey, Fellas, Get A Load Of Who's Ashamed Of U.S.!" Arthur Daley of the *Times* sighed, "Perhaps Liston is beyond redemption."

But the bombing had been on Sunday morning. Sonny's rage and distress had come three days later.

An Associated Press report of the following day quoted Geraldine as saying that, yes, Sonny had been upset by the tragedy of the Birmingham bombing. It quoted Sonny, too: "I have problems and them is my problems. I have to straighten them out myself."

He had fled Chicago the previous spring. He had run, but he could not hide. Two weeks after his sudden rage, a wire-service report from Chicago stated:

> Heavyweight boxing champion Sonny Liston was named in a $100,000 damage suit filed in Circuit Court Thursday by a 33-year-old Negro woman who charged that he had attacked her in an auto.
>
> The suit, filed by Mrs. Pearl Grayson, the wife of a Chicago policeman, John, claims that while Mrs. Grayson was riding as a passenger in an auto with Liston last March 29 on Chicago's South Side he "willfully and maliciously assaulted and beat and inflicted bruises upon her body and caused her personal injuries."
>
> Mrs. Grayson's husband served as Liston's bodyguard at Aurora, Ill., when the champion was training for his first title fight with Floyd Patterson, September 25, 1962.
>
> The suit includes $50,000 for assault and battery and an additional $50,000 for exemplary damages.
>
> Attorney Sheldon Mills, who filed suit, said no complaint was made to police at the time. He said he agreed to delay filing after conferring with Liston's business advisor, Jack Nilon, shortly after the alleged incident.

Then nothing more was heard, nothing more was said. In the speed of a moment, the report seemed no longer to exist; seemed to have vanished outright, before the scandal-hungry eyes of the press could rest upon it. It was as if the wire had never existed. There is no telling how far, if at all, beyond Chicago it reached.

Within a month, it was announced in Las Vegas that Liston and Clay would sign in Denver on November 4 for a fight to be held in February. As it developed, the fight would take place in Miami Beach, under the aegis of Frankie Carbo's old friend Chris Dundee, the big brother of Clay's trainer, Angelo Dundee.

Like the man said: *La commedia è finita.*

ASTROLOGY

IT WAS THE END OF THE ROAD. HERE HISTORY took the pen from the player's hand, where, for a moment, a heartbeat, no matter how tentatively, it had seemed to rest. What remained was epilogue and epitaph, chords like wind of death-song, of threnody.

America did not want Sonny as her champion. "It is hard to discern any merit in Liston," wrote Dan Parker in his column of February 13, 1964. And America saw Liston much as Parker saw him: "a sinister creature, full of hatred for the world." Liston had likened boxing to a cowboy movie. "There's got to be good guys, and there's got to be bad guys." The "bad guys are supposed to lose. I change that," he had said. "I win." But in his winning, he seemed invincible. There seemed no good, or other bad, that could conquer or stay him; and, in the cowboy movie of his championship, the good guys never had a chance. There was no showdown in the ring, no battle, no melodrama — only fast and predictable victory for the villain America despised. The cowboy movie of his championship was a box-office failure, and in a racket built on suckers' money, Sonny as a champion was bad, bad news.

Moose Grayson had said that there had been a "settlement."

Yes, said Foneda Cox. "They made a settlement with Moose."

By "they," he meant the Mob. "They paid Moose off. I don't know how much, but a lot. I think they even bought him a house. The Mafia picked up all of Sonny's tabs when Sonny got into trouble. I think maybe they got sick of it."

As the Clay fight approached, Liston was not only a bad draw and an unwanted champion. He was a man who could be exposed as a rapist at any time. This exposure would not only certainly cost him his title and end his career: with his record and reputation, he very likely could be returned to prison as well. Whoever had power over this exposure had power over Liston.

It was at this time that Ben Bentley quit, claiming that he was owed money and that the Nilons had reneged on an agreement to let him have the rights to the Chicago closed-circuit action for the Clay fight. "I don't blame Liston at all," said Ben.

Before the fight, the sportswriter Jimmy Cannon spoke with the former light heavyweight champion Billy Conn, whose career had spanned the years 1935–1948 and who was now forty-six years old.

"The first punch Liston hits him, out he goes," said Conn. "He can't fight now," he said of Clay, "and he'll never be able to fight. He hasn't the experience. The only experience he'll get with Liston is how to get killed in a hurry." Conn said — as Cannon noted bitterly — that Clay "took all the dignity away from the heavyweight title by acting like a big phony wrestler."

Look magazine ran a story entitled "Sonny Liston: 'King of the Beasts,'" in the February 25, 1964, issue. "In essence, Sonny epitomizes the Negro untouchable, the angry dark-skinned man condemned by the white man to spend his life in the economic and social sewers of his country." A photograph pictured him at home in Denver, sitting on a couch between two matching and ornate fringed lamps: "*The Listons pose for their first family portrait: from left to right, daughter Eleanor, 13, wife Geraldine, Sonny, his mother Helen and daughter Arletha, 17.*"

Of the Negro untouchable: "His pleasures are simple: he drives a two-toned 1964 Fleetwood Cadillac and likes *The Beverly Hillbillies* on television ('Whatever mah wife's watchin', Ah'm watchin')."

The night of the fight was February 25, 1964. It had been barely three months since the Kennedy assassination, and this was the first blood revelry that a post-hysteric America had allowed herself. The crowd that gathered at Miami's Convention Hall, and all the other crowds that gathered in the closed-circuit showrooms and theaters throughout America were there not so much to see a contest, for no contest was foreseen. This sense of the inevitable was evinced by the lackluster gate at Convention Hall, where only about half of sixteen thousand tickets, priced from twenty to two hundred and fifty dollars, were sold. What crowd there was seemed to be a part of a masque in the season of psychic plague, a ritual, a spectacle that pitted the embodiment of callow spirit and whistle-in-the-dark braggadocio against that of the Adversary of the American Dream. The air of festive anticipation was unsettling. The scent of dear perfume and fancy cologne mixed with that of cheap aftershave, smoke, and sweat. The oversized head of tough guy manqué Norman Mailer was no longer alone in blocking the view at ringside. Beside him sat fellow tough guy Truman Capote and Gloria Guinness of *Harper's Bazaar.*

Clay's pulse had raced to 120 during the weigh-in, and the adrenaline of fear seemed still within him as he entered the ring. That fight-or-flee rush drove him forward and into Liston with a frenzy, and he took the first round. Sonny began to grind him down in the second, but his blows were delivered with none of the awesome power that in the past had felled man after man. In the third, Clay opened a cut under Sonny's eye, drawing forth what Sonny had given no other man since the days of those whippings. In the fourth, Sonny connected repeatedly, but again, his blows seemed oddly restrained, and Clay came in again to bruise Sonny's fearsome face.

At the end of round four, Clay came to his corner screaming surrender. "I can't see," he wailed to his trainer, Angelo Dundee. "Cut off my gloves. Call off the fight." At the sound of the bell, Dundee pushed Clay to his feet.

In the fifth, Clay, who claimed difficulty seeing, had no difficulty in dodging Sonny's punches, which seemed at times designed not so much to hit Clay as to punctuate the air of his blind bob and weave. Clay reached out his left arm, rested his gloved fist against Sonny's nose, as if to keep the beast at bay; and, though Sonny's reach was greater, he never struck or swatted that arm away.

At the end of the round, Clay's vision returned, and Barney Felix, the referee, who had been about to stop the fight and award a technical-knockout victory to Liston, allowed the match to continue. After six rounds, the fight was even on points. When the bell sounded to signal the start of the seventh round, Liston just sat there, refusing to rise and telling of a numbness that ran from his left shoulder down to his forearm.

In the halls and cellblocks of the Jefferson City penitentiary — the one true stronghold of Sonny's popularity as a champion — the blare of radios was suddenly overtaken by howls of anger and disgust. The son of a bitch had thrown the fucking heavyweight championship of the motherfucking world. Shit, some reckoned: a thief for a penny, a thief for a pound.

A few days after the fight, there came to light a contract that caused no small amount of speculation. Long before the fight — the contract was dated October 29, 1963 — Inter-Continental Promotions, of which Sonny was a partner, had contracted with the eleven-man Louisville Group to purchase for fifty thousand dollars the rights to promote Clay's next fight after the Liston match. This was a staggering amount to pay for the future rights to a single bout by a fighter who was seen as facing almost certain defeat in his upcoming match with Liston. Jack Nilon, trying to explain the suspect pre-fight contract, said that "Clay represented a tremendous show-business property."

Liston later said that he had injured his shoulder in the first round of the fight. Jack Nilon said the injury came long before the fight, during training.

But the training and training camps of both fighters had been the object of much coverage by the press, and there had been no hint of any injury. During training just a year earlier, the news of a less debilitating injury, to Liston's knee, was pursued and covered as a major story, and that knee injury had been sustained off the training grounds and away from the eyes of the press.

When the Senate Subcommittee on Antitrust and Monopoly announced, on March 1, that it intended to investigate the contract between Clay and Inter-Continental, Nilon said, "We never dreamed Sonny would lose the title." The contract, he said, was just "a lucky fluke."

That was two days after the Internal Revenue Service filed liens totaling $2.7 million against Sonny: $876,800 against him and Geraldine; $1,050,500 against Inter-Continental Promotions, Inc.; and $793,000 against Delaware Advertising and Management Agency, Inc., a Nilon-run sister corporation of Inter-Continental.

Sonny was taken after the fight to be examined at St. Joseph's Hospital. Three hours later, it was announced by Dr. Alexander Robbins of the Miami Beach Athletic Commission that Liston did indeed show evidence of an injury to his left shoulder that was "sufficient to incapacitate him and to prevent him from defending himself."

Officials at the fight had withheld the fight purse on suspicions that things were not right. The announcement by Dr. Robbins served to counter those suspicions and expedite the release of the purse.

Later, a Detroit physician, Dr. Robert C. Bennet, would state that he had been treating Liston for bursitis in both arms and shoulders for the past two years. He said that Sonny had been taking cortisone shots for this bursitis almost continuously in the months preceding the fight. In his medical opinion, the bursitis was not connected to the injury that had stopped the fight in Miami.

"I think Liston's problem in the fight was that he swung and missed, severely stretching or rupturing his arm four or five inches below the shoulder," the doctor said. "In our post-fight examination, we could see the swelling and the blood."

Bennet was Joe Louis's doctor. When Joe had a dope seizure in New York in 1969, it was Bennet who helped to protect the fighter's image by covering the details of his emergency hospitalization. Bennet was also the physician for the Michigan State Boxing Commission. When I discovered this obscure circumstance, I could not but recall Truman Gibson's story about his encounter long ago at the offices of the Michigan commission, a story that also involved Joe Louis, as well as many other things.

Where were the doctors before the fight, and where were the doctors during the fight? Why would a man who had gone the distance in agony with a busted jaw in an insignificant fight — why would such a man fold in a world championship title match from a pain or a numbness in his arm? Why would a man with the most devastating right in boxing, a man impervious to punches, allow an injured left arm to move him to such passive and compliant surrender?

There are stories of the immense losses Ash Resnick incurred in Miami by betting on his friend. There are other stories of suitcases of money being sent by Ash to New York, where other, less ostentatious bets were made.

The night after Bennet's disclosure, Sonny was arrested back home in Denver. Doing over seventy-five in a thirty-mile-per-hour residential zone, he was carrying a seven-shot .22 revolver in his right-hand coat pocket, along with six cartridges and one spent shell. The arresting officer, Patrolman James Snider, asked him about the pistol.

"It's mine. I shot at my girlfriend."

He was in his Cadillac. There was a girl in the car with him. The cop told her to get the Cadillac out of there. He could barely force the handcuff around Sonny's wrists. Another cop arrived, and together they got him cuffed.

Sonny was drunk — he told the cop he'd had half a bottle of vodka — and he got belligerent during the ride downtown, asking the cop if he wanted to "mix it up" or "go round and round" and once trying to escape when the car slowed for a stop sign.

"I really didn't know who I had," Snider said, "until I got to headquarters and another patrolman said, 'Hi, Sonny.'"

Sonny refused to take a Breathalyzer test. He was charged with speeding, driving without a valid Colorado license, and reckless and careless driving. He was let off easy on the pistol. Under Colorado law, it was a felony for an ex-convict to be in possession of a concealed weapon, but it was charged against Sonny only as a misdemeanor.

On the following day, Sonny was served by federal marshals with a notice of a $115,000 lawsuit that Ben Bentley had filed against him the previous Friday in U.S. District Court in Chicago. The suit claimed fifteen grand in overdue wages and a hundred grand in lost income pursuant to Inter-Continental's failure to honor its commitment to grant him Chicago closed-circuit rights.

On March 23, State Attorney General Richard E. Gerstein of

Florida announced that, after a month's investigation of the Liston-Clay fight, it had been decided that there was no evidence of foul play. However, he said, several other circumstances surrounding the fight were "questionable." He spoke of "a well-known gambler and bookmaker" — he did not name him, but he was talking about Ash Resnick — who "enjoyed the full run of the training camp and was present in Liston's dressing room prior to the fight." Gerstein also said he wondered why Liston would pay fifty thousand dollars for the right to choose Clay's next opponent and promote his next fight "unless he or his managers knew the outcome of the fight in advance."

Kefauver was dead, but his spirit lived. On March 24, the day after Gerstein's guarded announcement, Senate investigators in Washington questioned Sonny's partners in Inter-Continental Promotions. The first called to answer was Garland Cherry, the Pennsylvania lawyer who held five percent of the corporation. He revealed that Liston had signed over more than half of his stock in December to Sam Margolis.

Sam was a big heavy guy, fifty-one, who smoked and chewed on a cigar as he sat before the committee.

SENATOR PHILIP HART: Mr. Margolis, what is your business?

SAM: I am in the vending-machine business.

SENATOR HART: Are you or did you have a partnership in a restaurant in or near Philadelphia in recent years?

SAM: That is, prior to the vending business?

SENATOR HART: Prior to your entering the vending business. What was the name of the restaurant?

SAM: Sansom Restaurant.

SENATOR HART: All right, who were your partners in that restaurant?

SAM: My partners was my wife, Carlo Musciano, and Frank Palermo.

SENATOR HART: What discussions, if any, did you have with Frank Palermo concerning Liston in either a fight or the promotion of it?

SAM: I don't know if we ever discussed it or not.

Sam was asked by committee counsel if he knew Angelo Bruno, the criminal overlord of Philadelphia:

"Do you know Mr. Bruno?"

"Yes."

"Did you have any conversations with Mr. Bruno about Sonny Liston?"

"I don't recall having any conversations with Mr. Bruno about Sonny Liston."

Under questioning by Senator Keating of New York, Sam said that he and Sonny had an agreement whereby Sam would receive half of whatever he could get for Sonny from the Nilon brothers in negotiating his position during the formation of Inter-Continental.

Keating asked if steps had been taken to put the agreement in writing.

SAM: No. I trusted Sonny.

SENATOR KEATING: Were you his manager?

SAM: No.

SENATOR KEATING: What was your title?

SAM: Friend.

Sonny had endorsed the shares before they were filled in with Sam's, or anyone's, name. The shares were now worth about a hundred thousand dollars after taxes. Sam had given fifty of the two hundred and seventy-five shares to his lawyer Salvatore J. Avena, who was one of two attorneys serving as counsel to him before the committee.

Keating brought up a meeting at Goldie Ahearn's Restaurant in Washington, D.C., on March 19, 1958, the night of a local middleweight fight between Jimmy Beacham and Willie Vaughn. Present were Frankie Carbo, Blinky Palermo, and Sam.

SAM: We did not have a meeting. We went there to eat.
SENATOR KEATING: Was Sonny Liston's name brought into the conversation?
SAM: I never heard Sonny Liston's name mentioned there at that time, Senator.

When Jack Nilon came before the committee, he was asked about the 1962 manager's contract with Liston that entitled him to a third of Liston's purses.

SENATOR HART: When did the change from thirty-three and a third percent to fifty percent occur?
NILON: I would say after the Clay fight, after it was signed.
SENATOR HART: Are you a licensed manager?
NILON: No.
SENATOR HART: How do you act as the manager in the Clay fight if you weren't licensed to be manager?
NILON: I wasn't the manager in the Clay fight.
SENATOR HART: Who was?
NILON: I had a second's license.
SENATOR HART: Who was the manager?
NILON: Actually, there was no manager.

At one point, Nilon expressed the feeling that he did not really "feel that I want to be a fight manager," upon which Senator Hart asked him, "As the manager of Liston under this fifty-percent agreement, what compensation would you receive, based on the Miami Beach Clay-Liston fight?"

NILON: I would receive — the gross sum estimated is probably four hundred thousand.
SENATOR HART: But you don't want to be a manager, nonetheless?
NILON: There is more to life than bread alone.

For years, Sonny had alluded to the inevitable. It was as if his fate were writ on a crumpled piece of paper, like those slips they had found on him in St. Louis in the summer of '59: an old and faded and irrevocable haruspicy folded away and sometimes forgotten amid those other slips, amid the lint and the nickels and the thousand-dollar bills.

"He told me, he said, 'Foneda, I'm gonna tell you. I've got to lose one, and when I do, I'm gonna tell you.'"

Though Foneda went most everywhere with Sonny, it was strongly suggested that he remain in Denver and not come to Miami for the fight. "They said, 'Well, you ought to stay here with your business.' And I said, 'No, I ain't worried about that. I got a cousin here that can run my business.'" But Foneda did not go.

"So, this is the only thing that I hold against Sonny, is that he did not tell me when he was actually going to lose. And I'm back here betting."

When Sonny returned to Denver, he seemed to Foneda somewhat distant but not unhappy. "He wasn't really upset." But, as Foneda saw it, Sonny had let him down, gone back on his word to him. "In fact," he said, "after that, I didn't go with him anymore."

Though they continued to spar and hang out together once in a while, the old days were over.

Sonny's bodyguard, Lowell Powell, was there on that stingy-brim night in Miami Beach, February 25, 1964, that night the unvanquishable Liston was vanquished by Cassius Clay.

When Liston failed to come out of his corner in round seven, the man in the stingy-brim hat knew what others did not know.

"I had bet a lot of money on Sonny. What we called a lot of money. Three or four thousand dollars was a lot of money, as far as I'm concerned. I was given odds that he would take Clay in so many rounds. I said, 'Sonny, I'm gonna put some more money on you.'

"He said, 'Don't put any more money on me, man. Two heavyweights out there, you can't ever tell who will win.' He said, 'You've got enough money bet.' That's as far as he would go with me.

"So, later on, after it all happened and he lost the fight, I said, 'Sonny, why would you let me lose my last penny on a fight and you knew you were gonna lose it? You could've at least pulled my coat.'

"He said, 'With your big mouth, we'd both be wearing concrete suits.'"

Myrl Taylor had been in Algoa with Sam Eveland in the old days and later on had gotten involved with the unions in St. Louis. Later, after another three-year stretch, he "wound up over all the laborers in the eastern half of St. Louis." He retired in 1993.

John Vitale, said Myrl, "liked to be around people. He always came to the fights." Not long before the Miami fight, Taylor approached Vitale. "I smell a rat here," he said to Vitale.

Vitale, one friend of the Teamsters to another, told Myrl: "Let me give you some advice. When there's two niggers and a million dollars involved, all you better bet on is that a nigger's gonna win."

"In other words," as Myrl said, "he's telling me, you know, get the fuck out of it."

As for Myrl's estimation of Vitale: "Well, he was supposed to be a big-time gangster, but he was actually a fucking informer for the fuckin' police. He had a code name and everything. But the Italians here, it was a different thing. People up in Chicago and shit like that, all the Mafia people, they killed somebody, they *killed* somebody. These people here, they never — they always just set 'em up and snitched on 'em. It was a different ballgame."

Sonny's mother, Helen, and eldest brother, E.B. Ward, put in a long-distance call to Sonny from Forrest City after the fight. As E.B. Ward recalled, it took the operator about thirty minutes to get him on the hotel phone. Ward asked him what happened.

"He said, 'I did what they told me to do.'"

Patsy Anthony Lepera was a gangster from Reading, Pennsylvania.

"In those years," he said,

> I was still making money through connections in Reading. One day, I got a call from Sammy to come down to his club. "We got something going." I walk in — there's Jimmy Peters the bookie and his brother Louis the Lug, the fight promoter — their real name is Lucchese. Joe Pastore is running the meeting.

Joe Pastore and me were good friends. When something was on, I used to get a piece of it. Now Joe tells us they got everything straightened out in the Liston-Clay fight. Liston is a seven-to-one favorite . . . he's going off the board. Philadelphia is sending up a hundred grand to bet, and Reading got to come up with a hundred grand, too. That's what the meeting is for. Okay, I'll go for twenty-five.

In a few days, we got the hundred together, and Jimmy Peters is working the money. He's laying it all through the coal region. Lots of bets were laid off with the Mob in Cleveland and Vegas. These guys took the other mobs.

Lepera watched the broadcast of the fight.

It's the seventh round, Liston stays in his corner, his arm hurts, he doesn't feel like fighting anymore, he sits there on the stool. It's a TKO. This guy didn't just take a dive — he did a one and a half off the high board. It was so bad, I figured we blew everything. It worried me — I already spent my end. But no, everybody got paid off. We had to give up forty percent for the information. I come out with seventy-five thousand.

Bernie Glickman, who had handled Sonny in his transition from St. Louis control, had come down from Chicago and was around the fighters' camps before the fight.

"Right before the fight, he called me up," his son Joel told me. "He knew I liked to gamble and he knew I loved Liston. He said, 'Don't bet. There's something wrong. I don't know what it is.' I'll never forget that. I didn't listen."

•

A Chicago bookmaker remembered that night, too.

> The biggest key to it, the biggest key was the odds. The fight was five-and-a-half-to-one here, and by fight time it was down to about two-to-one. One guy, he called me up from Vegas, he wanted to bet five grand on Clay. He was looking for four or five to one; but I'd already heard they were down to three-to-one, so I think I said I'd give him three-to-one. But for a fight to have dropped down like that. And if you knew anything about boxing, there was no way Clay could hurt Liston.

The oddsmaker Bob Martin:

> I tried to lay eight-to-one, and I couldn't play around Vegas, and a friend of mine in Miami called me and got me out for five hundred. So I lost four thousand. I would have landed for ten thousand, so I would've lost eighty thousand. I couldn't get on, so I don't know where the line moved.

Martin did not believe that Sonny took a dive. "No," he said, "no chance." He tempered that somewhat: "In my mind, no chance. If a guy takes a dive, there's gotta be a motive."

When the Man says move, you got to move.

Somebody told me to look to the east, to Mecca, for the answer.

Liston had his crew down there in Miami. Pep Barone and the Nilon brothers were there. Ash Resnick from Vegas was there. Sam Margolis, an old friend and partner of Blinky's who had brokered Sonny's deal with the Nilons, was there. His hero Joe Louis was there.

And Clay had his. Among that crew was Malcolm X. The two had met in 1962, and, although Clay's interest in Islam had already blossomed by then, it was Malcolm who cultivated, and, in Miami, completed, Clay's conversion. Malcolm at the time was fallen from grace with the Nation of Islam leaders in Chicago, and he had already begun to fear violence against him. He saw in Clay a means of reinstating himself and offered to deliver the flamboyant fighter, and his embrace of Islam, to the Savior's Day convention in Chicago on the very day after the big fight. The Chicago leaders were not impressed: they believed that Liston would win. But the thought of the power and publicity a Black Muslim heavyweight champion might bring cannot have been lost on them.

"They were rough people," Truman Gibson mused when I broached the subject. They were murderously rough, as Malcolm X knew long before assassins from the Newark Temple No. 25 did their work in the cold early days of 1965.

Perhaps, in a world that was no longer Carbo's, a threat of Muslim violence might have worked against Liston. He had long been apprehensive of the Black Muslims, as he was of all he deemed to be estranged from their rightful minds. But any involvement by the Nation of Islam would have been more likely part of a straightforward business deal. Clay was the first great fighter to emerge in boxing's post-Carbo age. He had, so to speak, been born to freedom. True, he was owned in part by the Louisville consortium, but he was virgin meat as far as Mob leeching was concerned. Soon, when his contract with the Louisville Group expired, he signed with a Muslim manager, Herbert Muhammad, a son of the Black Muslim leader Elijah Muhammad. Exalted as the Messenger of the Prophet Allah, Muhammad was a reformed alky born in Georgia of an itinerant Baptist preacher named Poole.

In the days preceding the fight, Clay had evaded questions concerning his reputed conversion to the Nation of Islam. On the day after the fight, he was ebullient with the profession of that conversion.

"I go to a Black Muslim meeting and what do I see? I see there's no smoking and no drinking and their women wear dresses down to the floor." (Not only a clean-cut young man, but one who knew that the gam was the devil's meat.) "And then I come out on the street and you tell me I shouldn't go in there. Well, there must be something in there if you don't want me to go in there." The separatist way was the way of nature, he said. "In the jungle, lions are with lions and tigers are with tigers, and redbirds stay with redbirds and bluebirds with bluebirds. That's human nature, too, to be with your own kind."

On that morning after the fight, proclaiming his conversion and announcing in victory his new name, Clay's jubilation was real. Knowing nothing of what Sonny knew, and having been a party to no conspiracy other than that of his own fear and bravery, he had no reason at all to disbelieve that he was, as he said, the greatest.

"White people wanted Liston to beat up and possibly kill poor little Clay," said Elijah Muhammad at that Savior's Day rally. "But Allah and myself said no. This assured his victory."

What a great title for a song, what a great title for a poem: "But Allah and Myself Said No."

Islam was a religion of slavery from its beginnings in the seventh century. The holy Koran looked upon slaves as the gifts of God, as those "whom God has given you as booty"; and the early, trans-Saharan slave trade in Africa was dominated by the Muslims. What a fine and fitting heritage, no matter how skewed and misknown, from which to enter the fight racket.

A tithe for Islam surely would not be too much to ask of a man of the faith so blessed as the champion now known as Ali. And from that tithe might be drawn a portion for Sonny. Clay was young, with a long future ahead of him. To a man who felt rather than knew his age, a cut of that future, a piece of every, increasing purse, might seem not a bad deal at all. But if the Nation of Islam had somehow got to Sonny, the unknowing Ali would have been sent into the ring praising the divinity and the blessing and the all-conquering power of Allah, rather than been constrained to not publicize his faith before the fight. To the Black Muslims, Clay's publicity value as a champion would be great, but were he to lose, having been known as a Black Muslim beforehand, his loss would be a loss for the power and image of the faith. The Prophet had not shared the future with the Messenger; and the Muslims, like just about everybody else, expected Sonny to bury Clay in the open night.

On February 16, 1963, a year before the Miami fight, the Court of Appeals in San Francisco had handed down its decision in a seventy-five-page opinion that confirmed the 1961 convictions of Frankie Carbo, Blinky Palermo, and the others. Alcatraz had been shut down, and Carbo was moved to another prison. Blinky lingered a while more on the outside, and was unincarcerated still the night Liston lost to Clay. It was not until June 5, 1964, that United States marshals took him from Philadelphia to begin his fifteen-year term in the federal penitentiary at Lewisburg.

The Devil gave, and the Devil took away. For Sonny, had the Devil not given to him in the first place, there would never have been anything to take away: because you could be the best, toughest, killingest motherfucking fighter in the world, but without the Devil it did not much matter a good goddamn, because it was the Devil's ring. There was no one left for Sonny to turn to; except to the Devil in himself.

•

"He who is by nature not his own but another's man, is by nature a slave."

Nature. Destiny. Fate. Guys like Frankie Carbo.

The writer Mark Kram recalls being with Ali many years later, in 1983, as they sat and talked by the trancing hushed-crackling flames of the fireplace in Ali's Los Angeles mansion. Ali became lost in silence, and, in that silence, he looked into the fire for quite some time. He turned to Kram and whispered to him: "Liston was the Devil."

In court on May 29, Sonny was let off gently on the speeding and gun possession charges brought against him in March. Municipal Judge Dan D. Diamond handed down fines totaling six hundred dollars. "You have been an idol of mine," said the judge. "God love you and bless you in your future. I'm sorry this had to happen." On an FBI memorandum reporting the judge's words, the Director, accenting those words with his pen, wrote, "Disgusting!"

On Christmas Day, Sonny was stopped for drunken driving and hauled to jail in a patrol wagon after becoming involved in "a shoving match" with the ten Denver policemen who had answered the arresting officer's call. He was wrestled into a cell, where he spent five hours of his Christmas. Counting a penny-ante speeding pinch that took place two weeks after the concealed-weapon rap in March, it was his third arrest in the months since the Clay fight.

He was sporting a close-razored moustache tight above his lip these days. He looked bloated some days, drawn on others. What little light had shone in those dead man's eyes could now hardly be discerned. He was described as "haggard" at the time of his arrest. While he now claimed to be either thirty — his date of birth as set forth in his license application for the Miami fight would have rendered him at that time a bit more than two months shy of his thirtieth birthday, though on the same application, he specifically stated his age as thirty — or his more customary thirty-two — a photograph taken of him early in November showed a man who appeared to have at least forty hard years behind him.

On January 30, 1965, a Denver jury found Liston innocent of the drunk-driving charges. When confronted with the police report that he had been staggering and stumbling while entering his car in front of a restaurant, Sonny explained that he had merely been just jive dancing to the music of his fine new 1965 Cadillac's fine new stereo tape player.

The suspicions and trouble stirred by the Miami fight were such that no state with a reputation for boxing would sanction the rematch. Art Laurie, who at that time was the chairman of the Nevada State Boxing Commission, told me that Senators Hart and Keating spoke to him personally about the prospect of holding the fight in Las Vegas. "They told me not to have anything to do with that fight, because our industry here was gaming, and that fight was going to stink out the place." They also told him that Sonny "only owned ten percent of himself." Laurie recalled that Ash Resnick, along with the promoters Mel Greb and Jack Doyle "came to my office and asked me for a date." (Greb and Doyle would later co-promote the Las Vegas Ali-Patterson fight with Inter-Continental.) "I said, 'That fight's not going to take place here.'" The governor of Nevada, Grant Sawyer, involved himself, and in the end, he told Laurie to use his judgment.

Laurie knew and liked Sonny. He had seen a lot of fighters in his time — born in 1918, he had been a heavyweight champion of the navy boxing team under Gene Tunney, and he later had refereed more title fights than any other official — but he had never seen a fighter with the brute force of Liston. Laurie was watching him work out on a sandbag one day in Vegas, and he saw something he never forgot: Sonny threw a left hook that carried such force that he blew the sandbag loose and sent it crashing to the floor. Furthermore, that force had wrenched open, straightened, and sent flying the S-hook by which the sandbag had been suspended.

Laurie said that "they" — and this, I now see, is what we truly need: a Gibbon, a full and glorious and detailed history of *them* — went for the money. "They got three hundred thousand dollars for the fight, and they bet it at seven-to-one. They got two-point-one million."

"The money was bet through Cleveland," Laurie said. "That's where they placed the money. That's what I understand."

Las Vegas was not alone in wanting nothing to do with this most suspect of sequels to the most suspect and infamous of heavyweight championship fights; and it came to be held, on May 25, 1965, before a sparse crowd at the Central Maine Youth Center, a schoolboys' hockey arena in Lewiston, Maine.

One thing is certain: in that rematch — it was Liston-Ali then, not Liston-Clay — when Sonny lay down in the first, he showed less acting ability than in the episode of *Love American Style* in which he later bizarrely appeared. That fight was not merely a fix — a fix that common lore attributes to physical intimidation by the legion of Black Muslims reportedly gathered there. These Muslims were, in fact, fewer than legion and were present to protect Ali from reprisal by the followers of the late Malcolm X, whose apostasy in breaking with Elijah Muhammad had been loudly denounced by Clay in his ever-increasing role as party-line mouthpiece — it was a flaunted fix.

When fights were tampered with, for the benefit of a fighter's career or the benefit of select few gamblers' pockets, or both, they were most usually rigged rather than fixed. Rigging was a simple and not illegal procedure whereby one fighter of greater capability — whether or not that capability was yet known to the general population of suckers — was pitted against another of lesser capability, who indeed might have been made to look better than he was in previous rigged fights. It was a straightforward matter, known as mismatching. (The 1954 *Boxing Reference Dictionary* of F.C. Avis offers the following definition of the noun *mismatch*: "a contest between two boxers of very different standards of ability." Sometimes mismatches occur unforeseeably, by nature, as it were; sometimes they occur by design.) As Truman Gibson said, all-out fixes were rare: when the same interests profited equally from a fight, no matter who won, what did it matter? Only when an extraordinary gambling payoff presented itself was a debt of fate called in. And only the designated loser knew. The preordained winner was never told, for the main burden of making the fix look real rested on him: for him, the fight must *be* real, and he must fight naturally and in ignorance. As a knowing accomplice, he would be not only a potential danger to the success of the fix, but also potentially nothing more than an unneeded and unwanted expense. Thus, the winner of a good fixed fight never knows that he is a party to the fix. It has been said that it is harder to throw a good fight than to fight one. But human vanity on the part of a victor does much to compensate in his heart and mind for any suspicion of inauthenticity on the part of his foredoomed opponent. The performance in Lewiston, however, was so bad that even Ali must have known.

Sonny — the eight-to-five favorite, despite the prior loss — could not repeat his Miami Beach routine of merely slouching on a stool while Jack Nilon announced his woeful incapacitation. For one thing, the physician at the prefight examination found no evidence of shoulder injury and declared him to be "the fittest man I have ever examined"; for another the most willing suspension of disbelief would not countenance it. And so, in the first round, when Ali hit him, he went down. Sonny, who had been knocked down only once before — by a fighter whom the risen Sonny then had proceeded to give the most ferocious beating of his life — here was felled by a blow so slight that few could see it: a short right that seemed intended only to fluster and to fend off, a short right followed by a left hook that missed.

"Liston collapsed slowly, like a falling building, piece by piece, rolling onto his back, then flat on his stomach, his face pressed against the canvas." This account, from a front-page story in the next day's *New York Times*, describes the halting, unnatural, and awkward amateur choreography of a man who is performing a fall rather than the sundering spontaneity of a man knocked down unawares.

It was a shambles. The referee, Jersey Joe Walcott, the Camden, New Jersey, assistant director of public safety and promotional shill of Inter-Continental, lost control of the goings-on after the knockdown. While maneuvering Ali into a neutral corner, Walcott failed to follow the knockdown count of the timekeepers at ringside. After the fight was declared over upon the count of twelve, Sonny rose only to find out that the fight, which was over, was still going on as far as Jersey Joe was concerned. Confused, he squared off, like Ali, as if to fight again, while Walcott simultaneously and belatedly became aware of the timekeepers' twelve-count. "Twelve? You counted to twelve?" he asked.

"Yes, twelve. The fight's over," they replied — whereupon Joe rushed across the ring and raised Ali's arm in victory.

The crowd stood and chanted, "Fake, fake, fake," again and again, until the last of them dwindled and dispersed in disgust.

"Fake, fake, fake." Some of them rushed the cordon of state troopers that surrounded the ring, yelling, "Fix, fix, fix," as Ali yelled back telling them to shut up, telling them that his was a righteous victory, a triumph of the "righteous life."

In reality, Ali seemed to have noticed the winning punch no more than anyone else. He would describe it after the fight as the "anchor punch," the secret weapon of Jack Johnson as passed on to Ali by Stepin Fetchit, the elderly comedian and old-time movie player who was now a part of Ali's ever stranger retinue. In time, it became known in legend as the "phantom punch." Studied frame by frame, the film of the only camera that captured it showed what those who saw it that night in Lewiston saw — among the many who saw nothing — a punch that seemed too ineffectual to knock down, or even to ruffle, the leviathan that was Charles Sonny Liston.

"I overtrained for that fight," Sonny would say.

Maybe it said something, too, that he trained no longer to the nasty horns and pistol rhythms of "Night Train," but to "Railroad Train No. 1" by Lionel Hampton, who was from Ali's hometown of Louisville. It was as if that song, "Night Train," which was the beat and synesthesia of his deepest pulse, had now been taken utterly and without outward sound into the secret part of him, that secret part that was indeed becoming the whole of him.

But it was the damnedest thing: for once, finally, he had been cheered going into that ring in Maine. What a hell of a time to have it all taken from you.

Six months later, in November, he was talking about recruiting Cus D'Amato to manage him in a comeback. D'Amato called Sonny "a challenge" and said there was "a distinct possibility that I could make Liston the heavyweight champion again if he divests himself of the people around him." When told of D'Amato's statement, Sonny said, "It's the onliest way." And that was that.

By Christmas, his home in Denver was up for sale. On March 29, 1966, Sonny bought Kirk Kerkorian's place in Vegas for sixty-four grand: split-level, pastel green, with a swimming pool and a backyard that looked out over the sixteenth fairway of the Stardust Country Club. The address was 2058 Ottawa Drive, in the exclusive area of Paradise Township, less than a mile from where his hero and buddy, Joe Louis, lived, at 3333 Seminole Circle, in a house bought from Johnny Carson.

The tie between Vegas and St. Louis was not a tenuous one. Later, during Sonny's final days, one casino owner was known to associate with Charles "the Blade" Tourine, who in turn was implicated in dealings with John Vitale in St. Louis. Still later, it would be said by police intelligence sources that between one and two million dollars in gambling revenues were "illegally diverted from the Aladdin Hotel's casino in Las Vegas" and "channeled to underworld figures in St. Louis." This report of November 1980, said: "as much as $50,000 was brought to St. Louis each month by couriers, often businessmen who went to Las Vegas ostensibly to gamble. The sources said that both these couriers and Aladdin employees delivered the money to John J. Vitale, an alleged underworld boss.

"Until last month, the gambling resort was owned largely by St. Louis interests. Wayne Newton, the entertainer, bought the casino for about $85 million."

Sonny's first fight after the downfall in Lewiston came more than a year later. In Stockholm, on June 29, he knocked out Gerhard Zech of Germany in the seventh round.

"Blood streamed from Zech's eyes and mouth in the sixth round," said a wire service report, "and the flow continued in the seventh until Liston mercifully knocked him out."

His next three fights were in Sweden as well: a third-round knockout in Gothenburg of Amos Johnson, on August 19; a first-round knockout against Dave Bailey in Gothenburg on March 30, 1967; a sixth-round knockout of Elmer Rush in Stockholm on April 28, 1967.

"This fighting is for the bird," he wrote to a friend in January 1967. From Sweden, in May of 1967, the Listons returned with a three-year-old boy, Daniell, who lived with them as an adopted son.

"I'm my own manager now," he declared in the summer of 1967. "When they try you for murder, they got to produce a body. But nobody can produce anybody who is managing me except me." Later, within the breadth of that same day, he said, "All I need is a manager. Somebody with a nice, clean record."

He talked about leaving Vegas, buying a farm somewhere, maybe Colorado.

In the fall of 1967, it was rumored and reported that Sammy Davis, Jr., was to be Liston's new manager. "Why would Sammy want to get involved with managing a guy nobody wants any part of?" asked Dick Young in his *New York Daily News* column of November 18.

A guy nobody wants any part of. "Liston, the bum of bums" — yeah, that's what some other columnist called him — "the nothing of all nothings."

For the first time, as if uncaring, he indirectly admitted to his control by Carbo and Blinky. Applying for a license to fight in California, a member of the boxing commission in Sacramento asked him about his history of managers.

"One's doin' fifteen years," Sonny said, "and another's doin' twenty-five."

The California commission turned down his application, but in February 1968, a California license was granted him.

In the spring of 1968, *Sports Illustrated* published an article called "What's Become of the Big Bear?" The author, Jack Olsen, described his attempts to draw words from the once infamous man who was now all but forgotten:

"Sonny lounged on a long window seat and tried his best to stay awake. 'Been huntin' rabbits,' he said with great effort, 'and when we hunts rabbits, we don't get much sleep. We leave at two o'clock in the morning." Olsen spends much of the time talking with Geraldine, then finally there is a question that Sonny rouses himself to answer. Olsen asked him if he lost any friends after the Clay fights. Sonny looked dead straight at him and dead straight said: "No. I had my friends in my pocket."

Back in 1965, he had been given a bit part in one of the two bad movies called *Harlow* that were released that year. In Vegas, he connected with a couple of more movie parts: Bob Rafelson's *Head,* which came out in 1968, and something called *Moonfire,* which came out in 1970. He did a 1969 Braniff Airline commercial with Andy Warhol, in which he sat in unsmiling silence, ostensibly aboard a Braniff aircraft, while Warhol, in the next seat, spoke to him about the "inherent beauty" of soup cans.

Punctuated by only one arrest (for drunk driving, in February 1969), Sonny fought a dozen fights between March of 1968 and

September of 1969. He won them all, eleven of them by knockouts. In December 1969, at Kirk Kerkorian's new International in Vegas, his former sparring partner Leotis Martin, a three-to-one underdog, knocked him out in the ninth.

There would be one more fight, with the Bayonne heavyweight Chuck Wepner, at the Jersey City Armory on June 29, 1970.

At the weigh-in and press conference at the Oyster Bay Restaurant in Jersey City a few days before the fight, a reporter asked Sonny if he would request a license to fight in New York, which had always been denied him.

"I'm on my way down," he snarled. "The hell with New York."

Wepner recalled that it was a surly motherfucker who looked down impassively at Wepner's hand when he extended it for a pre-fight shake before the press.

"Well, the first few rounds, the fight was almost even," Chuck said.

> I thought he was getting tired, and I started pressing him, and he really nailed me with that jab. He had a tremendous jab. And he started busting me up. After the fifth round, I was target practice. My one eye closed, my equilibrium was off. Broken nose, broken left cheekbone, seventy-two stitches. They iced me down for two straight days. I was in shock for three days, I really was.
>
> He could punch. And it got so bad near the end when the guy landed a jab — and he had a jab; he could step in and throw his shoulder, like, bang, with the shoulder right behind it, the way you're supposed to throw it — I could hear the bone shattering. The referee came in at the beginning of the ninth round and he said, "I gotta stop the fight, his eyes are all busted up." And I said, "I'm all right." And he said, "Well, how many fingers do I have up?" I couldn't see him, all I could see were blurs. Al Braverman had his hand on my shoulder. Al tapped me three times; I said,

"Three." He said, "O.K., you're all right, you can see." I came out for the ninth round and got banged around, but actually in the ninth I landed some. He was getting tired, definitely. He was even getting tired of beating the shit out of me.

Braverman, in partnership with Gary Garafola, was Chuck's manager. He was an acquaintance of Ash Resnick and had worked with Liston in Vegas. As Chuck said,

Al Braverman was supposed to be the trainer but was really only the cut-man, and Gary was the manager. Gary had Frankie De Paula, a couple other guys, and he also owned the Rag Doll up in Union City.

That's how I signed with him. I go up there to the Rag Doll, and they got this go-go girl dancing, and she was a knockout. Gail. Pretty sure her name was Gail. So, Gary Garafola, who owned the place, says, "When does your contract run out?" I said, "It runs out in about a month or two." He says, "What are you gonna do?" I says, "I don't know." He says, "I'd like to sign you." I said, "I don't know." So, I'm looking at the girl. Gary says, "You like her?" I said, "Do I like her? She's beautiful." He said, "Do you want her?" I said, "Do I want her?" He says, "You wanna sign a contract with me, you can have any girl here you want." I said, "Are you serious?" He said, "Yeah." I said, "I want her." He says, "Go in the office, I'll send her in." So, I go in the office, they've got these great big desks there, and I knocked everything off, pushed it on the floor. Five minutes later, she walks in and says, "Hi, I'm Gail. Gary told me to come in." I said, "Yeah?" She says, "What do you want?" I said, "I want everything."

I was loaded. Anyway, I come outta there, and I'm all perspiring and everything; I come out and Gary had the contract. He said, "Here's the contract." I said, "Give me the pen, boss, you got yourself a fighter."

Not long after the fight at the Armory, Garafola would be charged with the murder of his light heavyweight boxer Frankie De Paula. But Frankie's murder, Chuck said, "was over a broad. He was whacking somebody's wife, and they wanted him to stay away, and he didn't. I even told him." Gary was acquitted, went to the joint on another rap, and it was then that Braverman took over actively as Chuck's manager.

The Genovese team-player that oversaw that part of Jersey was James Napoli, also known as Jimmy Nap. He was, in Chuck's memorable phrase, "the local guy from the what-you-call-it. He had a lot to do with the fights. He was very involved in all the fights in them days."

The Armory fight went into the tenth round, and it ended only when Wepner, one of the great warhorses of boxing, could no longer see through his swollen and blood-drenched eyes. The referee was Barney Felix, who had refereed the Liston-Clay fight in Miami, six years earlier.

A few years later, Chuck would fight Muhammad Ali for the heavyweight championship.

"I would have to say that Liston was a lot tougher to fight. Ali didn't hit like Liston. Liston was the only man that ever hurt me."

Dave Anderson of the *New York Times* called the Jersey City fight between Liston and Wepner "a bloody sacrifice that evoked more sympathy for the loser than prestige for the winner."

Wepner's take was supposed to be fifty percent of the $37,600 gate, and from his take, he was supposed to pay out Sonny's guarantee of thirteen grand.

As he recalled, it was an even five grand, paid out to him in cash some days later at the office of the fight's promoter Willie Gilzenberg of Newark. "I gave Al a third. I wound up with thirty-something hundred." Three thousand and change left from what had started out as fifty percent of a thirty-seven-thousand-dollar gate. "Yeah. It was my biggest payday to date. By far."

Paul Venti, the knockdown timekeeper at the fight, shared a big musty dressing-room with Sonny.

> I didn't see Sonny Liston when I changed into my referee clothes, but when I went back after the show was over, Sonny was using a different corner from where I was. He got into his street clothes — brown suit, no tie, fedora — and I didn't want to bother him; I was in a different end of the room. And I was sitting on the stool of a piano that was there, and I was changing. So, now the guys came in from Bayonne, and they went over to Sonny.

Sonny was completely alone, Venti said, and the guys from Bayonne numbered either three or four.

"They had this white envelope, and they told Sonny, 'There you go. Seven grand. That's all we could come up with.'"

"'No, no, no,' he says, 'I came here with a deal to get fifteen thousand.'"

While the above-board guarantee was stipulated at thirteen grand, there may have been an understanding of an additional two grand to be paid under the table, a practice far from uncommon.

> "No, that's all we can give you. We're losing money on this whole thing. If you don't take it, then go home with nothing."
>
> He took a deep breath. When he took a deep breath — I remember it like yesterday — I moved away. I figured, hey, were gonna have some fireworks here, and these guys are kinda crazy from Bayonne. They're always at ringside.
>
> And, so, Sonny took a deep breath. "Count it," they told him. He looked through the money. He looked again. And he looked at the guys. Stuck it in his inside pocket and walked out.

Three men flew with Sonny from Las Vegas to the fight and back. Two of those men are still living; and both of them recalled that Sonny left town with either thirteen grand, as one of them swears, or fifteen grand, as the other remembered while conceding that, yes, it might have been thirteen. Ten grand of that money, one of them said, went to pay off a losing bet that Sonny had made on Jerry Quarry, another heavyweight in another fight, a dozen days before. (Quarry, who was twenty-five and white, had beaten Floyd Patterson in 1967. Although it was not yet public knowledge at the time of Sonny's bet, Quarry was to be the opponent of Muhammad Ali several months later in the fight that would mark Ali's return to the ring after an absence of more than three years. It is interesting that Ali showed up during the Wepner fight and purposely disrupted it, aggressively drawing attention from the fight in the ring to his own loud presence.)

Paul Venti's mind is lucid, and he is a very honest man. The same can rightly be said for the other two gentlemen. Could it be that, after leaving the Armory, Sonny might have taken it upon himself to have collected what was due him? There were in his corner no more of those guys, as Chuck would have it, from the what-you-call-it. The very fact that he had been treated as recounted in Venti's story evinces as much: that he was now a man without true intercessor, rabbi, or *cumpari*.

Venti, who was born in 1920, has been in the fight racket for a long, long time. "Frankie Carbo and Palermo," he said, "were running the fight game out of their cells. They were in jail, and they had a phone service at their disposal, and they made matches. They were running the Garden out of jail." (Lowell Powell agreed. "They could arrange anything.")

Things changed, Venti said, and things stayed the same. "Today you've got about six, seven organizations, and they don't have to tell you who their champions are. If you don't protect them, you just don't work again. It's happening today. They don't want a lopsided decision, but if it's close, they expect you to lean."

I remembered the rumors at the time of the fight. Liston, it was whispered, was going to go down for the Hudson County money.

"I wish," Wepner said with a laugh. "Maybe they didn't get the message through to him. I wish they had."

Johnny Tocco remembered sitting in a hotel coffee shop with Sonny a few days before the fight.

> A couple of shady-looking characters came in and motioned Sonny over. So, Sonny told me he'll be right back, and then he left. He was gone for hours.
>
> When I see him, I ask him who those guys were, and he just mumbled something. The next day, one of those guys comes up to me, shakes my hand, and says something like: "If your guy loses, don't feel bad. Chuck's a real popular guy here."
>
> Well, I went up to Sonny, and I said, "Hey, is something going on? Who are those guys? Sonny, are you just here for a payday? If somethin's goin' on, I want to know about it."
>
> Sonny said, "Aw, go to sleep. I'm going to knock this guy out."

Wepner, who was thirty-one at the time, said that, up close in the ring, Sonny "looked like he'd been around the block quite a few times. They said he was thirty-eight, and he looked like he was maybe fifty."

The money had run as dry as the rivulet that had trickled to nothing on that plantation slough. It was said that in November Sonny entered a Las Vegas recording studio and made him a rock 'n' roll record, and that he was hoping that it might bring him a few bucks when it was released. Nothing else was ever heard or discovered about that record.

Sonny was in an automobile accident on Thanksgiving Day of 1970. He was given emergency treatment at Sunrise Hospital, then released. Two days later, he was admitted to Southern Nevada Memorial Hospital, where, on December 1, he was reported in satisfactory condition. The hospital would not reveal the nature of Sonny's injuries. In a letter Geraldine wrote to a friend, she said, "he got cut on the head and nose kind of bad but we think it will be ok when it heal." He was released on December 4.

Something drew him to Los Angeles. There, on December 16, he was arrested on a freeway for drunken driving. He returned to Las Vegas.

Johnny Tocco, Davey Pearl, and Lem Banker were the three men who had flown with Sonny when he fought Chuck Wepner.

Tocco was a trainer who had worked with Sonny in the early days in St. Louis. He had moved in the early fifties to Vegas, where he had been operating the Ringside Gym on East Charlton since 1956. He was now serving once again as a trainer of sorts for Sonny.

Born in Paterson, New Jersey, in 1917, Davey Pearl had come to Vegas in September 1947. After blowing his last sixty bucks gambling, he had tried to politely bum a smoke from a guy who told him no, which "got me so mad that I made up my mind that I was gonna stay here and be somebody, and let that son of a bitch, if I ever run into him, know that he turned me down for a cigarette."

Davey tells this story sitting diminutive and dapper beside his diminutive and dapper and very identical twin, Lou. His package of Merit cigarettes is placed carefully before him on the table of a joint called Bagelmania, at Twain and Swenson, where he takes his breakfast coffee almost every morning; and, as he tells this story, he seems as if he would still be able, after more than half a century, to readily recognize that prick if he walked in, and would just as readily blow smoke in his face.

"That's what made me stay here. Plus the fact that I had no money." One thing led to another, and he found himself working the Flamingo, Bugsy Siegel's joint. "Ya hadda call him Mr. Siegel. Yeah. He got killed a few months after I started." From there, running shows, running joints, and working fights, he came to know them all, as many claimed but few did: from Sinatra to Dean Martin, from Carl Cohen, who knocked out Sinatra's teeth ("the number-one nice guy in Vegas," Pearl said of Cohen) to Moe Dalitz ("one of the greatest guys that ever lived. I cried when he died") to Meyer Lansky. "Dalitz, you had to respect him; Cohen, you had to respect him; but when Lansky said something, that was it. He was a nice guy, quiet as could be." Lansky was not a gentleman, said Davey, he was a *perfect* gentleman. They chartered a plane together, he and Lansky, in the summer of 1954, flew off to Frisco for the Olson-Castellani middleweight championship fight. Yes, Davey Pearl, the modest, down-to-earth, behind-the-scenes Vegas legend that the writ-big legends sought out and trusted, had a past that liars would pay to have as their own. In the fight game, he became a legend far beyond Vegas, as one of the most honored and respected referees in boxing. Told initially by the Nevada State Athletic Commission that he was too small to be a referee, Davey went on to referee thousands of fights, more than fifty world-title bouts among them. In 1997, he was inducted into the World Boxing Hall of Fame.

Sonny Liston, he said, was "one of the best friends I ever had in my life, if not the best." Times had changed. The days of gentlemanly tough guys were gone, and Davey was no kid anymore. But "after I was with Sonny," he said, "nobody fooled with me. You know what I'm saying? Nobody got tough. Nobody ever stepped outta line with me. There were guys here who were professional tough guys, and they'd maybe try to get in on the muscle, and I hated that with a passion. Well, nobody ever did that to me when Sonny was near me."

Davey remembered the time he cajoled Sonny into serving as guest referee at a boys club boxing tournament.

> Little kids; nine, ten years old. So, going into the ring, Sonny says to me, "Now I'll show you how a referee should referee." So, he gets in the ring and the kid is beating the other kid up badly. So he stops the fight. The loser was so mad he stopped the fight, he takes the glove off his hand and throws the glove at Sonny and hits him right in the face. I never got him back there again.

While never officially Sonny's manager — he accepted no money from him, though Sonny offered it — Davey was a friend who often performed the duties of a manager. They did roadwork together, ran maybe five or six miles on those mornings when Davey could rouse or find Sonny. Sometimes Sonny would be outside waiting for him. "The mornings that he wasn't outside, I knew he was trying to keep away from running, so I'd ring the bell. He hated for me to ring that bell. 'What the fuck you want? I ain't goin' today.' 'The fuck you're not goin.'" Sonny's respect for Davey seems in one way to have inspired the same reserved behavior that he showed among priests. "Everybody used to tell me he was a drunk," said Davey, who himself drank and smoked; but "I never saw him take a drink in all the years I was with him."

Some mornings, Sonny would not be at home when Davey arrived. According to another Vegas friend, Gene Kilroy, an associate of Muhammad Ali, Sonny on those mornings would be holed up often as not at Joe Louis's house, the two of them shooting craps on Joe's bedroom floor. Joe, according to Dean Shendal, was a craps degenerate, an alchemist who "turned money into shit." Truman Gibson, Joe's old friend, said that America's most beloved boxer had by this time become a smack and coke junkie who was fast falling apart. Truman remembered seeing him so strung out and fucked up that he was hearing voices come through an air conditioner. Louis was hospitalized for a breakdown in 1970; and, as Truman said, it was not until a stroke debilitated him that he got off the shit.

Lem Banker, another friend of Sonny's, was described, in a November 1997 profile in the *New York Times* business section, as "perhaps one of the most successful gamblers in Las Vegas."

Of his relationship with Sonny in Las Vegas, Lem Banker, who is now in his seventies, told me, "I was his best friend for the simple reason that I never tried to make any money off the guy." Like Davey Pearl, Lem seemed to evoke in Sonny that same respectful reserve brought out by priests. "He wouldn't drink in front of me," Lem said.

Banker said that, after returning to Vegas from the Wepner fight, "Ralph Lamb, who was sheriff, told me, 'Lem, I know you're friendly with Sonny. Tell him he's hanging around the wrong people on the West Side. We're gonna bust these guys. Tell Sonny not to hang out with them.'"

The West Side was the bad side, the black side.

"I started drinking in 1930 and stopped drinking in '87," said Charles Broadus.

Broadus, known as Doc, was involved with the Olympic heavyweight champion George Foreman at the outset of his professional career, in 1968. He brought Sonny together with the young fighter, and together Sonny and Foreman went to St. Louis.

"Sonny brought him over to my house," Lowell Powell remembered.

> I took him to the gym every day. The funny thing, Sonny sat next to me in the car, we were driving over south St. Louis to the gym, and this young boy, George Foreman, nineteen years old, and he was smacking gum or something in Sonny's ear, and Sonny said, "Will you stop smacking that gum in my ear?" He said, "If you seen the way I whupped that German, you wouldn't talk to me like that." That cracked everybody up, because Sonny wasn't used to people sassing him. He loved Sonny. Yeah, he loved Sonny.

Doc Broadus recalled running round the West Side with Sonny. "Me and him run together twenty-four hours. Only difference between me and Liston was I had to go to work and Liston would go to bed," said Broadus.

"We drank together," and chased down women. "Oh, shit, yeah." They hung out, too, he said, at the Zebra Lounge, which was part of Tocco's gym. "We had fun, we'd run together day and night. We had fun and enjoyed what we was doing, and that was that." As far as Broadus knew, Sonny never messed with dope.

The booze, the broads, all that shit. "Hey," as Dean Shendal said, "he was fucking around with thirty young broads." But no one who knew him — no one — believed that he was on dope.

According to Lowell Powell, his old friend and bodyguard from St. Louis, Sonny wasn't using the shit, but he was selling it.

"I learned a lot about Sonny's quiet business through Ash," Lowell said. "I guess Ash thought I knew a lot of things that possibly I didn't know. Sonny kept a lot of things from me. Well, a lot of things he couldn't discuss with me by virtue of my being a policeman," albeit a retired policeman.

"Ash was a good guy, yes. He loved money." And, as Lowell later said in idle reflection, "Money makes strange bedfellows."

And while Sonny was selling, he was also shooting his mouth off, threatening to talk about things. "Yeah," said Lowell, "that's what got him killed in my opinion. He started putting pressure down, he started selling narcotics."

Lowell received a long letter from Sonny. "I guess everyone was up set over the fight," it said, but it was good "to know I still have Friend. I know Friend ar much better then money." The letter ended, "I hope to see you when I get some money. I had not for got you."

On his way to visit his brother in Los Angeles, Lowell stopped in Vegas. It was perhaps little more than a week before Christmas.

> I came looking for Sonny and he wasn't at home, so I talked with Geraldine for a while. She said, "Sonny has gotten unruly." I said, "Isn't he coming home for dinner? I'll stay and eat with him." She said, "No, he doesn't trust me on food and things; he gets his little Kentucky Frieds and things, and you can catch him over there at the Hilton Hotel. You go to the casino, and if he's not there, you just stand there five minutes, and he'll come through."

The Hilton — it was still the International, really; Kerkorian's new management agreement with Hilton was in effect, but the name had not yet been changed — was only a few minutes from the Liston house. "I was there, I'd say, five minutes before he came up and touched me on the shoulder. So we got to talking and spent the evening together. We had just ordered new Cadillacs. I had got mine, he was waiting for his. He wanted me to stay, but I had to go. He drove me to the airport." He did not seem unruly. "No. He was in a very friendly mood."

On the day after Christmas, Geraldine left town to visit her mother in St. Louis. Sonny drove her to the airport.

While away, she would later say, Geraldine tried unsuccessfully to telephone her husband several times. She returned home to the smell of death on the night of January 5, 1971, at about half past eight.

In the glimpse of Sonny that she could bear before coming apart, she saw him lying back, stiff and bloated, butt-down in his skivvies on the upholstered bench at the foot of the velvet-covered bed: his upper body prone, his feet on the floor, his shoes and socks beside them.

Geraldine arrived, hysterical, at about eight forty-five at the home of her friend Bernice Heath on Aztec Way. With Bernice was a business associate, William Hartford. Without success, Bernice and Hartford tried to reach Geraldine's doctor, Kenneth Turner. They called upon another friend, James Custer, and the three of them accompanied Geraldine to her home, where, at about a quarter past ten, they found Sonny — what had been Sonny — just as Geraldine in her hysteria had described. At about eleven o'clock, they reached Dr. Turner's colleague Dr. William J. Cavin. He arrived at the house on Ottawa Drive at about twenty past eleven. It was Cavin who pronounced Liston dead at about half past eleven on that night of January 5, 1971.

Dr. Cavin did not examine the body. Judging by its abnormal swelling and rigor mortis, he concluded that it had lain dead for about a week. The police were called, and two detectives arrived at about twelve forty-five. They interviewed those present except for Geraldine, whose "apparent shock" rendered her unable to be questioned.

The subsequent Dead Body Report noted that, "Upon examining the mail in the house, it was observed that a Notice of Attempt to Deliver Mail dated 12-28-70, was observed laying on a table in the entryway to the residence. Also a newspaper dated 12-28-70 was noted." The newspaper was lying on the basement bar, next to Sonny's hat.

According to the report of Investigator H. Bowe of the coroner's office, "Decedent was in a bloated condition and gas was escaping from his nose. Blood appeared to have come from the nose and it appeared that blood had soaked and dried in the bedsheet at the decedent's head. Decedent's fingers appeared dehydrated."

The ID Bureau of the Clark County Sheriff's Office arrived to take pictures.

The body was removed by the coroner's office to Palm Mortuary, on North Main.

The sheriff's office stated that a quarter ounce of heroin was found in a colored balloon in the kitchen, a bag of reefer in a pocket of Liston's trousers draped over a bedroom chair. There was a glass of vodka on a nightstand; on a dresser, a holstered .38 revolver, a wooden cross, a stuffed rattlesnake, some loose change. The television set was on. Again duly noted was the December 28 *Las Vegas Sun* newspaper that lay by Sonny's hat atop the basement bar. Newspapers from the twenty-ninth and later lay stacked on the porch.

An autopsy was performed at Palm Mortuary later that day, January 6.

> The body is that of a well developed, well nourished middle aged Negro male measuring 73 inches in length and weighing an estimated 240 pounds. The body shows considerable postmortem changes. There is gaseous distention of the skin particularly the face, abdomen, scrotum and penis. Facial details are obliterated

> partially by this gaseous subcutaneous distention. The face shows a flattened appearance. The skin also shows some areas of bleb formation and skin slippage. The skin surfaces including the scalp show no evidence of recent traumatic injury.
>
> The left anticubital fossa shows a horizontal old scar which appears to have been traumatic in origin. This measures 3 cm in length. Immediately beneath the horizontal scar is a V-shaped scar with the apex at the horizontal scar, the arms of which measure 1 and 1.5 cm. in length. These scars have a somewhat nodular appearance and roughly follow the course of anticubital veins. These scars may have been caused by old traumatic injury but the possibility that they represent old needle puncture marks (in the V-shaped scar) cannot be absolutely excluded. There is no external evidence of a recent needle puncture perforation in this location. Dissection of both anticubital fossae show no abnormalities on the right. On the left there is a small extravasation of blood subcutaneously and in the dermal fat immediately beneath the skin. This is not associated with detectable hemorrhage about the exposed anticubital vein in this location. Portions of skin, subcutaneous fat and veins were taken for subsequent microscopic examination. Except for gaseous extention in the scrotum and penis the anus and external genitalia show nothing of note.

The term "antecubital," rendered incorrectly throughout as "anticubital," refers to the inner surface of the forearm.

The body cavities and organs revealed nothing out of the ordinary. Microscopic findings were said to include "an increase in fibrous tissue about the small blood vessels in the septums" of the heart. "The small arteries and the arterioles in the heart show considerable collagenous intimal thickening."

This description of microscopic fibrosis, or scarring, within the heart is an indication of the presence of small-blood-vessel disease.

While large-vessel disease is easily detectable in the living as well as in the dead, small-vessel disease is not, but, as with any fibrosis of the heart, it can possibly result in arrhythmia, which can lead to sudden death.

However, it is extremely unlikely to find normal large vessels and abnormal small vessels within the same heart, and instances of this rare condition (now known as Syndrome X) are restricted almost exclusively to women and, to a lesser degree, diabetic men.

According to the medical examiner's report, Sonny's death was due to "probable myocardial anoxia due to coronary insufficiency": that is, a deprivation of oxygen to the muscular tissue of the heart. The words "exact cause undetermined by autopsy" are appended in parentheses to the diagnosis of "probable myocardial anoxia due to coronary insufficiency"; but the implication is that this anoxia was caused by the narrowing of the fibrous small blood vessels described in the autopsy's microscopic findings: a narrowing independent of any large-vessel abnormality, as encountered only rarely and usually only among women.

There are two ways of interpreting this diagnosis. Either the examiner did indeed encounter in Sonny a very rare instance of Syndrome X in a male or, in need of a final diagnosis but lacking any other conclusive evidence, found it convenient to attribute death to a condition — small-vessel abnormality without accompanying large-vessel abnormality — that is all but undetectable in life and thus not a part of a routine medical history that could either refute or confirm such a condition as a postmortem diagnosis.

"Probable myocardial anoxia due to coronary insufficiency." Probable. Odd that after all these centuries of cut and croak, there should be no obfuscating medical term for that particular equivocation.

The immediate cause of death, as attributed to this "probable" cause, was diagnosed as "pulmonary congestion and edema." While commonly indicative of a heart attack, as here implied, this congestion and filling of the lungs with serous fluid is also indicative of a fatal heroin overdose.

"This autopsy," stated the report, "eliminates the possibility of homicide."

A confidential Homicide Detail report dated January 20 incorporates information from Sonny's physician, Dr. Richard J. Browning. During Sonny's recent hospitalization following his Thanksgiving auto accident, said Browning, the examination of Sonny's heart and lungs had been extensive and thorough. "His findings prior to the deceased's dismissal from the hospital," stated the confidential report, "were contrary to the Coroner's final diagnosis." The doctor also stated that in the five years he had known and treated Sonny, "there was no evidence of the deceased using narcotics."

It was Dr. Mark Herman who performed the autopsy under the supervision of Dr. James Clarke, the chief medical examiner. It was Dr. Mark Herman who was said to have seen, before he saw those other scars, the copper-colored whipping welts, old and faint, like one might imagine to have been those of a driven slave.

Those other scars. *"There is no external evidence of a recent needle puncture perforation in this location."*

The headline of the *Las Vegas Sun,* the day after the autopsy report: PROBE REVEALS LISTON MAY HAVE BEEN POSSIBLE NARCO VICTIM.

A day later, the *Sun* ran a small piece under the heading "Narco Agent Last Person Known to Have Seen Sonny Liston Alive":

> The last person known to see Charles (Sonny) Liston alive was an undercover narcotics agent.
>
> Sheriff's detectives said yesterday Liston, known as the "bad man" of professional boxing, was visited at his home Dec. 30 by

the agent. They refused to divulge the nature or reason for his visit, but did say Liston was apparently in good health at that time.

Lawmen believe the 38-year-old heavyweight may have died from an overdose of drugs. Puncture wounds, similar to needle tracks, scarred the well-muscled arms and small quantities of heroin and marijuana were uncovered inside the $70,000 luxury home at the Sahara-Nevada Country Club.

No name: "the agent." Agent Nobody.

"They refused to divulge the nature or reason for his visit, but did say Liston was apparently in good health at that time."

A date of death established by the date of a newspaper left beside a hat, December 28, and the date of a newspaper left on a doorstep, December 29. Then an unnamed visitor, a phantom agent, to establish well-being on December 30 — an "agent" never to be heard of or from again. How difficult would it be, really, to place day-old or week-old newspapers on a dead man's doorstep? Does bestowing the title of agent on an invisibility give credence to words attributed to that invisibility? *Undercover agent.* Undercover of what? Undercover as in undercover manager, as in under cover of the night? Why would a man who could not read lay a paper beside his hat in the privacy of his own home? Who was the boy who delivered those papers that piled up outside the door? It would seem that he could be brought forth, or was he, too, an undercover agent. Under what premise did the undercover agent gain entry to the abode of the living? *Excuse me, sir, I'm an undercover agent, may I come in?* The newsboy and the narco. Maybe they were one. Unnamable. Unknown.

Pieces of Sonny's brain, heart, lungs, liver, and kidneys had been sent to the California Toxicology Service in Los Angeles for independent examination. The report showed that "traces of morphine and codeine were found in body tissues but not in sufficient amounts which could be considered as causing death." These traces of morphine and codeine "corresponded to the amounts which would normally result from a breakdown of heroin in the body."

Why was the evidence of heroin present? How accurately, after the passing of an unknown number of days, could the component traces of the breakdown of the heroin reveal the quantity of heroin that originally had been present? These questions were not addressed, and they were not answered.

The *Las Vegas Sun,* January 20: "Liston Death 'Natural'":

"Although traces of heroin were found in the corpse of former world boxing champ Sonny Liston, local experts have ruled the 38-year-old heavyweight died from natural causes."

Case closed. And closed, too, the coffin. Services were held at Palm Mortuary Chapel on the Saturday afternoon of January 9, 1971, with the Reverend Edward P. Murphy presiding. The Ink Spots sang "Sunny." Folks laid down flowers. His little adopted boy looked as though the world had ended or, worse, had taken on the colors of all the sadness that ever was. Of Sonny's kin from the old days, only J.T., the brother known as Shorty, made the trip. The silver-steel casket was taken to Paradise Memorial Gardens, and Sonny was laid, fist and feet, beneath the dirt.

Case closed.

Someone suggested I get in touch with Ralph Lamb, who was the sheriff at that time.

"I don't know anything about him except that he fought here," Lamb said.

"I was not in charge of the case," and "I don't know who was. It was a long time ago."

A long time ago.

Natural causes. Some who knew him accepted this. A few felt that perhaps Sonny did indeed die on dope. "I think he was using and he overdosed," said Gene Kilroy. "I think he was depressed because he was running out of money. I think either he did himself in or he accidentally did himself in." Dean Shendal tended to agree with Gene. "Listen," he said, "this town, you'll hear Rip Van Winkle never went to sleep. There's more bullshit in this town than there are bullshitters. I don't know where it all comes from. Some of it comes from guys like me."

Most who knew him protested that his phobia of needles precluded this. That fear was by all accounts lifelong and intense, evident as early as his prison days and as recently as his November hospital stay, when he expressed anxiety and distress at having been injected unawares.

"He never took a shot," said Sam Eveland of Sonny in those prison days. "He would catch pneumonia before he would take a shot. That's how scared he was of needles."

The *Philadelphia Daily News* writer Jack McKinney, who was one of the very few intrepid sportswriters to champion and defend Liston, said, "Sonny was deathly afraid of needles. He and I had the same dentist in Philadelphia. His name was Dr. Nick Ragni. When Sonny went to Ragni for a root canal, he wouldn't even take Novocain."

Lem Banker told me that Mickey Duff, the British promoter who handled Sonny's first overseas tours, noted that Sonny refused all inoculations or blood tests, that "he didn't want anything; he was afraid of needles." Banker also said that Sonny refused to take a needle when he got his California boxing license, before his fight with Henry Clark, in 1968.

"Look what they did!" Johnny Tocco remembered Sonny raving when Tocco visited him in the hospital after his Thanksgiving automobile accident. "He was pointing at some little bandage over the needle mark in his arm. He was more angry about that shot than he was about the car wreck." Sonny was still bitching about that shot two weeks later, Tocco said. "To this day, I'm convinced that's what the coroner saw in his exam — that hospital needle mark."

"He was," as Lowell Powell put it, "as scared of a needle as a goat is a butcher knife."

The one unsettling and ambiguous stroke in this picture, the fact overlooked by, or unknown to, those who attest to Sonny's fear and avoidance of needles, is that he was alleged to have undergone, and likely did undergo, cortisone-shot treatments in 1963 and again in 1964. Furthermore, there never was a junkie who did not start out afraid of needles. But Sonny's extreme reaction to injections during his hospital stay in November 1970 indicates that Sonny at this late time was far from seduced, indeed repulsed, by the charms of the piqûre. And if it is true, as Foneda Cox claimed, that the 1963 knee injury was feigned, there were no cortisone shots at that time; and if one were to regard the after-the-fact account of a bursitis-ridden shoulder as part of an obfuscating explanation brought forth after the first Clay fight, one might suspect, too, that there had been no cortisone shots in 1964.

Chuck Wepner, who fought Liston five months earlier, told me that Liston certainly did not box like a junkie.

"He didn't look like a junkie to me. Although his eyes were bloodshot, but that could be from anything. That could be from just not sleeping much. I think he partied and drank a lot. They said that the guy, you know, a lot of the fights, he didn't really train that hard, and he partied and he did what he had to do and he went in and knocked guys out."

If anybody could have got him to banging the shit, it was his buddy and only hero, old Joe Louis.

Many simply called it murder.

"A friend of mine called me, said, man, they found Sonny dead," Lowell Powell recalled. "I said, 'I'll be damned, they got to him.'"

On the West Side, and on the Strip, in joints in Chicago and joints in St. Louis and joints in New York, you hear different things. He got involved in a big dope deal. They had his money, they figured who needs him. He got involved in some shylocking operation, fucked with the wrong people. Different things, all sorts of things. Of course, killing Sonny would have been no mean feat. The moment his killers started toward him, as somebody said, "that woulda been all she wrote." The consensus was that they put something in his drink, then gave him a hotshot.

The police seemed eager to be shut of the whole mess. Drug overdose, natural death: each verdict was welcome and readily accepted in turn, no further questions asked, no matter how many questions the reports left unanswered.

If Sonny was killed, as most who knew him believed, his killers concealed their act with sophistication and skill that were extraordinary in the extreme — or with the common and ordinary complicity of those entrusted with the revelation of their act. Las Vegas, "a friendly environment for the right people," was also historically a very murder-friendly place.

Liston was surrounded by, as they say in Sicily, the friends of friends. His life in this regard had been very friendly. The Teamsters, the Boys, this one, the other one: everybody was friends. Sonny knew this guy, and this guy knew Vitale, and Vitale knew this guy, and Kerkorian knew this guy, and Sonny ends up in

Kerkorian's house. Better homes and graveyards. You drive a car for some Syrian guy in St. Louis, and some other Syrian guys end up with the Aladdin, and you end up in Vegas, and Ash ends up at the Aladdin, and you end up with Ash, and the Aladdin is funneling money to Vitale. Round and round she went, one big circle of friends. Made sure folks who couldn't read got their newspapers delivered right to their door; sent around agents without names to check that you were all right and well. Friendship. It was a beautiful thing.

The gossamer web becomes clearly visible. But the spider is nowhere in sight.

The men who could have helped Sonny, even if only to see, were no longer there.

In the end, they would fare better than he. Frankie Carbo, released from prison early due to illness, would die in a Miami Beach hospital bed, age seventy-two, on November 9, 1976. Blinky Palermo, released from prison in the fall of 1971, would have the balls to apply for a new manager's license, and would die, without that license in a Philadelphia hospital bed, age ninety-one, on May 12, 1996.

"Oh, he loved Blinky," Davey Pearl said with a smile that was wistful. "He told me once that of all the guys that he had, Palermo was the nicest to him."

"I just heard he OD'd on drugs," Chuck Wepner said. "Then, later on, years later, I started hearing stories that they knocked him off. He wasn't a well-liked guy."

Dope, shylocking. Money. Whatever it was, it came down to

money. From that nickel on that winter night in 1950 until the end, it came down to money. Not only in his world, but in the only world there is: it came down to money.

Lem Banker, who is convinced that Sonny was murdered, spoke of an ex-cop imprisoned at Carson City who claimed he was offered a contract by Ash Resnick. The story is that Ash and Sonny had a big falling out. Over money. Banker doesn't believe the story: "Ash didn't have Sonny killed," he said. "Ash did a lot of things, but he wasn't a murderer." And I don't believe it, either.

Davey Pearl seemed hesitant to call Sonny's death a murder outright, but as he spoke, other feelings seemed to emerge. "Dealing with the wrong people, there's always a chance of getting killed," he remarked. Then: "The police don't even know who killed him."

Johnny Tocco believed that Sonny died from natural causes: "I think he had a seizure, or something that caused some kind of convulsion, like a stroke." This diagnosis, based on nothing, seemed to be that of a man unwilling to accept that his friend's death could have been brought about either by heroin or the wages of his unknown, "quiet business," or both.

As someone had told me to look to the east, so someone told me to look to the calendar.

If a deal had indeed been made whereby Liston was to receive in secret a percentage of all of Ali's future earnings, that deal would not have been worth much. Since early 1967, when the government came down on him for refusing to serve it, Ali had been inactive. There were no earnings. But when Ali, in late 1970, began again to fight, it was not for the sort of purses that fighters had known. (In 1965, the year of the Liston-Ali rematch, Liston declared a taxable income of slightly over $109,000; the IRS set it higher, at slightly over $199,000.) In December of 1970, Herbert Muhammad undertook for Ali the brokering of an unheard-of five-million-dollar deal for a fight with Joe Frazier.

By the time that fight was fought a few months later, Sonny lay beneath the Las Vegas dirt of the Garden of Peace at Paradise Memorial Gardens, beneath a bronze plaque that bears his name and the words A MAN.

I no longer believe in the secret-percentage angle as the cause of Sonny's death. A deal unwritten was a deal that need not be honored, except among the honorable. And a threat to expose a deal unwritten was no threat of all, especially when it came from one who could ill afford to unsettle the ghosts of his own past.

I believe, in the end, it had more to do with that starless astrology of the soul of a man who "died the day he was born," with the nature of certain January nights, with the domain of that god who beheld beginning and end at once.

Many Januarys ago, he had stalked the night for money; and there came a time, after fame and wealth and the stain of them, when money was gone again.

It was what he knew. Dirt, fist, feet. He befriended no priests in Vegas.

As always, there was money in the street. There was money in dope, there was money in shylocking. I believe that it was to that money that Sonny turned. Whatever it was — dope, shylocking, both — he may not have been content with the old plantation deal of "workin' on halves"; and that may have been his end. Or, whatever he was doing, somebody did not like it. He was, after all, a man whose mere presence seemed to inspire cops to run him out of town, threaten to baptize his ass with lead, or seize him for "corner lounging." I think it can be said with confidence that to accept the premise that Sonny was murdered is, by necessity, to accept the involvement and the malfeasance of cops in that murder, one way or another, either directly or through cover-up, either acting of their own accord or according to the command of a higher power.

But, as much as I should like to meet that unnamed undercover narcotics agent, that newspaper delivery boy; as much as I should like here to have as expositive Virgil the ghost of Big Barney Baker, of Ash Resnick, of the unnamable who knew, I feel that the truth might be far more mundane.

I look back to a sentence that I wrote over a year ago, a sentence that appears in the earliest of these pages: *Only he and the men who killed him knew the date of his death.* Looking at it, I realize that it can be easily and cleanly deleted, plucked from the page, with no effect on the words or meaning that surround it. But I choose to leave it there, because it expressed my feeling at that time, and because, unlike a statement proven untrue, it very well might express not only my past feelings, but also the truth, which, in this matter, will never be known. And since it was in the winding passage from that sentence to this — the passage through the unseen sediment, detritus, and sludge beneath the course of this book, and through the articulation of that course as well — that my feeling, for no specific reason, evolved and changed, I think it would render inorganic what has been organic. As the phantom narco, Agent Nobody, said: Exposita without logic, it makes the world go round.

If someone wanted to kill Sonny, he or she could far more easily and with far less risk have put a bullet through his skull in the street any night of the week.

I think he took too much dope and died. The fact that no gimmick was found means nothing. He could have shot up elsewhere, then been overcome by the overdose at home. Maybe he did not even bang the shit. And no one knows how long he had been dead when they cut those dead-tissue samples from him. How could the measurement of lingering traces of dispersing morphine and codeine reveal the amount of heroin present in a body at a time of death that was unknown?

Sonny's friends did not want to admit that he was doing dope. There was never an indication that he was. What sort of an indication was to be expected from one who might not even be addicted?

"No, he doesn't trust me on food and things; he gets his little Kentucky Frieds and things."

As Sonny had said, he wanted to model himself after Joe Louis, "who I think was the greatest champion of all and my idol. He did everything I want to do." Maybe they were shooting more than craps together.

The mystery of a death serves only to distract us comfortably from the mysteries inside ourselves. Ultimately, the true cause of Sonny Liston's death was the mystery in him. He rode a fast dark train from nowhere, and it dumped him at that falling-off place at the end of the line.

The only true mystery is one without an answer. That we should be put here for a sigh then blown to nothingness like a harl in an idle wind — that is mystery enough. Sonny Liston was an embodiment of that fatal mystery, which claims us all and leaves no track marks in so doing.

Call it Shango, call it Syndrome X. There is only one real cause of death, and that is death.

"He's dead, that's all," as Davey Pearl said. And, like the man said, he was born that way.

ACKNOWLEDGMENTS

As the worn phrase has it, this is a dark tale. It could not be otherwise, as I knew when I took its first breath into me. It was a tale untold whose telling long had beckoned me. And while the nature of that beckoning is to be found early in the pages of this book, it should also here be said — an acknowledgment of another sort — that given the choice between the sunny side of the street and the umbrous, I have perhaps more often than not chosen the latter.

In my work on this book, I encountered those who cleared the shadows with light, and those who overcast light with shadow. Enlightenment, enshadowment. Which leads to which? And, in the end, are they one and the same?

I don't know where, or with whom, to begin to express my thanks for those encountered, casters of shadows and of light; where, or with whom, to begin to express my thanks for those who helped in so many ways. There are those, characters in the tale of Liston's life itself, who opened to me. These were the men and women who took me to where I never could have gotten, for to descend into a lost and secret underworld without the guidance of the souls who knew it is to be a stranger to the soul of that lost and secret place itself. As serendipity has it, in my alphabetical log, the first of these guides of my descent is a Virgil — the welterweight champion Virgil Akins, who came up with Sonny in the old days in St. Louis. Others spanned the time and places of Sonny's fatal astrology: Lem Banker; Ben Bentley; Jesse Bowdry; Doc Broadus; Foneda Cox; Sam Eveland; Larry Gazall; Truman Gibson; Joel Glickman; David Herleth; Gene Kilroy; Jim Lubbock; Claude E. Lyles, Jr.; Tom Lynch; Bob Martin; Ezraline Lynn Mable; George Morledge, Jr.; Davey Pearl; Lowell Powell; the Reverend Edward B. Schlattman; Dean Shendal; Myrl Taylor; Ezra Baskin Ward; Mattie Ward; and Chuck Wepner. Many of these — renowned and obscure alike — are deserving of books unto themselves, such have been their lives, which I have sought in the course of this tale to glean and convey, sometimes in glimpse, sometimes in depth.

Without men such as Foneda Cox, Truman Gibson, Davey Pearl, Lowell Powell, Ezra Baskin Ward, and Chuck Wepner, this book could not have been what it is; and, while their importance is, I hope, manifest in the pages that follow, I should like here, in thanking them, to reiterate both that importance and my gratitude for their generosity. It was an honor to come to know them, as it was to know others, also of considerable importance, whose request for anonymity I have respected.

I write this on a cold night as one millennium, a dead wisp in that supernal breeze that we call time, becomes another. It is black outside, a little after half past four, when the joints too are dead. In the background — fuck the neighbors — the melancholy violin and viola, the mean self-threnody of Iggy Pop's "No Shit," from his brutal, beautiful, and courageous *Avenue B*. I remember a night a few months back, at Manitoba's, a joint on Avenue B. I was there to read poetry, and Chuck Wepner, one of the last of the stand-up guys — a guy who fought not only both Sonny Liston and Muhammad Ali, but also, for charity, a Kodiak bear — had come in to introduce me. "This guy," he said, "writes like Sonny Liston hit." That night, this night, the blackness and the cold and the threnody of feeling one's own death and declaring that the only godly prayer in the face of that death is the decision to not to take any more shit, not from anybody — this fills me now, at this moment, as the long night, black and cold, of the book that follows still lingers, the labor ending even as it did, with a laugh in a crowded, smoke-filled room on Avenue B; ending, like all else, with a death that never comes because it is always here. And so here's to Chuck Wepner — water glasses raised high, as I think as I write this we're both still on probation, he in one state, I in another — Chuck Wepner, who took the blows; Chuck Wepner, who wouldn't rat out the Devil to God Himself, and who therefore is closer to God than any fucking asshole who believes that the laws of man are but filth compared to those of the soul.

What language, for shame, with which to precede my thanks to more genteel souls — then again, who knows, they might be killers and rapists by night — those underpaid, unlaureled heroes of that filigree of wisdom that is knowledge: Claudia Anderson, senior archivist of the Lyndon B. Johnson Library; the staff of the Arkansas Department of Health, Division of Vital Statistics; members of the Arkansas State Historical Society; Mary Barns of the St. Francis County Circuit Court clerk's office; Margaret Booker, librarian at the Missouri Department of Corrections, Jefferson City; Tedi Burris of the Ernest & Julio Gallo Winery; workers at Carson City Vital Records; Richard Cawthorn of the Mississippi Department of Archives and History; Mary L. Eldridge of the U.S. Department of Commerce, Bureau of the Census; Don Cline, the superintendent of operations, Missouri Department of Corrections, Jefferson City; the Cross County Library; Jimmie James of the Cross County Historical Society; Evelyn Bell Crouch; the Forrest County Public Library; Jessie Hemphill Golden; Talmage Golden and Pauline Hall of the Montgomery County chancery clerk's office; Noel Holobeck of the History and Genealogy Department of the St. Louis City Library; Sarah Johnson of the Montgomery County Tax Assessor's Office; the Little Rock Central Library System; Tim Kniest, director of public relations, Missouri Department of Corrections, Jefferson City; Frank McEwan of the records division of the St. Louis Police Department; the Mississippi Department of Archives and History; the Mississippi Department of Health, Division of Vital Statistics; the Mississippi Historical Society; the workers of the National Archives in New York and Washington, D.C.; the Nevada Office of Vital Statistics; the New York Public Library; Christy Relyea of the office of the Clark County Assessor; Tina Rose of the Circuit Clerk's Office, Montgomery County, Mississippi; Neal Rudnick of the Las Vegas Library; the St. Francis County Courthouse; the St. Francis County Museum; Kathy Smith and the staff of the St. Louis City Library; Linda Seelke, archivist of the Lyndon B. Johnson Library; members of the Wynne, Arkansas, Historical Society.

Several prominent figures in law enforcement — all of them of that most old and rare school: good cops, in every sense of the word good — took me not only into their confidence, but often selflessly aided me in my search, leading me to people, places, and truths that I likely would not have found without them. Among these men are William Anderson and James Hackett of St. Louis, and Matt Rodriguez of Chicago. In Jim Hackett, whom I met on the verge of his retirement from high office after a long and distinguished career in the force, I found a rare, kindred spirit of kindred sensibilities. It was as if we were from the same neighborhood — in a way we were, though thousands of miles apart — and as we became friends, we were never really aware of *becoming* friends, for it was as if we had always been such. It was my impression that Jim, longing for the old down-and-dirty, hands-on detective work of his early years, took up the Liston case as an invigorating opportunity to return to those days of digging and searching in the light and the dark and shaded copses between them, where he knew that the emanations of human nature often lay. Whether the impression I here convey is right or not, one thing is sure: my thanks to Jim Hackett are considerable, as are my thanks to fortune for bringing me to know him. He is another stand-up guy, who, in his own way, like Chuck Wepner, faced forces and took blows that many of us cannot imagine.

Of inestimable value was the devoted help of another scattered crew of great characters. I want here in particular to express my most heartfelt thanks to Chris Dickinson and John McGuire. *Heartfelt.* What a dainty, moribund, and demure-sounding word. Fuck *heartfelt.* These people are as good as they come, and I can't type their names without seeing them smiling, and without my sitting like a fool smiling back.

Jules Feiler went far beyond the bonds of friendship to serve as a catalyst in so many ways. Alan Katz, in an act of great kindness, shared with me copies of the Federal Bureau of Investigation files on Liston; and knowing of his intense and dedicated interest in Liston, I hope I have returned that act of kindness in part with this book.

There are so many, for the writing of this book was a maze, an endless Latin sentence of a puzzle pieced together only by the decipherment of inflections. A litany of names does no one justice, but if people are willing to sit and stare at stone slabs bearing the countless names of countless dead fucks, I hope that you, who have bought your ticket to what follows, will pause to consider those others whom I here cannot forget:

Jim Agnew; Frank Barbarotta; Irl Baris; Jerry Blavat; Chris Calhoun; Steve Calt; Timothy Chanaud; Tim Channell; Dave Cohen; Pat Daily; Lisa Derrick; Gary Dretzka; Gerry Feltmann; Heather Fink; Frank Fortunato; Terry Friedland; Shecky Greene; Charles Greller; some guy named Gus; Paul Hempil; Ted Hemphill; Nick Ippolito; Eddie Jaffe; Sarah Jumpner; Hank Kaplin; Ed Kelly; Greg Kot; Mark Kram; Irv Kupcinet; Art Laurie; Frank Liston; Roger Lee Liston; William Liston; Mike Manetti; Joe Mazzola; Jake McCarthy; the Reverend Jack McGuire; Mickey McTague; Richard Meltzer; William Nack; Tim O'Connor; Michael Ochs; Monsignor Artie Peet; Sarann Knight Preddy; Mark Ratner; Tony Romano; David Roter; Jim Schwenke; Hubert Selby, Jr.; Dr. Allen Spivack; Laren Stover; Kenn Thomas; Mike Tocco; Paul Venti and the guys at the club; Cliff Van Langen; Sarkis Webbe, Jr.; David Zinsser.

As a companion journeyer through the labyrinths of all matters arcane, Jeff Roth, as always, is to be thanked.

Dr. Allen S. Yanoff, one of the most distinguished physicians in New York, examined for me the conundrum of Liston's autopsy report. Through the years, I have been thankful for this fine man and fine doctor many times for many things, and for this beneficence I am thankful once again.

Throughout my work on this book, and especially in its early stages, I was blessed to be assisted by Carrie Knoblock, a master of the research sciences whose resourcefulness, expertise, thoroughness, and diligence exceed any simple statement of gratitude and praise, no matter how superlative.

This book had its origin as a story written for *Vanity Fair,* and, regarding that origin, I want to acknowledge Graydon Carter for allowing me the freedom to write it, George Hodgman for not editing what I wrote, and Sara Switzer for taking care of business. Abby Royle, who transcribed the interviews conducted for that story, went on to transcribe the many, many more that followed.

In the final stages of the book, I was fortunate to work with an exceptional copyeditor, Jay Boggis, and master reader, Greg Rahal, astutely chosen by Peggy Freudenthal, the copyediting manager of Little, Brown; and was fortunate, too, to have been aided by the sharp eyes and keen classical literary sensibilities of Catherine McRae.

Above all, I want to thank Michael Pietsch and Sarah Crichton of Little, Brown; and along with them, as always, my agent, friend, and conspirator, Russell Galen. As for my assistant, Sarah Fabbricatore, I pause here to summon words. But this is no time for artful metaphor, and there are no words to be summoned, only the words that come freely forth. She is my right arm. She is my protectress from what keeps the breezes from entering me. Is that metaphor? It feels not to be. In any case, enough. Let's just do it, as that eminent littérateur Chuck Wepner would have it. Let's just write like Sonny Liston hit. She's the best. After me, anyway.

These are my last acknowledgments. Never again. Too much trouble. Let that be a warning. Don't ever help me, because it won't get your name in a goddamn book.

Now, here's to Sonny.

INDEX